MY BAYOU

MY BAYOU

*New Orleans through
the Eyes of a Lover*

Constance Adler

Michigan State University Press
East Lansing

♾ The paper used in this publication meets the minimum requirements of ANSI/NISO Z39.48-1992 (R 1997) (Permanence of Paper).

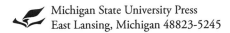 Michigan State University Press
East Lansing, Michigan 48823-5245

Printed and bound in the United States of America.

18 17 16 15 14 13 12   1 2 3 4 5 6 7 8 9 10

LIBRARY OF CONGRESS CATALOGING-IN-PUBLICATION DATA

Adler, Constance.
    My bayou : New Orleans through the eyes of a lover / Constance Adler.
        p. cm.
    ISBN 978-1-61186-032-0 (paper : alk. paper) 1. Adler, Constance. 2. New Orleans (La.)—Biography. 3. Saint John, Bayou (La.)—Biography. 4. New Orleans (La.)—Social life and customs. 5. Saint John, Bayou (La.)—Social life and customs. 6. Hurricane Katrina, 2005—Social aspects—Louisiana—New Orleans. 7. Adler, Constance—Marriage. 8. Self-actualization (Psychology)—Case studies. 9. New York (N.Y.)—Biography. I. Title.

    F379.N553A35 2012
    976.3'35064092—dc23
    [B]
    2011024666

Cover design by Charlie Sharp, Sharp Des!gns

Book design by Scribe Inc. (www.scribenet.com)

green press INITIATIVE Michigan State University Press is a member of the Green Press Initiative and is committed to developing and encouraging ecologically responsible publishing practices. For more information about the Green Press Initiative and the use of recycled paper in book publishing, please visit www.greenpressinitiative.org.

Visit Michigan State University Press on the World Wide Web at:
www.msupress.msu.edu

The way of love is not
a subtle argument.

The door there
is devastation.

Birds make great sky-circles
of their freedom.
How do they learn it?

They fall, and falling,
They're given wings.

—RUMI, TRANSLATED BY COLEMAN
BARKS, *THE ESSENTIAL RUMI*

What's going to become of lovely New Orleans
That rotten old town that everyone loves?

—GRAYSON CAPPS, *NEW ORLEANS WALTZ*

CONTENTS

WHAT THE PELICANS SAW

THERE IS A MUDDY TRICKLE OF WATER THAT RUNS THROUGH MY neighborhood where I walk every day. It's called Bayou Saint John, named for John the Baptist. Fitting that such a twisty, curious waterway should be named for that eccentric cousin of Christ. The Choctaw people were nice enough to show the way to the explorer Jean Baptiste Bienville. It was the shortcut to the Mississippi, saved them miles of purgatorial struggle. History is undecided whether Bienville named this waterway for the saint or himself. Both stories fit, and it doesn't matter. My sense is that he considered this *his* bayou. He could name it whatever he liked.

My own baptism into reverence for the bayou took place on the morning that, by the calendar's reckoning, was Ash Wednesday. Carnival had just climaxed, and having moved over that ecstatic peak into the downward slide toward a somber meditation on our mortality, the day called for wearing a gray smear on our foreheads to remind us that fun is fine, but death is where it's at. Amidst this atmosphere of decay and dust, I stepped into my pink paisley rubber rain boots and headed out to the bayou with a brown paper bag and one yellow rubber dishwashing glove (for the right hand) to pick up the garbage that had accumulated along the waterline. It was a good time for cleaning, not just because it was Lent, but also because the bayou was particularly clogged with junk at this time of year. I don't know where it got deposited, but it all seemed to float down here to my neighborhood between the Dumaine Street Bridge and the Magnolia Bridge.

My companion Lance, himself a muddy trickle of a dog, ran ahead of me. When he's in a good mood, Lance trots like a show pony, tail waving like a flag, mouth turned up at the corners in a giddy smile. When he's in more of a brown study, Lance runs like a jackal with nose to the ground, and ass slightly tucked as if he expects someone to kick him at any moment. I have never kicked Lance, never placed angry hands on his body. This dog lives a life of undiluted pleasure, punctuated by rare admonitions for petty crimes, such as chewing ballpoint pens that leave big ink stains on the living room rug. The worst punishment I have given Lance is to speak in a sharp voice, which is enough to send him into a crumpled state of abject remorse. This skulking posture of Lance's must come completely out of his imagination.

As I walked and picked, I found a lot of waterlogged plastic grocery bags, little white plastic rings from soda-bottle tops, cigarette-pack cellophanes, drink straws. Surprisingly few condoms. Not sure if I should be glad of that or not. Glad for me, at least. Then I reached down into the murk because I saw a white patch of something, maybe a sandwich wrapper. But no, it was the white belly of a dead turtle. Was it a plastic bag that killed him? I've heard that turtles die from trying to eat plastic bags, which resemble fish sometimes in the way they balloon out as they drift below the water. I couldn't stand to look at the turtle, but I couldn't look away either. I could see the seams that held together the plates of his shell, his thumb-shaped head, and his legs flippering uselessly in the gentle sway of the water. It made me think of that passage in Michael Cunningham's *The Hours* when Virginia Woolf's nephews find the body of a bird in the garden. "Oh, thinks Virginia, just before tea, here's death."

I left the turtle to his slow decay and continued the task of cleaning the bayou. Farther along, I leaned over to grab what I realized—too late again—was a full diaper that someone had secured into a close bundle before dropping it into the bayou. As I lifted it from the water, the odor of baby shit and mud reached my nose. Too bad. I had gotten this far with it; I had to keep going. A commitment is a commitment. I had to pick up whatever I found that was not supposed to be here. That was the Lenten promise I had made to myself.

As I stood there with a dripping, muddy, rolled-up diaper in my gloved hand, two pelicans soared past. They flew like stealth bombers. The sight of the birds stopped me in my boots. It happened every time. I would pause in whatever I was doing and watch them. They held me in their flight.

Whenever the pelicans showed up, they bestowed a surprising air of benediction on the bayou, a visitation from some other world. Clearly they're not from around here, you say to yourself when you see one of these prehistoric giants floating effortlessly on an updraft, poised in midair against a backdrop of rooftops. These birds belong in a more spacious realm.

Why would these gorgeous wild creatures come to our cramped quarters? Why would they offer their blessing in this squinched city dwelling, with all our crankiness, preoccupations, and busy everydayness? Certainly not because we are good. The pelicans fly equally above the deserving and the undeserving.

They come every year around November to take up winter residence in Bayou Saint John until the end of spring. I am not sure where they spend the rest of the year—probably farther out into the Gulf or in Lake Pontchartrain. For several of the colder and windier months of the year, the brown pelicans live here in this bayou, which flows through a crowded, built-up neighborhood. They float low in the air, gliding on their huge wingspans just inches above the water's surface. It's a great gravity-defying trick of aero-engineering that still looks like pure magic to me. The pelicans make the ducks and herons and cormorants look like they are still practicing flight. These local birds, who appear just as harried and spent as the people, seem to belong here, pecking and paddling around in this citified waterbed while the pelicans make great sky circles with their wings.

Among the linocuts that Walter Anderson made from images he gathered while living on Horn Island is one that displays the artist's view of a pelican as she flies overhead. Of course the choice seems obvious now, but it is an unusual perspective. Usually, artists paint birds in flight from a perspective that shows them in a representational manner, so we can see their plumage and bone structure. They look pretty in a conventional sort of way. The average person would probably be immune to Anderson's peculiar vision of the bird, as the perspective is foreshortened, which warps the image slightly. Then again, Anderson saw a lot of things that no one else could see, and so it's not surprising that he would appreciate the potential beauty in the underside of a pelican. I don't think you have to be eccentric like Walter to see it, but the underside of a pelican does have an allure. I call it "stately absurd."

The pelican in flight holds her head back, pushing out her plumed breast, which is rounded, pompous, and awfully serious. She owns the bayou, and she is stately absurd as she coasts on the air in the manner of a B-52 bomber. She is graceful until she attempts a landing. That is always a wobbly, crashing affair, more comedy than precision; yet her command of the air remains awe-inspiring.

The pelican's breast also reminds me of the harrumphing bosom that Margaret Dumont presents in Marx Brothers movies. I felt sorry for this actress, since her character had to play the solemn foil. Her role consisted of a lot of gasping indignation and holding an erect posture as she thrust the bulwark of her bosom around while Harpo and Groucho swarmed over her like a kooky plague of ants. Just like Margaret Dumont, the pelican betrays no awareness of how funny she is as she floats high above our heads, which is the only reason she gets away with it. The pelican's stateliness would never hold if the Marx Brothers could fly.

Another important difference between Margaret Dumont and the pelican is that the pelican is a savage killer. I had the opportunity by lucky timing to stand on the Magnolia Bridge one afternoon when the sky was high and brilliant, while a group of four or five pelicans came through.

They were doing what they always do—cruising for fish. As soon as one spotted her prey below, she tucked her wings against her body so that her flight turned sharply downward, and she plunged beak first from fifty feet in the air. As she crashed into the water, she kicked up a great fountain of froth. Amidst the splash, it's almost impossible to see her split-second adjustment as she hits the water, unless you watch this performance several times over. Just as her beak reaches below the water to the place where the fish swims, unaware that death plunges from above, the pelican opens her mouth and scoops the unsuspecting fish into her rubbery pouch. Then, in minutely coordinated movements, she rights herself onto the surface of the water, her massive wings flapping a downdraft to get her balance, while simultaneously her neck wattles convulse with the fish, now fighting for its life, as it disappears into the darkness inside her. When I observed this brilliant combination of anticipation, keen sight, timing, and athletic prowess, I realized that cartoons were only a slight exaggeration of what happens in the so-called real world.

On this Ash Wednesday, as I watched the pelicans soar past me on their giant wings, I marveled at their ability to be at once magnificent and comical. I accepted their benediction and glimpsed the mystery and magic they brought with their wild grace. The birds prompted an unaccountable shift. My feet were literally sinking deeper into the mud where I stood, and yet I also felt myself sinking into something else that didn't have a name yet. The pelicans offered an invitation to descend into this place. To deepen my relationship to my bayou and the city it flowed through.

I interpreted this descent, inaugurated at the beginning of the Lenten season, as a call to stewardship. When I saw an aerial photo of the bayou—the pelican's eye view—I was struck by its resemblance to a spinal cord. How intriguing that geography has determined the bayou to be the primitive backbone for this city. It carries the vital spinal fluid that animates the land around it. Bayou Saint John is the reason New Orleans exists where it does today. Were it not for the convenient passage between lake and river afforded by this innocuous, muddy trickle, the French explorers who established New Orleans would have gone elsewhere. So we have Bayou Saint John to thank for putting us here.

When the pelicans came that day in February, Hurricane Katrina wasn't due to arrive for another six months. I couldn't have articulated a complete awareness of the threat that loomed over my city, my bayou, my home. Didn't know how soon would come that crashing, fierce storm that brought it all closer to my heart. Yet, on that day, I sank into a more encompassing embrace of my home and my role in it. I received my vocation. Some task was called for with urgency not yet apparent. I would document the body enlivened by this spinal cord. My sense of stewardship consisted of a simple assignment: Pay attention. I would walk my daily walk along the bayou and see what I could see. Sure, picking up the trash was always a good idea, but my self-appointed job would be to love this bayou by attending to it with my vision and imagination. I would give roundness and shape to whatever transpired here. I would breathe life into this body with my words.

SLIP INTO GRACE

EVERYTHING HAPPENS ON THE BAYOU. LOVE, SEX, VODOU, MARRIAGE, birth, baptism, death, and daring rescues. If you spend enough time walking there, you will witness all manner of dramas, both high and low. Then, every so often something completely startling comes hurtling onto the scene. For instance, from time to time we find a car upended in the bayou. Usually these arrive at the bend of Moss Street near the yellow house where the Vietnamese nuns live. The water is shallow there, and the road makes a tight turn. So drunk drivers who take it a little too cocky and too fast often go right over the edge, and the next morning we'll see the back end of a Camaro or a Dodge sticking straight up from the water, the front end lodged in the muddy bottom. Whenever I find side mirrors and headlights littered on the embankment along that curve, I know there has been another car-dunking. There is nothing anyone can do about it. No one can change the shape of the bayou. It wants to turn that way. So the city has put up a steel barrier and orange caution signs, with arrows pointing the way around this sharp turn. Still, no amount of signs can penetrate the misty confidence of a drunk driver in New Orleans.

There have been a few people who ended up in the bayou, not from drunk driving, but some star-crossed turn of the wheel. These things happen. More often than not, a valiant passerby or the police manage to fish them out of the drink. Some are not so lucky. It's hard to walk along the bayou and not think of the people who have died in it. There is a pleasant tree-shaded portion of the bayou half a block past the Esplanade Bridge where each year a floral wreath appears. It marks the place where a car plunged into the water with two young people in it. The girl in the passenger seat drowned. Someone who loves her and misses her places the wreath there on the anniversary of her death.

In 2003, a woman went missing for a couple of weeks. No one knew what had happened to her until there was a prolonged drought. A man on his bicycle stopped on the Mirabeau Avenue Bridge because he saw a hand sticking up out of the water. The newspaper story reported a "human hand." What *other* kind of hand might there be? I wondered. Soon the police figured out that this was the missing woman. Apparently, she had driven off the road, into the bayou, where her car sank out of sight. She died there and remained until the drought brought the water level low enough that the biker could see her. It appeared that she had been struggling to escape from her partly opened window. They found her strapped into her seat with the seatbelt. When I read this detail of the seatbelt, I imagined her to be a careful driver, conscientious about safety, so unlike most drivers in New Orleans.

Here is something I haven't been able to get out of my head. Two summers ago, a young man, who was walking along the bayou, stopped to help two little boys who were fishing near the Dumaine Street Bridge. Their cork bobber had come loose from their line. The young man waded into what at first seemed like shallow water to retrieve the bobber, but then he slipped on the sudden downward slope of the bayou's muddy bottom and fell into deeper water, where he drowned. This young man was unable to swim, and yet he had volunteered to go into the water to help the kids. The two little boys, who couldn't swim either, stood helplessly while the young man died. Later the police found his shoes on the concrete bulkhead that lines the bayou—his wallet and house keys tucked inside for safekeeping.

Why does someone drown? It doesn't make sense to me. For most of us, our bodies float on their own if we let them. Our lungs are filled with air. Our fat, our bones, this stuff we are made of is buoyant. If you are in water and do nothing at all except tilt your head back, you will float. If you keep completely still and release any effort from your limbs, then you will hover in the water as if held by invisible hands just below the surface, while a small portion of your face, encompassing your eyes, nose and mouth, will be exposed to the air so you can breathe. And this is the important point: Stop *trying* to do anything, simply *be* in the water, and you will float. I have done this for long stretches of meditation—not in the bayou, but at the deep end of a pool. I allow myself to hang in the water and then drift without making any effort to propel myself. I don't know what causes me to move in the water at all. Maybe my own heartbeat is the motor. But I don't sink to the bottom of the pool.

So why does someone drown? Perhaps he doesn't believe he can float. And then he panics. In the grip of a terrifying belief crisis, the drowning man claws and churns at the water, trying to gain firm purchase on something that is not solid. He cannot make decisions about what to do in water because he doesn't believe in the medium itself. Does not believe that it is possible for him to have a relationship with something that offers no resistance. His hands and feet pass through the water as if nothing is there. Yet there is something there, something that will kill him if he cannot stop fighting and negotiate a different way of being with the water. When you're in water, it's actually your own fear that kills you, not the water.

Infants will swim instantly and instinctively if you just put them into a pool. I've seen it on film. Eager and open-eyed, they go like new frogs, kicking behind, paddling in front. The usual explanation for an infant's facility in water is that a young child, who is preverbal, has only sense impressions in his head, without the distinctions of past, present, or future that grammar creates. So the infant, newly emerged from his original watery home, feels just fine in the water and knows what to do without being taught, because water is familiar and intimate to him. He hasn't been alive long enough to forget how nice it was in that watery womb, nor does he have the ability to conceive of a past that is gone. To the infant mind, the water, the air, the breast milk, the soft fluffy blanket, his own body, the sunlight—all of it is the same undifferentiated flow of stuff. So there is no reason to fear water any more than he would fear sunlight or fear his own hands.

Of course, no one knows what happens in the infant mind. It's all guesswork. Babies can't tell us, so we have to imagine it. What I have always imagined is that just as the infant sees no difference between water and himself, he also sees no difference between his life and his death. It is only later, when he learns language and falls from grace, that he sees himself as separate from water and everything else. This initiates his belief that his life is something to be preserved.

I have watched older children learning to swim, kids who are in the six- to eight-year-old age range. What I find fascinating about this process is that these kids won't even trust their own parents, who stand in the pool with loving arms extended, cajoling the terrified child to come in the water. They may speak to their child in the most reasonable and comforting tone of voice and say all the right words: *Don't worry, I'm right here. I won't let go. I promise I'll hold you the whole time. I won't let your head go under.* None of that means anything to the kid clinging to the side of the pool. He won't go. He won't let himself slip into this stuff that isn't solid, that he has forgotten how to be with. His fear of water and death is so strong that it overrides his trust in his parents. Nothing will convince him. Every kid has to face this alone and make the decision in his own time and in his own way. The first time a kid tries to swim—more than any of the conventional benchmarks—is the true coming of age. This is the moment when he realizes that there is something bigger than his love for his parents. That is his love for his own life.

When he does eventually let go of the side of the pool, he has to leap over his own cognition that is telling him: *Don't go in that water. You'll die.* Who knows why he does it? It's not because anyone talked him into it. No, something calls him back into this water that is not air and not solid, and he churns his arms and legs until they remember, remember, remember what they used to know. Gradually his body understands something that his mind would not allow when he was clinging to the edge of the pool. His arms and legs return to moving in concert with the water. And he slips into grace.

I don't have a clear memory of the precise moment that I learned to swim. I think a swim coach may have taught me the rudimentary movements at the community pool in the small New Jersey shore town where I grew up. Then my father taught me the rest by throwing me off the dock behind our house and into the bay. He stood at the edge of the dock with his hands on his hips and shouted, "Okay! Now, swim!" This was how we learned things in our house. I swam because I was terrified I might die. This was not the only time it crossed my mind that my father might kill me.

Later I had to pass a swimming test in the bay in order to participate in sailing summer camp. I flunked the test the first time because I just couldn't stand to tread water for any length of time. The water was dark, and it scared me. There might be creatures down there that could come up through the darkness and get me. I had learned to swim laps freestyle, and so I felt relatively okay moving quickly through the water. I reasoned that as a moving target, I would be more difficult for the creepy bottom-dwelling creatures to catch. But the part of the test where we had to hover in the dark water, paddling and staying afloat in one place, freaked me out so much that I couldn't do it.

The camp counselor said I could try again after practicing on my own for a couple of weeks. So each morning I sat on the edge of our dock while my mother stood over me, yelling and threatening me with punishment if I did not go into the water and swim laps to the bulkhead and back again. I stuck there, crouched and cowering, for a long time, staring at the murky water. I had read a story about flesh-eating barnacles that grow on bulkheads. I believed that if I swam to the slimy bulkhead and tapped it (I had to tap it for the lap to be counted as legitimate) that the flesh-eating barnacles would get me, and I'd leave portions of my fingertips behind with each lap. This is the doom of children who read and imagine. Of course, I couldn't tell my mother this, because she wouldn't hear it. Her face was a hard mask of spitting fury as she blocked the narrow dock with her body. I was cornered. The only way out was to go in the water. So I dove and swam.

It's pretty amazing to me now that I enjoy swimming at all, considering what my parents did in their misguided efforts to teach me to swim. I can't say I have recovered from this early introduction to dark water. I am never at ease in water where I can't see what's going on below. Most of my serious swimming I do in a crystal clear pool, where I can be reasonably sure there are no creepy bottom-dwelling creatures, and if there were, I'd see them coming because I wear goggles. Nothing gets the jump on me when I'm swimming.

Yet, despite my nervousness around dark water, I can't seem to stay away from it. This gurky bayou, with its dark descent to a bottom no one but the turtles can see, is the reason I chose to live in this neighborhood in New Orleans. When I walk along its soggy edge, I feel a pull in my gut. Deeper than mere pleasure, it is a sense of simple rightness. If I had to put my finger on the source, I'd say it is the scent of decaying marsh grass. This is the smell of things falling apart, unraveling to a mealy base form, as the gentle destructive water takes all things back into itself and drags them down to the bottom, where they gradually become indistinguishable from all other things. From tree branches to dead ducks, all eventually break down into the parts that are most useful to the water. The bayou takes it all back and in the process releases a powerful scent. Hydrogen sulfide. Similar to rotten eggs, this is a familiar fragrance from the back bay in southern New Jersey, the cradle of my girlhood. Once that scent gets into your nose, no other place ever smells like home.

Allow me to say a few words about New Jersey—much derided, little understood. I haven't figured out yet how the mere words "New Jersey" have become such an easy punch line, but it seems they have. You don't have to come up with a joke that is actually funny; as long as you put "New Jersey" in there somewhere, people will laugh automatically—people who have never set foot in New Jersey. I'm sorry, but I just don't get it. And I don't care if I sound defensive about this—I don't see what is so goddamn funny . . . Instead, I offer our unofficial state motto. "New Jersey: Look before you laugh."

In my New Jersey, it is always summer, bleached out by sun and salt. We had real winters, of course, with snow and frozen pipes, but the significant New Jersey exists as a warm island floating in my imagination. It's a place where school has let out, and I can hear the distant buzz of lawn mowers through wafting white curtains as I recline on the pink shag carpeting of my bedroom floor with a pile of books that will hold me through this luxurious stretch of time. Notable among these are Nancy Drew Mystery Stories, *Anne of Green Gables, Harriet the Spy*—my own personal pantheon.

My sisters and I head out each day for the beach a few blocks away. Like tightrope walkers, we pace out a cautious bare-footed path on the white painted lines that cross the blacktop of Atlantic Avenue, so as not to burn the bottoms of our feet. I am so captivated by the shape of my own shadow on the street that I almost lose my footing and fall into the fiery pit. Then we scramble up and over the bulkhead, stopping at the bottom wooden step. That surface is cool enough to stand on. We pause and look to the rolling waves of the ocean about fifty yards ahead. Then we run across the hot, loose sand, our feet stinging. We hop and leap, taking the longest strides we can, the pain coming a little late with each step. For a second, I almost think I can stand it, and then *yow!* it hurts. It's a race to the water, and we hurl ourselves onto the cool wet sand. Every time I think I won't make it, but I do.

We would never say that we lived in "New Jersey," but always identified our region as "South Jersey." It seemed necessary to distinguish that we lived in the lower half of the state. We saw ourselves as different from the northerners. That upper part of New Jersey had the reputation for great industry, wealth, organization, and punctuality, while we in the southern part were noted for our easy summery living, sensuousness, ghost stories, and poverty. I promise I am not retrofitting this idea. All the usual assumptions about lifestyle, character, and economics that in popular belief typify the split between the northern states of the Union and the southern states of the Confederacy, between northern Italy and southern Italy, between North America and South America, also applied in microcosm to the North Jersey and South Jersey of my childhood.

So I have always possessed a sense of myself as a southerner, even though citizens of states below the Mason-Dixon Line would enjoy a loud laugh at the idea of a Jersey Girl making this claim. Nonetheless, I believe this accounts for how I ended up here in New Orleans. The two places, my two homes— New Jersey and New Orleans—have much in common. One of the cheap jokes that people like to make at New Jersey's expense is to refer to my ancestral home as the "armpit of the nation," a suggestion that New Jersey stinks. Well, if that's true—and I'm not saying it is—we would have to say that New Orleans is the crotch. More specifically, it is a woman's crotch. New Orleans's location at the end of the Mississippi River where it opens wide to release its flow of mud-rich water into the Gulf of Mexico, the fertile Delta silt that has produced so much life—all these characteristics demand the comparison.

This region where New Orleans reigns, sometimes to her detriment, is soft, yielding, vulnerable, and manifestly feminine, sexual, and procreative.

Putting aside the commonplace derogatory associations, consider for a moment the armpit and the crotch. Both noted for their moist environment, which gives rise to their complex and robust fragrance. Sometimes loved for their gamy nature, sometimes denigrated as filthy, these body parts possess the ability both to arouse and disgust. In the interstices of that attraction and repulsion lie their power and mystery. Just as the quality common to the armpit and the crotch is their dampness, so too as places on the map is their geography ruled by the pervasive presence of water.

We lived in a small town called Longport, "The Pearl of Absecon Island," where the Intracoastal Waterway flowed past our back door. This wide, choppy body of water was a major character in our family history. We were never far beyond its presence, which filled the view outside our dining room window. The bay had many moods: calm and flat at summer sunset, frozen into raging whitecaps at the coldest point of winter. Always there, always making itself known to us through smell, sound, touch, and taste, like a fellow animal. It has saturated my consciousness and shaped my response to the world ever after.

Deeper than story, the impressions of my childhood spring from the sensual reminders of the bay below my bedroom window. The clap, clap as the water, disrupted in the wake of a boat, came up against the bulkhead. The singing of the halyard as the wind whipped it against the mast of my father's sailboat. The aching, lonely screams of the gulls. The funky odor of tar and seaweed clinging to the pilings on the dock. The chill shock of the water engulfing my body when I jumped off the dock. The blue-green bubbling murk that filled my sight for the moments I was submerged. The sting of water rushing up my nose. The taste of salt spray on my lips, and the intoxicating scent of my own skin after I'd been on the bay all day, sailing to the marshes in my Sunfish.

All these come to mind as I walk along Bayou Saint John. My attachment to this bayou in New Orleans flows out of the early childhood imprinting I received by the bay in South Jersey. Even though my present home lies twelve hundred miles away from that original dark water, if I close my eyes and just listen and sniff, the humid air along Bayou Saint John stirs me in a place that can't be mapped. I may spend the whole of my life navigating the borders where water laps against my thoughts. And why? Because it feels right to be at the edge of this dark water. Not in it, but near it. I maintain a respectful coexistence with the water. I am afraid to be immersed in it, but I know I belong to it.

DREAM STATE

A POPULAR CONVERSATION OPENER IN NEW ORLEANS IS TO ASK, "So how did you end up moving here, anyway?" Just about everybody has a romantic tale to tell, usually involving an affair with a dark-eyed stranger who then disappeared with a few bars of haunting music. Some people come for Jazz Fest and never leave. Or in the case of a friend, she and her husband went broke while visiting New Orleans one summer and so had to stay because they didn't have enough money to get back home. That was twelve years ago. They're still living here, now thriving and raising their children.

A common theme I've noticed among these tales is that New Orleans tends to be the place where people bottom out. They come here because too many other things in their lives are not working and they've run out of options. All those people you've heard about slipping through the cracks? Well, they end up here. There are no more cracks to slip through in New Orleans. Once you've settled into this bottomland, you can rest easy in the knowledge that there is no farther you can fall. There is a certain pleasure in giving over to that slide.

My own journey started over fifteen years ago when I was in New York. At the time, I believed Manhattan would be my home for good. I was an ambitious young journalist, determined to live in this hub of publishing. New York was a huge, ongoing street drama. I loved the shouting, the rudeness, the constant rush and shove. It excited me. I was at the center of the world and couldn't imagine wanting to be anywhere else.

Then one night I had a surprising dream. It was one of those dreams that was so vivid, all the details and dialogue so sharply delineated, that I woke from it with the distinct belief that I had literally traveled to another place while sleeping and lived inside a complete story. In the dream, I took a train from New York to New Orleans. When I arrived, I went for a walk down a quiet street, lined on either side with tall, elegant houses and ancient oak trees. I don't know how this dreamscape had made it into my subconscious image bank, because at that point in my life I had never seen the actual New Orleans in a waking state. In the dream, a woman walked beside me as we went beneath the canopy of oaks, whose branches met overhead and dappled the street with shadows. Green sunlight filtered through the leaves. The woman turned to me and said, "You know, you might become an interesting writer if you move to New Orleans."

(Note she said *interesting* writer, not great writer. Before this dream, it would not have occurred to me that it was better to be interesting than great.)

When I woke from the dream, I wrote it down in my notebook and puzzled over it. I didn't know what to make of this message. It seemed important, but what was I supposed to do? Just pack up and leave because a dream told me so? Not likely. Besides, I was still hooked on New York and didn't see any reason to leave.

Several months after the dream, I had an occasion to see the actual New Orleans for the first time. The magazine I was working for at the time sent me there to do a story. I stayed in the French Quarter, half a block off Bourbon Street at the Hotel Maison de Ville, which had a secluded brick courtyard brimming with philodendron and fan palms. The time was a few weeks before Christmas, the off-season for New Orleans tourism, and the Quarter was nearly empty when I arrived. A dead town, it seemed, as I drove past silent, shuttered houses girdled with creeping moss.

The atmosphere shifted when I got to Bourbon Street, which never dies, and never sleeps either. The music from the bars kept me awake all night. So I had no choice. I got out of bed, got dressed, and walked the streets. As Walter Anderson (sometimes called "the Van Gogh of the South") once wrote, "Everything I see is new and strange." That was how I felt when I saw New Orleans for the first time. I was like a dry sponge, and I absorbed the damp air along with each fresh shock to my dulled senses. Every corner I turned brought me a sound or color that I can still summon from memory: the sudden trumpeting of the paddleboat horn sounding on the Mississippi River, the dirty white paint on the shop fronts along Decatur Street, the brick side of a house slowly undressing as the aged mortar fell away, the deep hush of the night air, as if the city held its breath when I crossed Rampart Street into the Quarter.

During this first visit, I learned that in an earlier age, the Louisiana Office of Tourism had put out the slogan "Dream State" to promote the 1984 World's Fair. It was an apt phrase that should have stuck but didn't. From the moment I arrived in New Orleans, everything I saw had the almost alarming clarity of a dream image. Each seemed freighted with significance deeper than a surface understanding would yield. I felt called to pay close attention.

Drawn by the angle of the light that fell in a casual slant against the whitewashed buildings, I walked toward Royal Street one afternoon. I had never seen sunlight *recline* in such a way. There were two people making music in the street. A man sat on an overturned plastic tub and huffed into a harmonica. Beside him, a woman played a washboard strapped to her chest. Her hands made a syncopated blur along the tin ridges, a rapid clicking metallic sound like insects dancing, and she swayed to her own rhythms. Her loose hair flew around her arms. Her pink lipstick shone in the light. The woman leaned back and closed her eyes. She couldn't tell if anyone in her small audience was dropping money into the basket. She turned her face into the late afternoon sun and strummed her washboard. She was lost in her music, blind to the world outside her song.

As I watched her and listened, I realized that I wanted to be lost like that. I wanted to give up caring what I looked or sounded like. To be released from the tyranny of striving. I admired this woman's freedom. I liked how she lived in her skin. And I suddenly got it. Here was the thing missing from my own skin. Me. I was just a big thought balloon floating down the sidewalk. I was twenty-eight years old, and I had not yet descended into my own skin. It was a good insight, but I still didn't know what it would take to get there.

19

On the last day of my visit, I walked toward Esplanade Avenue at the back end of the Quarter. When I got there I stopped, and it seemed everything around me and in me stopped as well. Here was the street I had seen in my dream several months before. In an instant, I recognized the quality of stillness in the air, the trees and shadows. The dissolving vapors of my dream life had pressed through the veil into the concrete realm of my waking life. This was too freaky, even for me. So I just stood there, my busy mind startled into blankness.

Esplanade Avenue was quiet save for the clip-clop of hooves as a man in a horse-drawn cart rolled past. It was not one of those fancy carriages that convey tourists through the Vieux Carré, but a long wooden flatbed, a working cart. The man had been selling fruits and vegetables from the back of it. Now he and his horse were done for the day. The small man sat folded over himself and wore deep grooves in his tough brown face like a walnut, unsmiling. He held the reins in a loose grasp with one hand and leaned his chin on the other. The horse appeared to know his own way home.

I stood at the edge of Esplanade Avenue and felt I was at the edge of my life. The sunlight, heavier than normal, pressed into the top of my head. The quiet of the street stilled my rising urge to flee. The sudden appearance of the hurried, mindful horse and the small, dark man—all these elements made the air rich with potential and produced a sensation that I stood at a threshold. I was between the worlds.

Tennessee Williams has written that in New Orleans, "An hour isn't an hour but a little piece of eternity dropped into your hands." It's true. This place has the power to make time stand still. It forces you to notice RIGHT NOW and gives sharpness to details that would normally escape into the quotidian flow.

I knew that I was onto something big. Here was evidence that dreams may come alive in the physical world. Most smart people, in the wake of such a revelation, would have followed the suggestion given by the dream. I was not that smart. After my visit to New Orleans, I returned to New York and stayed another four years. I had structures in place that supported me and kept my life rooted there. I had a job, a boyfriend, a great apartment. It took time for those structures to fall away before I could finally work up the guts to follow the dream's directions, leave New York and move to New Orleans . . . Boy, I sure do miss that apartment.

During the transition phase before the actual leap to New Orleans, while I observed the shambles of my days drifting to the ground around my feet, I was also surprised to notice that there was much about New York I didn't like anymore. For one thing, I had begun to dislike the stories I had to write in order to make a living. A turning point arrived when an editor called me and asked me to do a story on "The Five Best Ways to Burn Fat." The suggestion left me stunned by its utter vacuity. I couldn't think of a single thing to say in favor of this story idea. Perhaps I was in a rash mood, but in that moment, this story assignment seemed to typify the whole New York magazine world. This was as good as it would ever get. So I told the editor, since I would never read a story about the five best ways to burn fat, I was probably the wrong person to write one. She never called again.

Also, the city lacked quiet. All that hurly-burly that I had loved so much in the past was giving me a headache. I felt polluted and a little crazed by the constant noise. In addition, I didn't have a garden. It became important for me to start growing things with the accompaniment of the Earth's own music. To plunge my hands into soil and hear the natural sounds muffled beneath the urban clamor. I wanted more green space. New York had become a clanging, concrete prison.

So in tears I arrived at the realization that my love affair with Manhattan was over, and I had to find a new home. But where could I go after New York and not be bored? I bought a plane ticket to New Orleans. My dream from years earlier had remained at the back of my mind, and I hauled it out of storage. Now seemed like a good time to test it out. I would go for another visit to New Orleans to see if it felt like a possible next home. Perhaps I had imagined the whole dreamscape-come-alive thing that had happened the first time I went there, but the memory still attracted me.

I stayed in a rambling old bed-and-breakfast in the Garden District hosted by a woman who wore voluminous flowered dusters, piled her hair in an oily gray bird's nest, and screamed whenever the telephone rang. I rented a bike and rode all over the city, taking the measure of the land. When I wasn't biking, I walked uptown and downtown, looking and drinking in the greenness of everything, the obscene abundance of foliage swelling over fences, tree roots erupting out of the cracked sidewalks. The life that roiled beneath this city was too strong to be contained by anything so ordinary as concrete.

Everywhere I went, I struck up conversations with the people I met, telling them my vague plans and asking what they thought. They all told me to come to New Orleans and gave me advice on neighborhoods. I was not convinced. The city was pleasant enough, but I didn't feel ready to make a commitment to moving there. I wasn't clear on what would lead me into such a decision, so I walked the streets like an innocent fool, waiting for a sign.

Toward the end of my week's stay, I stopped at a coffee shop in the Garden District. I studied my street map while I sat at one of the outdoor tables. The map showed there was a Constance Street nearby, and I decided my visit would not be complete until I had walked on my namesake street. At the table next to me there was a couple, a man and a woman, who laughed and flirted with each other. They were loud and irritating. So I folded up my map and set off on my journey.

I had walked a few blocks when a car pulled up beside me. The window rolled down and a woman called to me from the passenger seat. It was the woman I had just seen at the coffee shop. The man she had been laughing with was driving.

"Hi there!" the woman said. "Listen, I noticed back there that you were looking at a map. So I guess you're not from around here, are you?"

"No, I'm here for a visit. Why do you ask?"

"Look, we just wanted to help you out. That direction you're heading . . . it's a bad area. You don't want to be walking this way."

"I don't?"

"No, you really don't." The woman's voice was more strident now. "Turn around right now and go back the way you came."

Puzzled, I looked farther down the street. I didn't understand what she was getting at. This peaceful block didn't seem any different from the block where we had all just been drinking coffee. What was the cause for such alarm? Chasing me down in their car to deliver this dire warning? Then it dawned on me what she probably meant. I must have been walking toward a block where African American people lived. *That's* what made it bad in this woman's view. Okay, now I disliked her even more than when she had been irritating me in the coffee shop.

I have never been good at controlling my face, and so I thanked the woman as politely as I could, while struggling to mask my distaste for our conversation. They peeled away from the curb in a big hurry. Maybe they were offended that I didn't appreciate their Good Samaritan effort. Or perhaps they were afraid for their own safety. Either way, I didn't care. I kept walking in the direction I had begun.

Years later, I recalled the woman and her words as if they were parts of a dream. Taken as an archetypal encounter, her message resonated in a much larger way. *Turn around and go back the way you came.* Sometimes dreams will throw a trickster figure in your way, a test to see if you are brave enough to follow the challenging path. There is no salvation without temptation. That's how I saw this woman. She offered the lure of a kind of safety, the illusion that the familiar is better. She represented fear-based thinking, terror of the darkness, the false belief that the unknown must be dangerous. I didn't want that anymore. If I obeyed the woman's instructions, then I would return to an unsatisfying past. I wanted to change my life. This was *my* dream, and I would not go back. I wanted to discover things strange and new. I continued my walk towards Constance Street.

When I got there, I found it to be a lovely street. Modest, gentle, graceful—all the qualities you would expect from a street so beautifully named. I made a left turn onto Constance, ambled along for a couple blocks, and then for no reason at all made another left turn and walked up that block. I was enjoying the sound of the breeze riffling through the oak leaves. A few steps farther, I came to a tall two-story house with a wide front porch and a pink flowering vine curled along the fence. The door to the house was open. A woman stood on the porch, jangling keys in her hand. There was a "For Rent" sign in front of the house. I stopped at the gate and smiled at the woman.

"Are you here to see the house?" she asked.

I opened my mouth, and the word "yes" came out.

The woman with the keys was a real estate agent. She had been waiting on the porch to show the house to someone who had not kept the appointment. I happened to wander by while she was still waiting for this no-show.

Next thing I knew, I was getting a tour of the house. It was perfect. It had dark hardwood floors and those airy nineteenth-century ceilings that stretched up for, oh, I don't know, twelve or thirty feet. The bedroom faced two floor-length windows that opened onto a balcony. There was a fenced-in yard for my dog to run around in, a side gallery and a garden below for the basil, rosemary, and mint. The rent, by New York standards, was crazy cheap.

That afternoon, I signed the lease. The next day I returned to New York, packed up my apartment, said goodbye to my friends, and announced I would be moving to New Orleans. One friend of mine, a journalist who would never disentangle himself from New York, said, "Well, I guess New Orleans is probably the only city in the world you can move to that won't make your New York friends think you had sold out."

My departure from New York also represented a break from my origins, or so I hoped. None of my siblings had ever lived more than a couple hundred miles from our ancestral home in New Jersey. Here I was moving over twelve hundred miles away, and to a different time zone as well. This sent shock waves through the family. To this day, my mother remains incapable of acknowledging there is a time difference between New Jersey and New Orleans, or that I am a vegetarian. Both these facts reside in the "unacceptable" file.

A few days before I left, I visited my family. When the time came for me to leave, and I was walking out the door, my father grasped me by the upper arm. "Don't go," he pleaded.

"Dad, I'm leaving right now." I tried to twist out of his hand. He tightened his grip. He was hurting my arm.

"Don't go!" He said it again, louder this time. I had never seen such undisguised fear in his face before. I didn't know where this was coming from. He should have known, of course, that this sabotage attempt only fueled my determination to go. I had to get away from this love that strangles. He seemed like another obstacle put there to test my strength.

In the end, I won. I wrenched myself free, literally and otherwise, from my past and my father's grasp. Birth is never easy, nor is rebirth. So it was with this bumpy exit that I landed on the path to my new life.

I arrived in New Orleans in August, height of the hurricane season. This month and I must have some kind of karma together. It seemed that just about every major event of my life in New Orleans would transpire in August, when the heat was like a coat of cement. On the evening that I first drove into the city, my poor dog panting in the back seat of our car that lacked air conditioning, a terrific storm tortured the purple sky. The stream of traffic on the I-10 overpass took me past the tops of buildings. To my left, I saw a warehouse, probably struck by lightning, had caught fire. The licking flames reached up to the guardrail of the highway. A car horn honked. Distracted by the fire, I looked to my right and saw a man driving along beside me, waving, smiling, and trying to get my attention. *Gosh people are friendly here.* Then the man lifted his pelvis off the seat to display what would normally be hidden inside his now unzipped pants. He gestured toward his priapic majesty with affable pride, clearly expecting me to agree that no one else in the world possessed one quite like this.

What a memorable welcome. And what a wild kingdom I had chosen as my new home. Everything I had known, everything I had assumed to be true and safe about the world had fallen away like an old, dried scab. Underneath I was fresh and sensitive to whatever came next.

The house I had found near Constance Street was just the beginning of my adventure. Over time, I bounced to other apartments, jobs, and boyfriends. Nothing stuck, but I had a hell of a lot of fun. Walking with spectacular otherworldly creatures in the Krewe of St Anne on Mardi Gras morning, midnight swims in the lake, steamy gin-soaked afternoons under the rain rattling the porch roof, lots of pesto that I made from the basil growing in my garden, the buzz of cicadas swelling the summer dusk, the mourning doves calling at daybreak, the metallic taste in the air of a thunderstorm rolling in from the Gulf. The furry leaves of the fig tree outside my bathroom window brushed the screen that allowed a light breeze to waft over my skin while I reclined in a tub of tepid water and turned the soil of my thoughts.

Yes, everything was strange and new, and the experiences that this place

25

gave me ran the pleasure scale from soothing to exhilarating. At times, the city threw something in my path that left me gasping with shock. For example, New Orleans is the only place where I have heard the phrase "nigger lover" used as a direct address. It happened on Halloween night. I was driving down Saint Charles Avenue with some friends to a party. We were in costume. I was a witch, as usual. A car drove along beside us. It carried two men and two women, who looked like they were in their late twenties. The car swerved toward mine, and the driver was yelling something at us. We couldn't make it out, so my friend in the passenger seat rolled down the window.

"Nigger lover!" the guy shouted. "Yankee, go home!"

His words struck like a snakebite. My friend quickly rolled up the window to shut out this noise. I sped off to get away from the car. Our jolly evening was poisoned. *Come on, this can't be real.* I felt as though I had fallen into some kind of nasty comic book. If the scene hadn't been so ugly, it would have been absurd.

For a while I puzzled over how this guy had chosen me as a target. Then it came to me. My car, an inheritance from my family, was still registered to my parents' home and had New Jersey license plates. That must be how the guy had sussed out the "Yankee" part. Then, of course, it's just a short hop from there to "nigger lover." Why, everyone knows the State of New Jersey is a veritable hotbed of "nigger lovers." People in New Jersey stroll along the boulevard all the time and greet each other by saying, "Hey, don't you just love niggers?" And then replying, "Oh, yes! Niggers are my favorite!"

I just couldn't grasp it rationally. People didn't really *say* that anymore, did they? Certainly not without quotation marks. The phrase, which I had never heard spoken aloud before, had an almost quaint, prehistoric quality to it. Aren't we past all that by now? Apparently not. Just like the man said, "The past is never dead. It's not even past."

Most disturbing was the guy's virulent tone of voice, the way his face contorted with the effort to propel the words like bullets, and his friends howling with obscene glee in the backseat. All these pointed to a deeper well of loathing than I had ever known up close. I finally put my finger on why the phrase disgusted me at such a profound level. It joined "nigger," a word designed to cause pain, humiliation, and fear, to the word "lover," a word designed to cause happiness. It was a vicious misuse of the word "love." A rape through language. My ears felt dirty from hearing it.

I had gone looking for a new life, and I found it. In addition to offering her many delights, this city also taught me that anything at all might rise up from her chthonic ground of being. New Orleans makes no guarantee of sweet dreams only. This episode was a reminder that in this "Dream State" the city functions as the subconscious. Its essence remains undiscovered country. Underneath the life here, there stirs a dark chaos that defies explication. The city thrums with this unstructured creative power that is a rich mine for all the sensual pleasure and heart-stopping beauty. Yet we must not forget that this chaos will give birth to all the raw passions. Rage, joy, attraction, arousal, aggression, fear, ecstasy, loathing, lust, love. Whatever seeks expression most urgently will come roaring out of the darkness. It is a pure source of psychic material without filters to keep down the scary stuff. New Orleans taught me that when you embark on an adventure, if you truly want to change your life, you have to be willing to absorb all the shocks, both pleasurable and ugly.

This was the alchemical swamp I lived in. It introduced new elements into the laboratory of my being. In so doing, it tainted and changed me in ways that I would spend years sorting through, trying to see myself whole.

Although I loved New Orleans, still I was restless, not sure where I wanted to be. By then, I had spent well over a decade moving every year or so, either to a new apartment or to a new city: Philadelphia, Baltimore, New York, then New Orleans. In one house where I lived for two years, I never bothered to hang pictures on the walls. I had grown accustomed to my light-footed ways, my loose commitment to dwelling places. This pattern held true after I got to New Orleans. I left for a year to attend graduate school, where I got a degree in creative writing. All my New Orleans friends assumed I'd never come back. But then when school was done and I experienced the typical postgraduate vacuum, I had to fill it. So, I moved back to New Orleans because I couldn't think of anywhere else I wanted to live. Besides, by then I had warped into a shape that fit New Orleans and none other. No decent city would have me.

Upon my return, I moved into the neighborhood around Bayou Saint

John for the first time. Here the city captured me in its spell for good. I had traveled twelve hundred miles to find a place that smelled like the place I had always known. My feet got stuck in the mud. I knew that at last I would stay put for a while.

I AM SAVED, AGAIN

One June morning, I was walking home from the informal play date I take Lance to in the park next door to Cabrini High School. It was the beginning of the steamy season. Everything was swollen and green. The surface of the bayou barely moved. The air was thick with the distant promise of a thunderstorm. For this little while, the bayou was bright and hot.

As I walked in the wet, uncut grass, Lance loped ahead, off the leash, nose to the ground, looking for something rancid to eat. It was too hot for jogging, but there was a die-hard runner passing us, a square-built man with a gray regulation crew cut and USMC T-shirt. He was running like a machine. It made me sweat just to look at him. Lance got himself tangled up in the jogging man's feet, but then earned a pat on the head by being charming about it. *There's a man who loves dogs*, I noted, and then continued following Lance in my customary dream bubble, not fully in the world. A gradual awareness nosed into my reverie that I had been hearing an intrusive sound for several minutes, but it hadn't fully registered yet. So I stopped and listened with more attention. There it was again. Fierce splashing and that unmistakable high-pitched yelping that I know so well. Dog in distress!

For some weeks now, I had been hearing persistent rumors from more than one source that there were alligators living in Bayou Saint John. I thought it unlikely, because this bayou doesn't seem like the ideal

29

environment for alligators. It's a wide-open space; there wouldn't be enough places for them to hide, not enough food, and too many people around. I'm no expert on alligators, but I am pretty sure they'd rather stay away from us.

Whether the rumors were true or not, the possibility of alligators swimming in this bayou had led me to decide that Lance would not be permitted to swim in it ever again. I also warned other dog owners not to put their dogs' lives at risk. It may sound cruel to deny my dog a cooling swim in the bayou, and certainly Lance would agree. He is an avid chaser of sticks and tennis balls into the bayou, although I have noticed that he won't go into the water by himself—only if another dog goes in first. It's as though he wants a swimming buddy to prove it's safe before he will commit himself to a full immersion. My dog seems to have the same timorousness around dark water as I do.

During the hottest weather, the bayou is a popular swimming hole for dogs from blocks and blocks around. We humans stand there watching. *We'd* never go in that gurky water. Instead, we take vicarious refreshment from the spectacle of our dogs diving and splashing. There are few things more pleasurable than watching a dog, caked in mud, slavering after a tennis ball, take one more frenzied plunge into the bayou. We all pray for that freedom and joy, and yet seldom have it. Still, I can't stomach the chance that an alligator might swim up from the depths to take a chunk out of my dog's gut. So Lance has to maintain a respectful coexistence with the water too.

(Later, I amended my prohibition against swimming in the bayou because I felt sorry for Lance that he couldn't join his friends for a cool dip on hot days. Lance is now permitted to go into the water up to his armpits, but no farther.)

Alligators were the first thing that came to my mind on this summer morning when I heard splashing and yelping. My worst fear had been realized. An alligator was eating a dog! In my bayou!

I turned around and squinted across the water. On the far side, against the high concrete bulkhead, I saw the splashing. Sure enough, a dog was struggling to pull himself out of the bayou, scrabbling his toenails on the rough surface. But the top edge of the bulkhead was too high for him to gain any purchase there. I looked to my right and then to my left. I had to make a quick decision about which bridge to use to get to the other side of the bayou. I was standing about halfway between the Dumaine Street Bridge and the Magnolia Bridge. I started running toward the Magnolia Bridge, yelling over my shoulder, "C'mon Lance! Let's go!"

I ran about twenty steps, not an easy thing when you're wearing sandals in long wet grass, before I realized that it was actually a shorter distance to the Dumaine Street Bridge. So I turned and ran back in the opposite direction, where I passed Lance, who had not budged. He was sitting in the grass and watching me with a baffled expression. Why had his pleasant morning been disturbed? I snapped the leash onto his collar and tried to pull him along. I implored him: "Lance, get moving! Quick! We've got to help that other dog!"

Lance dug in his toes and balked. *No, we don't gotta anything*, he seemed to be saying. *This is* my *walk, and I'll take it the way I want.* I gave the leash a sharp tug and urged him into a grudging trot behind me.

Before he came to his princely existence of undiluted pleasure, Lance was a beat-up, woebegone piece of trash I picked up on the street. I may be making up this next part, because with dogs as with infants, we don't know for sure what they're thinking; we can only speculate. But I believe it is precisely because Lance had such a harsh puppyhood that he is so unenthusiastic about saving other stray puppies. Now that he lives the fat life, he doesn't have much sympathy for newcomers who might compete with him for the abundance of snacks and good fortune that has been flowing his way for years now. Far from prompting largesse of spirit, Lance's rough early days seem to have made him a savvy survivor, pragmatic to the point of brutality. He takes the attitude that *he's* found *his* gravy train, so now all those other lost dogs, they can just move along and find their own soft touch.

By the time I reached the Dumaine Street Bridge, I was not only completely winded and drenched in sweat, but I had also figured out that there was no alligator involved in this scenario. This dog had just fallen into the bayou and couldn't get out on his own. Some parts of the bayou's edge are grassy mud that gradually slopes downward. Dogs can easily walk in and out of the water there. In other parts, there is this high concrete bulkhead where the water is immediately deep, and there is no congenial slope for a dog to stroll up to the bank. A dog who didn't know better could struggle to his death here.

Clearly dogs cannot be held responsible for what they don't know. Yet, their lapses in judgment continue to cause a lot of trouble for us humans. Particularly me, it seemed. As I came off the end of the bridge, hampered by the reluctant Lance I was dragging behind, and we closed in on the jogging USMC man in front of us, I recalled a similar incident that happened when I was ten years old. It was summer, and I was hanging out in our yard, gradually becoming aware of an anguished howling that filled the air around me. Once I started to listen to it, I realized that I had been hearing this sound for quite some time. It had slowly leached into my awareness, as if I were waking up to it from a deep sleep. I was shocked to learn that it was possible to hear something without listening.

Once I became aware of the howling, I began to look for the source. I couldn't see anything. Nothing in our serene backyard could be making this sound. It seemed to be coming out of the air itself. I walked around the house, up and down the bulkhead along the bay behind our house, and saw nothing. Meanwhile the howl grew more anguished. I couldn't imagine what could create a noise so drenched in fear and despair. The sound shredded my heart each time it rose on the air. I wondered why no one else in my family heard the howling. How could they be deaf to such suffering?

Finally I figured out that the howling grew a little louder when I was near the water. So I went onto our dock, kneeled down at the edge, and looked underneath. There, caught in the crossed planks between the pilings, was a black and white dog. And he was howling for his life. He must have fallen into the bay somewhere and then drifted or swum with the current until he got tangled up in our dock, where he decided to stop trying to save his own life and ask for help instead.

Even though I was only ten at the time, I knew what to do. I called the dog to me. He let go of his fragile perch underneath our dock and let himself into the deep and unresisting water again. The water that I'm sure terrified him. But he trusted me enough to do it. He let go of this relatively safe place because he believed I would bring him well and truly home.

He started swimming toward my voice. I called him "sweet" because I didn't know his name yet. I stood up and ran back along the edge of the bulkhead still calling the dog. And still he swam toward my words as I ran. I knew what I was doing. There was a ten-foot drop between me on the bulkhead and the dog in the water. So I had to get him to swim over to our neighbor's dock because they had a ramp that went down to the water's surface. If he could swim to me there, I'd be able to reach down and grab him.

The dog was so tired from his long struggle in the water before he arrived at our dock, yet he gave it one more try. He swam to me. What a brave and strong and smart dog! I ran and shouted encouraging words to him. Somehow he understood. If I live forever, I'll never know how dogs can understand our words, but they do.

By this time, my mother had gotten into the act. She ran behind me as I pulled the dog through the water with my words. It made her uncomfortable that something big was happening in her domain that she was not controlling. She wanted to put a stop to it, or slow it down. I heard her anxious, strident voice, and none of it swayed me. As I clambered over the fence between our yard and our neighbor's yard, my mother shouted, "Watch out, he might bite you!" I leaped away from her. Her voice did not pull me the way this dog's howling did, echoing the desperation in my own chest. This dog and I had a destiny to keep.

I ran down the ramp, my sneakers sliding on the seaweed to the edge of the water. The dog could see me closer now, and he quickened his sturdy dog paddle, closing the few remaining yards between us. I reached down, grabbed the scruff of his neck, and lifted him out of the water. In a single fluid gesture, one of the most unselfconscious acts of my life, I folded the dog into my body and wrapped my arms around him. The dog pressed his black snout into my neck as if I was the whole world, and I was. His entire being, drenched in relief, sank into my chest and my belly. I had never felt a person hug me in the way this wet dog did. Finally I knew what love and gratitude felt like, and for a few minutes before my mother showed up, the howling stopped.

It's hard to say if I remembered all this as I was running on the Dumaine Street Bridge. Or if this connection occurred later when I began writing.

I'd say that this story mixed with sense memories always hovers just below the surface of my mind. Like the submerged car parts and grocery carts in the bayou, they can be easily reached if the circumstances are right and you know where to look. So it may have been the emotional force of that dog rescue during the summer of my tenth year that fueled my dash along the bayou in New Orleans in the spring of my forty-third year. Certainly, little else could get my creaky, out-of-shape self to move that fast in that heat while also wearing sandals.

As I ran up behind the USMC man still grinding at his even pace, I was gasping for breath, and yet I managed to say, "There's a dog drowning up ahead." Without the slightest surprise or pause in his gait, the man instantly accelerated his running. He knew what to do. I could see years of military training in his quick and able response, his surge of speed. While I limped behind, he scanned the surface of the water, spotted the flopping, yelping dog, and zeroed in on him. By the time I caught up to them, the man was trying to reach the dog, but the dog wouldn't let him. He didn't trust anyone at that moment. When the man grabbed for him, the dog paddled away, still yelping, and then swerved back toward the bulkhead and scraped his toenails on it. He kept swimming along the wall. Now he was trying to get away from us. This animal was crazed with fear, not capable of understanding that we were trying to help. Even so, I got down on my knees to try my hand at it.

"Careful he doesn't bite you," Mister USMC said behind me as I reached. Well, I'd heard *that* before. But I knew what to do. I just had to get a solid fistful of the back of his neck and I could scoop him out of the water. I managed to place my hand on his neck, felt the wet fur and dense flesh there. As he slipped out of my fingertips, I noticed this was a solidly packed puppy with a great muscled future ahead of him—part rottweiler, most likely. Sure enough, the brutish mongrel turned his head and snapped at my hand. He missed. But I could see he still had his milk teeth.

The man told me to give him Lance's leash. He would make a lasso out of it. Great idea! We were a team now. I ran over to Lance, who was observing all this drama with bored detachment. He was still not fully supporting the rescue effort.

The man fashioned a slipknot out of Lance's leash and dangled it in the water ahead of the puppy, who swam right into it. He then drew the loop closed on the puppy's neck and swung him up, casting a sparkling arc of bayou water through the air, and deposited him on the grass, where he lay on his side, stunned. This got Lance's attention. True to his nature, Lance closed in on the nearly drowned pup. He darted in and out, nipping at the puppy's back legs, trying to rouse some reaction out of the poor inert animal. I shooed Lance away and knelt beside the puppy.

He lay in the grass, his body deflated, no fight left in him, no way of knowing what had just happened to him, or how he had suddenly moved from the water into the air and then dry land. His posture was one of deep, uncomprehending exhaustion, as if he had just been born a second time, brought through the darkness against his will, and set back onto the wheel of life without any hint of how or why he'd gotten there—or what he was supposed to do next—which is how each of us comes into this world, after all. The pup lay still on the grass, only his wet, furred ribcage huffing. He lifted his head and looked at me with sorrow, as if to say, *Why did you bother? I'm just a dog.*

I was worried he might not be able to breathe well enough, so I made a move to loosen the leash from his neck.

"That dog is gonna bite you," the man warned me.

"It's okay," I whispered to the puppy. "I promise I will never hurt you." I reached down to the knotted leash. He let me touch the back of his neck. I tugged the loop over his head and released him. The puppy didn't do anything for a few seconds. Just looked at me. Then, like a pistol shot, he sprang to his feet and pelted across the street, around the corner, and disappeared, running in that foot-flopping way of puppies, not looking where he was going, just running for the sake of getting gone. I didn't realize until he had disappeared that I had expected him to stay. I felt sad. Lance looked after him with his usual philosophical absence of regret.

"That dog sure didn't want to stick around here," said Mister USMC.

"I hope he knows his way home," I answered.

A DOG'S LIFE

THE BAYOU IS A NATURAL ALTAR FOR RITUAL AND CEREMONY, A MAGNET that draws people to its edge to conduct their spiritual transactions. Or anything that requires a special concentration of energy. On my daily walk I once stumbled across a man, wrapped in saffron robes, who sat at the edge of the water with his legs folded beneath him in lotus position and his hands resting lightly on his knees. His eyes were closed, and his lips moved in silence. There is a Krishna temple a few blocks away on Esplanade Avenue, and this man no doubt walked from there to the bayou for his morning meditation and chanting. I called him the Bayou Sadhu.

Another sunny afternoon, I watched a young man, naked to the waist, stand at the edge of the water while playing a *berimbau*, an Afro-Brazilian instrument that usually accompanies the swirling feints and thrusts of combatants in the martial art of capoeira. This slender boy was alone as he played his music and hummed a soft song. His back gleamed with sweat as he stared at the water with perfect, unselfconscious focus. The neighborhood business of cars along Moss Street, dog walkers like me, all sorts of noisy city distractions flitted around him. His gaze never wavered from the bayou. His music flowed uninterrupted. He was in the depths, all right. Dragged right down to the basement of his soul.

Each year on Yom Kippur, my neighbor Rachel walks to the bayou and contemplates her misdeeds from the previous year. Then she places bread on the water. The bread has absorbed these sins and takes them away, leaving Rachel cleansed to begin a new year. The bayou takes it all back and changes it into something else.

One of my favorites was the man who came buzzing past the bayou on a motorbike one morning as I paused near the Magnolia Bridge to drop Lance's morning deposit in the trashcan. He pulled up onto the grassy edge near the water and stopped, allowing the engine to shift down to idle. He wore a helmet and had a gray beard. He was dressed in a short-sleeved blue-and-red plaid shirt, black pants, and shiny black shoes. Everything about him suggested that he faced an unexciting day at the office. He probably worked in one of those hermetically sealed tall buildings where the worker drones grow wan from the lack of natural light and air. The man sat with his hands folded in his lap, while his motorbike thrummed beneath his straddled legs. He closed his eyes and lowered his face in an attitude of prayer. He remained in that pose for a few minutes, still and silent, in the dark inner space of his own contemplation. Then he kicked his cycle into gear and roared down Moss Street.

It pleased me to know that I was not the only one who saw the bayou as a holy place. When our friends Kellie and Stephen told me they planned to bring their one-year-old son, Jake, to the bayou to baptize him, I understood why. Kellie had been living near the bayou for years. Like me, she had fallen into a deep, mystical attachment to it. We had only talked vaguely around this shared sense of the bayou, but when she told me she wanted to consecrate the life of her new child in this water, I understood without explanation that the bayou would impart to this little boy both an initiation and a protection. My imagination went to work, and I constructed the scene. She would hold Jake by the heel and dip him into Bayou Saint John—in the manner of Achilles's mother, who dipped her son into the River Styx to give him immortal strength. For the rest of his life, I believed this golden, curly-headed Jake would possess the fierce heart of a warrior. Though just as powerful, Bayou Saint John would grant a different quality of strength to Jake than the Styx gave to Achilles. Jake's immersion in the bayou would give him valor in the face of mystery. His battle would move against the fear that brings on numbness and sleepy disregard for all the sharp beauties that surround us. Jake would go into the dark water with eyes open to see what he could see.

My husband and I became engaged while standing on the Magnolia Bridge. Although it spans *my* bayou, this is *our* bridge. The escapade started one cold and windy January night with dinner at our favorite restaurant. As we were driving home from the restaurant, Sean stopped the car, turned to me, and asked, "Do you mind if I put a blindfold on you?"

"Not at all! Please! By all means, go right ahead!" My usual answer.

So he tied a scarf around my head, blanketing me in complete darkness. Then he kidnapped me! He began to drive in a serpentine pattern all over the city, arbitrary left turns here, capricious right turns there, trying to throw me off. I tried to keep track in my head, sensing each turn and visualizing where we might be going. Part of me always wants to get ahead of surprises, even the nice ones. When we paused at what must have been a red light, I rolled down my window and, blinded as I was, shouted to what I believed was a car in the next lane, "Hey! Are we anywhere near the I-10 overpass?" No answer. I was lost in the dark.

Finally Sean brought the car to a full stop somewhere and asked me to wait. "How long?" I asked from behind my scarf.

"Oh, about ten minutes."

"Ten minutes! Could I have something to read?"

My future husband got out of the car and went round to the back, where I heard him make rustling sounds. I also heard clinking sounds. Then he was gone. Ten minutes can feel like ten years when you have been blindfolded, even if you have been blindfolded by someone you like a lot. When he came back to get me, I was about ready to spoil everything by tearing the scarf from my head and yelling at him. But he persuaded me to go along with the game a little while longer. He took my hand and guided me over surfaces that felt like pavement, then grass, down a curb, and then across a street. I drew on my store of sleuthing tips gleaned from Nancy Drew Mystery Stories, and took careful note of whatever evidence of my surroundings I could sense through my own footsteps. Even so, I couldn't place where we were.

Then he removed my blindfold. Ta dum! We were standing on the

Magnolia Bridge, over Bayou Saint John, just a few blocks from where we lived. After all that intrigue, all that driving uptown and downtown, our journey had brought us home.

He had set up a beautiful altar on the bridge, decorated with silk pillows, a large vase of flowers, and a circle of about thirty votive candles. As we stood there, the wind blew out the candles and knocked over the vase of flowers.

"One day we're going to laugh about this," I said. We were already laughing. I still had no idea what was coming.

Sean and I met when I showed up at the yoga studio where he taught. A friend of mine asked me to accompany him to a "chanting class" there. I had no idea what this was, but I said, "Okay. Sure, I'll try it." When I got there, I sat down on the floor with the other people. Sean was dressed all in white, and he clasped a drum under one arm. He perched cross-legged on a high bolster so he was a little bit above the rest of us. Sean explained that the class was based on a devotional practice that originates in India, called *kirtan* which consists of people gathering to sing in a group. The songs are mantras or prayers to various Hindu deities, which when chanted repeatedly, bring about significant changes, both in the world and in the person speaking the mantra. The practice is based on the simple idea that words have power. I couldn't have agreed more.

On this night, my first experience of Sean, he sang a mantra to Shiva, the destroyer. First he coached us in pronouncing these unfamiliar words: *Om Namaha Shivaya*. Then we all just fell into it, repeating them in unison to the accompaniment of Sean's drum and led by his strong voice. We were tentative at first, but the other voices gradually grew in force and volume around me. I sat with my eyes closed and tried to keep up with the pace. Before too long I noticed an increasing roar coming from the direction of where Sean was sitting. It was like a dam opening to allow a thundering rush of sound. I opened one eye to peek at him. He sang with such effort that his face had turned bright red. I closed my eyes again and allowed the buffeting storm of his voice to surround me. It was magnificent and filled the space. Sean's singing was larger even than Sean himself.

Much later I realized that he had been pouring it on for my benefit.

The peacock fanning his tail feathers. That was okay. I enjoyed it, and it worked. I have always had a weakness for show-offs.

After class, I thanked him. Sean tilted his head to one side and turned the high beam of his twinkly gaze upon me. But I didn't follow up on this flirtation and stayed away for a year. Something about Sean unnerved me. I sensed that his was no mere casual twinkle. It had purpose and promised a great deal more than I was ready for. For the most part, I wasn't ready because I was disgusted with men at the time. The details aren't important. Let's just say there wasn't a jury in the world that would convict me for saying that a lot of them turned out to be complete idiots, and leave it at that.

During my year of skulking around the outskirts of this potential relationship, I occasionally walked past the yoga studio where Sean taught, each time checking to see his name on the schedule of classes. I didn't actually go inside until after the death of my dog Henry. These events were connected.

Henry was a great chesty black Labrador with the heart of a lion and a head like a box of hammers. This dog had a superb sense of style, always hogged the limelight, and was an enthusiastic kisser. He also possessed a complex set of neuroses that made life with him thrilling to the point of insanity. For example, he picked hellacious fights with other dogs for no reason except that he enjoyed the exercise. He also suffered from a thunderstorm phobia so acute that he would plunge through the windows of my apartment in a crazed attempt to escape from the storm. Once he pried the burglar bars from a window with his teeth, tore the screws from the wood and bent the thick metal bars, so he could bash through the window glass. The dog was strong.

Henry had these window-jumping panic attacks only if he was alone. If I happened to be away from him on a stormy day, I would rush home at the first flicker of lightning, often to find a pile of broken glass on my porch and drips of blood, my dog's blood. Then I'd find Henry by following the trail of blood along the sidewalk. I got to be an expert at window glazing. After a while, when Henry had figured out that he could smash through a window and not die, he'd smash through windows during clear weather, just for the fun of it or because he felt like taking himself for a walk. Henry reminded me a lot of Bill Clinton—a huge pain in the ass, but so devastatingly handsome and charming and filled with such high self-regard that he effortlessly forced his way back into my forgiveness—ever in my heart, no matter how egregious his sins.

Life with Henry was not all hell. One of my favorite memories of him was when we went swimming in a pond hidden in the pinewoods of Mississippi, about an hour's drive from New Orleans, where some friends had a weekend getaway. There was an afternoon when Henry and I were there alone. Nothing between us and the trees but glorious hot sunshine and gritty cool water. Henry and I, both of us completely nude, spent hours of that day crashing into the water and chasing after a stick I had thrown far out into the center of the pond. We raced to where the stick floated, the two of us swimming side by side. I swam faster than Henry, tending to scoot through the water like a minnow while he trucked along more like a water buffalo. But I always let Henry get the stick. It seemed important to him that he should get the stick. Then I held onto his tail as he towed me toward shore. Henry clenched the tree branch (about the size of a baseball bat) in his strong teeth and made a frothy V-shaped ripple in the pond. The sunlight gleamed on his wet pelt. His muscled shoulders and big paws worked the water, and he snorted through his nose like a steam engine. I trailed in his wake, languid as a summer dream on my back in the muddy pond, while my big black dog pulled me back to land. Then we would do the whole thing all over again. He loved it.

Our long tour of veterinary medicine began one day in early summer when I looked at Henry and knew there was something not right about him. In his salad days, Henry had weighed in at ninety-eight pounds of unyielding gristle. Lately, he had slimmed down, although his appetite was as robust as ever. He still chased a tennis ball with the mad fervor of a serial killer. Still threw himself into the bayou like a man on fire. Even so, I took him to the vet and demanded that blood be taken and tests done.

"Test him," I said. "There is something not right."

Sure enough, the vet found lots of things wrong with him. Henry had reached nine years of age, and his body was not working. There was the heart murmur, the hypothyroid, the arthritis, the cataracts, and the non-regenerative anemia. For reasons that no one could explain to my satisfaction,

Henry's bone marrow had stopped producing "baby red blood cells," as the vet described them. His elderly red blood cells were sloughing off without replacements, leaving Henry with not enough blood.

Our vet is a beautiful dark-haired woman named Nicole. She looks like a supermodel and has a mind like a library. I have learned a lot from her over the years. Like many vets, while she appears coolly unimpressed with humans, she melts into helpless, goofy affection around dogs. They return her affection in buckets. (Lance will slip his tongue into Nicole's mouth every chance he gets.) Henry was crazy about her. She, I believed, was secretly in love with Henry herself. How could she not be? He had this devastating effect on all women. Nicole reassured me that it was not time to worry yet.

"It could be any one of a number of things," she said. "Let's eliminate all those possibilities before we go to cancer."

I couldn't pretend even to myself that Nicole had not said the word "cancer." Instead I put the word on a back shelf in my mind where it waited for me to return. Nicole and I were both eager to try lots of different possibilities. She told me that Henry's limp most likely came from the arthritis in his shoulder.

"Only have arthritis. Don't have cancer," I commanded him. Henry had always wanted, in spite of himself, to be an obedient dog. He was silent and patient with us as we progressed through tests for lead poisoning and a few other things that might be killing his baby red blood cells. He continued to lose weight and cooperated with taking his medications. The pill bottles lined up on my kitchen counter: acepromazine, soloxine, prednisone, piroxicam, and much later it was torbutrol for pain—but I'm getting ahead of myself. I felt like I was running a nursing home. The pills caused side effects. The steroids helped with his limp, but then he lost control of his bladder. I couldn't reproach him. He was so embarrassed. He sat in the kitchen doorway, his gaze lowered in shame, as I pulled the refrigerator away from the wall to mop up the yellow puddle that had pooled beneath it.

"You know, guy, I've been meaning to clean back here anyway," I told him. "Look at the dust bunnies! It's filthy. Really, it needed a good mopping." He was too smart to be fooled by my lie, but I think he appreciated the effort.

None of the tests showed anything to explain his loss of red blood cells. In the end, after weeks of searching for the answer, Nicole was able to diagnose Henry by petting him. During one of his checkups, Henry was perched like a nervous king, unsure of his throne, atop the high metal examining table. Nicole was running her hands over his body, to calm him and because she liked touching him. Her hand stopped when it passed over his shoulder. She found something that had not been there the last time she had examined him. In a short time, it had become as plain and dense as rock. Henry had a tumor embedded in the bone.

Once she pointed to it, I could see what was growing there. His right shoulder was larger than the other, so much so that it caused his elbow to bend inward from the added effort of supporting that side of his body. This, after all, had caused his limp. Who knows when this evil goblin began riding on my dog's shoulder. I touched my hand to it. The lump felt different from the rest of him. It lacked his supple vitality. Instead, it felt as unwholesome as I knew it was, like an inert chunk of cement emerging from his body.

"I'm sorry," Nicole said. "I don't need to run any more tests. I can tell what this is just by the feel of it." It was the tone of Nicole's voice that scared me. No longer reassuring me with a light air, she spoke with a toneless finality that she must have learned in her veterinary practice. She was reverting to strict medical training: This is how you give bad news to the humans, who are, after all, the ones who produce the messy emotional stuff. The animals themselves don't notice how the entire world changes after terrible words are spoken. True to my species, I sat down and cried. For his part, Henry looked with a worried expression at the floor, still only concerned that he might fall off the high metal examining table.

"I knew it," I said. "I just knew there was something wrong with him."

"That's what it means to love a dog," said Nicole. "You and Henry have an intuitive connection. You'll always know what's going on with him." Her eyes reddened, and her voice had lost some of its flatness. She was becoming a soft human again. She probably had to have a lot of conversations like this one. I felt sorry for her.

Despite the clear evidence on his shoulder, I wanted more. So I took Henry for x-rays to confirm with pictures what was happening inside his body. I stood beside Nicole as she tilted the gray, smoky pictures toward the fluorescent light from the ceiling. Together we looked at the inside of his chest while Henry sprawled on the floor, enjoying the air conditioning and licking his feet. Nicole drew an outline with her index finger of Henry's lungs on the x-ray. Then she drew my attention to the spray of whitish shadows. It had metastasized from his bones, and now he had lumps all through his chest, she explained. At any moment these lumps could cause his lungs to fill with blood.

"How could this happen?" I whispered.

"Because it's cancer," said Nicole. "Cancer is fast."

She told me that when the time came, I could bury him under my house if I wanted to. "It's illegal, but everyone does it," she said. "The main thing now is to keep him comfortable. As long as he's eating and walking, he's okay." Nicole also gave me the phone number of a company called Pet-A-Care that would cremate his body, if I preferred that option. I was crying so hard when she gave me the card that I couldn't read it. I don't know how I drove home.

A month later, on Thanksgiving Day, Henry came to dinner with me at a friend's house and was strong and lively. He chased our host's cat; he ate turkey and pumpkin pie; he swiped a hunk of bread out of someone's hand. He was rude. He was himself. He even dragged me onto the levee for a walk after dinner. It was probably this strenuous walk that started him on his downward turn. Later, during the night, he woke me to let him outside so he could vomit and pee. And then he collapsed on the grass. I carried him inside and put him down onto a futon I had dragged onto the living room floor and covered with a feather blanket.

In the morning, he was gasping so hard that Nicole made a house call. She told me that Henry was trying to die. She gave him a shot of Lasix to get the fluid out of his lungs. Henry ran outside and peed about two gallons, and then miraculously he calmed down. He was himself again, breathing normally although still shaky. Nicole also gave me a bottle of torbutrol to sedate him if he became distressed.

"I can put him down right now if you want," Nicole offered.

The understanding that it would be my choice and my responsibility to hasten Henry's death, so that he would not suffer unduly, had been on my mind since Nicole had found the tumor. At the rational level, I was willing and prepared for it. The only question was when to make this choice. I believed I owed Henry some of his own preference in the timing. He should live as long as any reasonable person (that would be me) could see that he was able to enjoy life. Because that's the whole point of a dog's life, right? To have pleasure. So, ever since his diagnosis, I had been clinging to the idea that as long as Henry could walk and eat, I didn't have to kill him.

But now it was time. Still, I didn't want him to die when he was so panicky and struggling. I felt encouraged by the effectiveness of this drug Lasix, and told Nicole that I wanted Henry to be stable first. That way we could schedule a time to put him to sleep, so he could go to his death when he was calm. I wanted him to slip away without pain or fear. Only later did I understand that I was trying too much to control Henry and orchestrate his death. I had overestimated my power in this situation. Henry had other plans.

I started him on the torbutrol at five that afternoon. He had begun gasping again—a rapid, agonizing rasp—and was getting agitated. I put my ear to his chest, and it sounded like high tide coming in every time he tried to expand his lungs. The medication took the edge off his anxiety, but then his blood pressure dropped so low that he kept going into shock. So I wrapped him in my sleeping bag, and he vomited on that. Whenever I got up to do something like put the sleeping bag in the wash or get towels to clean the mess, he tried to follow me by dragging himself off the bed and onto the floor, where he would vomit again. It took me a while to figure this out, but he was probably erupting with anxiety whenever I turned my back on him. So I stayed with him and gave him water to lap from my cupped palms.

Nicole called from home that night, and I told her that Henry and I had both had enough, and I would bring him into her office first thing in the morning for her to put him down. She told me to be there at eight o'clock. I lined up the pills on the table by the bed and figured I could dose him with the sedative every two hours and that would get us to eight o'clock the next morning. I told my mother when she called that I was contemplating putting a pillow over his face and finishing him that way because I couldn't stand the ragged sound of his breathing another second. My father, who is a surgeon, got on the phone and told me to dose him with all the torbutrol I had.

"Give it to him!" my father shouted. "Make him comfortable. That's all you can do now." His voice shook with emotion, surprising to me because he had never liked my dog. My father had greeted the news of Henry's cancer with malicious pleasure. "Oh, he'll be dead very soon," he had said. Then I remembered my father's mother, who had died of lung cancer in a hospital in Germany—far away from her beloved son. The myth my father had crafted around his mother's death is that she had asked one of her friends, a nurse in the hospital, to "slip her something"—an extra high dose of something, morphine most likely, to help her die. My father believes his mother chose her death, rather than wait passively for it to claim her, because it was too much of a coincidence that she had died on the anniversary of her birth.

When it came time for his midnight dose, Henry bit me on the thumb hard enough to draw blood. He had lost his tolerance for having pills shoved down his throat. This was the first time Henry had ever hurt me. I sucked my bloody wound, kissed his head, and apologized. Fortunately he didn't live long enough for me to try his two o'clock dose.

The end was subtle in contrast to all the drama beforehand. I was sitting beside him and writing in my journal. I could feel his rib cage pulsing against my thigh when I noticed that his breath had slowed. I hoped he might be falling asleep. But then I put my hand on his chest and listened as his breath got even slower. His chin lowered with a slight twitch. As I pressed my hand into his body, Henry's life rippled beneath my palm with such delicacy. It felt like a long, soft hiccup.

This was no theoretical concept, no safe metaphor. This was a punch-in-the-gut endpoint, but with the sound turned off. Imagine a silent car crash. His breath stopped. His blood stopped. Henry stopped.

I heard a shout. "Thank you God for giving me this dog!" Was that my voice? I didn't know where it had come from. The words had jumped from my mouth with their own will and force. I curled over Henry and pressed my face into his neck and inhaled that smell I loved so well—something like dusky chicken soup—just behind his velvety ears. Henry always had puppy ears. I drew my fingers through his thick black fur. *Please once more.*

His luxurious, warm coat filled my hands. Now I heard shrieking. This time I knew it came from me.

I lifted my head to look at my surroundings. I was the only one there. Blind with tears, I stood up from the bed and staggered around the room, unsure of what I was supposed to do next. It seemed necessary to tell someone what had happened, to make preparations. This was the other part of my responsibility for him, right? So I called Pet-A-Care. The woman who answered the phone was surprisingly lucid and patient with me, given that I had undoubtedly woken her from a deep sleep. That it was two o'clock in the morning had escaped me.

"My dog is dead," I said in my new, unrecognizable voice, a half-shout, half-whisper. "I mean he just died. Just now. Will you come and get him?" Somehow I had formed the idea that Pet-A-Care would come immediately to retrieve him. I didn't know how this worked. The woman explained with great kindness that she would come as soon as the sun came up.

My conversation with the Pet-A-Care lady caused me to realize that I should not make any more phone calls for the time being. So I'd have to be alone with Henry for a few hours more. I went over to the bed to check on him. He was still dead.

Henry's last act as the life departed his body had been to deliver a bowel movement, which I discovered when I lifted his tail and found a discrete brown turd clinging to the short hairs. "That is so like you," I said, as I wiped him clean with a paper towel. Henry appeared to be sleeping, so I covered him with the blanket, tucking it around his neck as if he might catch cold.

I had to get out of the house. I had to get away from my seeming-to-sleep-but-actually-dead dog. So I pulled on my coat and shoes and walked to the bayou.

There, at the edge of the dark water in the dark night, I paced out my gathering grief. I opened my mouth and made noises I had never heard before, moaning through clenched teeth, half-formed guttural phrases. A howl rose from my throat into the sky.

"Alone," I called. "There isn't any more."

I leaned into a chill wind, my face twisted and wet, and looked at the city around me. There were signs of life despite the hour, traffic sounds.

But for the most part I could imagine the rest of New Orleans slept, while I screamed into the bayou, "I don't have a dog anymore! He's gone!"

I stood by the edge of the water and felt the weight of this cold new thought: Now I am a person without a dog. It sank all through me, and I knew it was true. The generous, silent bayou accepted the words I had placed into it, and only glinted sharp fragments of moonlight in response. I walked for a while, dogless and unfinished.

When I returned home from the bayou, I walked in the door and saw Henry had changed while I was gone. I forced myself to pull back the blanket and touch his side. There was none of the familiar soft, fleshy give. It felt as though his hide encased a stone replica of a dog. His ears weren't the same either. This stuff he was made of wasn't him, now. He didn't look like he was sleeping, either. Finally, it was time to cover him completely. I pulled the blanket over his face that wasn't his face anymore.

Then I went to bed and dozed and woke, waiting for the sun to come up. All night I heard Henry's toenails clicking on the floorboards up and down the hallway. I expected to see him lumber around the doorjamb. Henry never walked when he could lumber. But these tricks of the mind passed in time.

Sometimes I wonder if I did my best for Henry—that maybe I should have let Nicole put him down when she first offered. Perhaps, but then I did give him such a heavy dose of Torbutrol that night. No doubt that hastened his death. After all my difficulty around this decision, it turns out that I probably did kill my dog. Although his passage was excruciating, I am glad he died at home in bed with me, where he most loved to be. And that he received help by my hand, rather than by means of a needle slipped into him while he lay on a cold metal examining table at the vet's office. No one wants to think about this when they adopt a puppy, but sooner or later the most loving thing you may do for your dog is kill him. If you have the courage to love a dog, you must also find the courage to help him through the doorway when the time comes. Those are the terms of the contract.

In Henry's case, what little courage I may have found within me was accidental and a product of desperation. But I learned so much from him through his death. He taught me the rules of love. Henry showed me what

Rumi meant when he said, "If it is love you are looking for, take a knife and cut off the head of fear."

Even though I probably helped him die, the myth I have crafted around Henry is that he died in his own way and his own time. While I sat with him, I read to him: "Do not go gentle into that good night. / Rage, rage against the dying of the light." (It was generous of Henry to allow me this indulgence, as he had always preferred Yeats.) And he did do exactly that. Fierce and strong until his last moment, his eyes were open to the light. Henry went to his death with as much deliberate zeal as he had ever gone through a plate-glass window. He was his own dog, God bless his soul.

A lot of people think of their dogs as their children, which makes sense. But I always think of Henry as my first husband. His size and power and attitude of entitlement—all these qualities made him more of my peer and partner than my child. His death, coming as it did after nine years of passionate engagement, left me feeling like a bereaved widow. I walked around as though half my brain had been amputated.

A lot of time went by where all I did was lie in my bed and cry. I'd stare at the ceiling and wonder with a genuine curiosity what would happen if I did absolutely nothing. If I just stopped trying, how long would it take for my whole world to completely unravel? Someone would have to force me out of my apartment. (I have no idea how I paid my rent during these months.) Failing that, I might die of starvation and melt into the mattress. Who would come for me? I considered not moving at all. I had no reason to get out of bed. There was no one to take on walks.

Eventually I tired of this line of thinking. I got out of bed and took myself for walks around the bayou. It felt a little pointless to do this without a leash in my hand, but I tried it because I had nothing else to do. That's when strange things started to happen.

Stray dogs began crossing my path. A lot of stray dogs. It got to be ridiculous. It seemed that I couldn't go anywhere without some flea-bitten, half-starved, homeless, bedraggled, oddly formed, beaten-up, lame excuse for a dog presenting himself to me as if he were a gift from Heaven. It was as though someone had posted my name and address on the dog underground bulletin board, along with the message that a space had just opened up. One morning, I was sitting on my couch, reading the newspaper. I had left my front door open. A beagle came onto my front porch and scratched at the screen door. She had a direct air about her, made another insistent scratching sound when I didn't answer. She looked at me through the screen with an expression on her face that seemed to say, "Hello, I'm here to apply for the job."

Whenever possible, I helped these strays move on to humans who wanted them. I didn't want them, and the whole kooky situation had escalated to a point of such grand absurdity that I suspected someone was throwing dogs at me. It reminded me of another mysterious set of events from my past that had been too weird to dismiss as coincidence. While I was living in New York, there was a period of time when I kept finding broken typewriters in my path. Again, I did not look for these encounters; they just dropped down in front of me. First I found a typewriter sitting on the steps of my apartment building. Two nights later, I walked past a trash can on the street corner, and then a minute later when I came back and passed the trash can again, there was a typewriter, slightly damaged, perched on the edge of it. In the space of a minute, someone had dropped off a needy typewriter for me to find. Shortly after that, I heard a knock on my apartment door. When I opened it, I found an elderly, broken-down Olivetti sitting in the hallway right at my doorstep. No sign of human life. Just a typewriter.

As with the other typewriters, I took this one in, repaired it, gave it a bath, cleaned its ears, fed it, changed the ribbon, and then donated it to Saint Luke's Thrift Shop. Clearly these typewriters served a purpose in my life, and I eventually got the message—I'm not completely stupid. Yet, I had divined that it was my job to send them back into the world, refreshed from their stay with me. I enjoyed the romance of finding them and caring for them, but they had to go. I had no room for them in my home.

With this more recent spate of stray dogs, again I resisted them all, refusing to make eye contact because if you meet their gaze, it's over. They suck your brains right out. I was strong in my resolve to remain dogless. The neighborhood of my heart that allowed dogs was still closed to traffic. No one was getting through. I mean no one.

Dogs are different from typewriters in a lot of ways. For one thing, they're pushy. The stronger my resolve grew, the stronger the dog encounters became. One night, as I took my stroll along the water, sure enough, right on schedule, a stray dog came up to me. He had long ears like a rabbit, short legs like a badger, and loopy black and white markings similar to a Hereford cow. In other words, he looked like a joke of a dog, as if someone had made a playful composite of all the most unlikely parts to form a dog. This guy didn't seem to know he was odd looking. He looked me right in the face and wagged his tail in the universal signal for "Aren't I cute?"

"Sorry, not interested," I said, and kept walking. He followed me, this time running in a rapid circle around me, and then made a low bow, his forepaws extended and his butt high in the air. Okay, this was outright flirting, and I was not in the mood.

"Get lost!" I snarled. And then regretted it. That is a rude thing to say to a stray dog. Undaunted, the dog leaped on me, slamming into my thighs, and then danced away, bowing and wagging, daring me to chase him. Then he ran in a circle around me again, his tongue hanging out like a slab of ham. He laughed his dog laugh, merry and bright, enjoying the game he had just invented. Then he body-slammed me again. I gathered he considered himself irresistible. I also couldn't help but notice that he still had his testicles. No wonder.

"I told you I'm not ready!" I shouted at him. "It's too soon! Go away and stop bothering me!" His feelings didn't seem to be wounded by my harsh words. Instead, he gave up wooing me and trotted across the street with his proud head and tail raised, as if he had pressing business elsewhere. I watched him go off into the shadows, reuniting with the ever-flowing stream of stray dogs, and I felt relief. This was not my dog. He belonged to someone else, or maybe he belonged only to himself. I had done the right thing by sending him away; however, I did reflect on the scene with some worry. I was yelling uncontrollably at a strange dog on the bayou as if we were former lovers. Something had to be done about the situation.

Several more months would pass before Lance and I met at a jazz club on Frenchman Street called The Spotted Cat. That's right, I found a stray dog at The Spotted Cat. For this reason I considered naming him Kitty at first, until a friend of mine talked sense into me. In the end I named him Lance-lot because my friend said he had an air of nobility about him. That noble air was due to exhaustion and hunger. As soon as Lance got a few meals into his belly, his true goofball nature emerged. Seems he left his dignity back on Frenchman Street.

I wasn't looking for someone to fill the opening left by Henry that night, but when I first saw Lance walk into The Spotted Cat, I felt a slight thaw in my resolve not to allow a dog back into my life. It was just a hint, but I noticed it. To begin with, I couldn't take my eyes off the puppy on the other side of the room, nosing around, looking lost, looking for someone. A strange mix of foreboding and excitement rose within me. I knew what I was in for, both short-term and long-term. Yet still there was a splinter of hope, an opening to happiness—yes, even a little bit of life perhaps. And there I went. My frozen bulwark of pain started to buckle and crack, and then I tipped right over. I couldn't stop it. An irrational wave of optimism swept over me. In defiance of all good common sense, I realized I would do this. I would take care of another dog.

This puppy was a good candidate, but just to be sure, I decided to test him to see if he was mine. So, I squatted down on my heels and cupped my hands around my mouth. "Hey, Shit-head!" I yelled through the bar noise. Lance's head snapped up as though he recognized my voice, as though he knew his name, as though he had been looking for me. Just for me! Like a puppy-shaped cannon ball, he shot through the crowd and threw himself into my arms, all wriggling butt and soft brown eyes and absurd skinny legs. Tired and happy, grateful to stop looking, he settled against my neck as though he had always been there. Nothing in heaven or earth could move him from that place. I sniffed the back of his silky ears. Yep, it was the right smell, the right feel. We had a match.

Even before Lance's arrival, I had begun to take some new steps away from the pain over Henry's passing. A friend of mine, whose father had recently died, suggested that I try yoga. This had helped her cope with that loss.

Of course, yoga. It just so happened there was a yoga studio a few blocks from my home. I knew about it because I had already been there and shied away from Sean. It was time to come back. I had left skittish and returned shell-shocked to the yoga class that Sean taught. He called it "Serenity Yoga," and it was what I needed. There I laid down my burden of grief. By moving my body through these twisty poses, turning and pulling my muscles, the pieces of my sadness shifted and dissolved into the no-thought all-space stillness at the end of each class. Slowly I came back to myself and to life. I saw the color of the sky again. I could taste food. Smell the earth after a rain. Gradually, I also began to notice the warm, fur-covered yoga teacher at the front of the room.

God, I hope he's not afraid of thunderstorms.

Turned out Sean was not afraid of anything. Or so he told me when I warned him what a difficult person I can be. He said he didn't care.

"You're a brave man," I said, playing cute.

"I *am* a brave man," he replied, straight like an arrow. I was struck by the bravery in the statement itself. It took guts for a man to claim his own courage. I was moved by the strength in his sincerity. And taken aback. I had been clowning—my usual way of approaching the truth—but Sean had answered in complete seriousness. I tested him to see what he might be afraid of. Paper cuts? Nope. Worms? No way. Chopped liver? Not an issue; we're vegetarian. He was not even afraid of me, or the roadblocks I threw in his way.

How did we get anywhere with this romance? It was deceptively simple. I came to yoga class one evening, and had decided it was time for Sean to ask me out. It didn't seem necessary for me to discuss this with Sean beforehand. He was supposed to know the agenda by reading my mind. So class went on in the usual peaceful manner, and at the end I remained sitting on my yoga mat, expecting Sean to perform his duty. Instead he became engaged in conversation with some other students. Sean's apparent failure to ask me out on a date, in the precise moment that I had decided he was supposed to ask, caused me to rise from my yoga mat and disappear into the bathroom, where I vented a hissy monologue that went like this: *Why do I always have to do all the work in relationships! What do I have to do for this guy? Draw him a map? Fine! Well that's just fine!* All this was accompanied by a lot of flouncing around the bathroom and balling up paper towels.

Having thus clarified the situation for myself, I left the bathroom and sailed with quiet dignity across the studio floor. As I passed Sean and his throng of admirers, I waved and spoke in an overly bright tone of voice, "Well, goodbye. See you next week." Then I walked out of the studio, showing only my stony profile.

I had just started my car, and was sitting there with the engine idling, when the screen door to the studio sprang open with such force that it slammed against the side of the building. Sean leaped down the front steps and ran into the street. He was barefoot. A light spring rain had begun to fall. (Why do the most important and beautiful things seem to happen when it's raining?) The early evening sky made a pinkish-gray backdrop for Sean's dash down the blacktop that gave off tendrils of steam from the cooling rain. As he got closer to my car, he held up the palm of his hand, fingers spread wide like a traffic cop, giving the signal for "STOP!" I guessed that was meant for me, so I stayed where I was.

Sean ran up to my car. I rolled down my window. Sean bent down and inclined his face to look me straight in the eyes.

"Connie, would you like to go out sometime?" he asked.

"Yes, I would, as a matter of fact," I answered, still not quite finished with my huff. "My number is in the phone book." Then I rolled up my window and drove home.

THEN COMES MARRIAGE

SEAN AND I BEGAN OUR COURTING AND MATING RITUALS IN THE vicinity of Bayou Saint John. At the time, Sean lived on one side of the bayou and I lived on the other. We often walked along the water in the evening after dinner. It was a sweet time. Seemed like everyone was in love.

During one such evening walk, we stood on the Magnolia Bridge and witnessed the courting and mating ritual of the nutria. The nutria were hanging out on the concrete base of the bridge, where they were half-submerged in the water. I have to admit I can't stand nutria. They creep me out. Giant rats from South America, nutria do not belong in these parts. Some guy imported them here in the 1930s with a grand plan for selling their pelts as a poor man's alternative to mink. Soon they escaped from his farm and disappeared into our wetlands, where they quickly adapted and reproduced at an astounding rate. One female can produce several litters a year, spawning dozens of babies. Then she sets her whole family to work destroying the marshes. The nutria's appetite for marsh grass has fatally altered the ecosystems of the outlying regions along the Gulf and con-tributed to coastal erosion, which in turn has made us more vulnerable to hurricanes and flooding. On top of all that, nutria are ugly, and they move in a guilt-ridden, furtive scuttle, making it obvious they are up to no good.

Once it became clear that the nutria had to go or Louisiana would sink into the Gulf of Mexico, there was an attempt to create a market for nutria meat. Unfortunately restaurants had a hard time selling nutria burgers or nutria steaks. Everyone knew they were rats—great big ugly rats. There is no way you can dress up that idea and make it palatable to diners.

The Jefferson Parish sheriff put a price on their tails: four dollars. So civilians could do a lively trade trapping the pests, while the sheriff's deputies hunted them with rifles at night, when they were most active. I have never had the impulse to harm an animal before I met my first nutria, but I have thought about joining the Jefferson Parish deputies on their nighttime hunts. There is something about the nutria that awakens a deep visceral disgust in me that, given the right circumstances and a weapon, could escalate into a murderous act. I feel they should not exist, and I resent their invasion of my bayou.

Anyway, back to sex. On the night in question, Sean and I and Lance witnessed two male nutria attempting to attract the cooperation of a female nutria. This operation required that the first male make his move by swimming in a circle around her and make a low coughing noise. Or maybe it was more of a soft barking sound. He would swim in a circle from her front to her back, coughing and barking while she gazed off as if absorbed in some important happening in the distance. Then the first male made a grab for her hindquarters. Depending on his skill, I gather, she would let him hang on for a few seconds, but then she'd shake him off as if he were an irritating pest. Then the second male, sensing a momentary advantage, would glide out of the shadows and swim the same circle around her, coughing and barking, passing before her as if she were the grand marshal in the Nutria Sex Parade. She'd let him have a try at her hind end, but then she grew annoyed with him, too, and shook him off. The boys traded back and forth like this for quite some time—without getting anywhere, as far as we could see. They appeared to achieve some sort of, well, "union" if you can call it that, but not in a way that I would consider complete or satisfying, even if I were a rodent.

Totally absorbed, we watched this display for nearly three-quarters of an hour. Lance was fascinated too. We hung over the railing of the bridge and whispered excitedly to each other.

"Okay, this time I think she's gonna let him just go for it."

"Oh, no! Guy, try it again."

As we watched, I tried to interpret the behavior. I came up with the idea that the males' purpose in circling around her was that she could get a good look at them, to determine if their DNA would be a good addition to hers. She was probably looking for certain attributes: a healthy coat, good swimming skills, agility, strength, and persistence under duress. In short, she was waiting to see which of these two was more dedicated to her hindquarters before she was going to let anyone get inside there in any lasting or meaningful way. Either that or she was just a dumb nutria slut, ready to take on any male who happened to swim by, coughing and barking.

What is it about sex that changes your whole life? One minute you're a clear-headed person, in full possession of your faculties and independence. And the next you feel like a snail without a shell. Quivering, mewling, prone to tears, and having recurrent dreams about the brakes on your car not working. All of this has to do with the sudden entrance of this man into your previously well-ordered life.

See, what happens is that just as soon as you give a man the slightest encouragement, he MAKES YOU FALL IN LOVE WITH HIM, and gets you to the point where YOUR MIND IS NOT YOUR OWN ANY LONGER and all of a sudden it matters if he calls or shows up, and then just as you let your guard down and trust him enough to let yourself be vulnerable with him, he GOES ON VACATION FOR TWO WEEKS by himself WITHOUT YOU.

The situation leaves you in a ticklish quandary because technically he is allowed to go on this vacation without you, as he made the reservations before he even knew you that well. Furthermore it's almost a quasi-business trip, as he will be attending a yoga workshop and retreat. In any case, he had planned this trip months earlier, long before the two of you started dating, and so according to the regulations established by the Geneva Convention, he is permitted to go on the trip by himself, even though he is now officially your boyfriend. So you are not legally entitled to complaint; however, this does not mitigate your right to whine. Or to feel abandoned and bereft.

Here was how I handled it. I went for a walk around the bayou. A long walk. The presence of the water and my circling of it, step by step, seemed to pull my anxious heart and mind into a slower, deeper rhythm. After a time the bayou worked its spell over me, and I reached a calmer place, something more like being than thinking, that allowed me to drive Sean to the airport with good will. His flight left before dawn. I came home and did what I always do: I tried to find the right words. Here is the letter I wrote to him.

For Sean on the occasion of his journey to New Mexico:

On the drive to the airport, it is still dark night. We are humming along in silence, my car making the most noise. I listen worriedly for bad brakes. More tiredness than either of us has the energy to talk about. I look over at you and see that you are staring into the road ahead. I think, "His hand is on my thigh, but his head is in New Mexico." I imagine that you are already formulating your intentions for this retreat. Or you are just planning your next nap. Or you are in a sleep-deprived trance state, below thought. I can't tell.

It occurs to me that I don't know anything about you. Your face is a face I have grown close to in the past few weeks, and yet I don't know what goes on behind your face, until you tell me. And even then how can I know what is happening from moment to moment? Things could change. Something could emerge that I did not anticipate. There is nothing more surprising than another person. No adventure more dangerous.

I drop you off at the airport and you look like a kid going off to summer camp with your knapsack and your tent and your sandals. I can't stop myself from asking questions like: "Did you remember your bath towel?" and "Where is your wallet?" I kiss you good-bye and get in the car and then begin driving east on I-10 into the sunrise. The clouds stand out in sharp relief as the sun, still below the horizon, begins to light the sky behind them. This configuration throws the clouds into shadow, making them a dark blue, close to the color of your eyes but not quite.

I realize even as I write this letter that I am flying into the dark with you in much the same halting manner that this old car of mine trundles through the night. There are splashes of light from the streetlights, and a limited circle of light from my car's own headlights. But for the most part, I am throwing myself into the dark. In faith. In trust. As promised. It's scary, but the alternative—staying home and never going anywhere—is far worse. This resembles something I've heard a famously blocked writer say. That she started writing again because the pain of not writing became greater than the pain of writing. I'm hurtling through the dark toward you in written form. My mind is racing; my fingers on the keyboard can't move fast enough to keep up with my thoughts. I want someone to catch me, to listen to me. Will you? Will you? Will you?

I picked him up at the airport two weeks later. He was even furrier than usual because he had been living in a tent and had not bothered to shave. We had a tentative reunion, the space between us filled with the awkward awareness that we didn't know each other that well, and yet we were intimate. So we had to search for that reconnect after a separation that had occurred too early. On my part, I chattered like an idiot. Sean was beatific, said little, and chuckled softly to himself in the passenger seat of the car as I drove us home through the night. Again, we were driving in the dark. As I drove and chitchatted about my activities during his absence, the back of my mind sorted through possibilities. *Okay, so this is it, right? This is where he tells me that since he's had time to think about it, he doesn't want to be in a relationship. It was nice, it was fun, but it's not what he wants. Or maybe not. Maybe something else. Right, so what's going on here? Do we have something? A relationship? Anything? Will you say anything at all, or are you just going to sit there and chuckle softly to yourself?*

At a certain point, Sean disrupted my flow of alarming thoughts when he leaned across from the passenger seat and licked my bare shoulder. It was going to be okay.

Two years later, we got married on the Magnolia Bridge, in a flurry of marigolds and a gentle mist. It was early October. We had a costume wedding. My husband's attendants were Superman and Zorro. My attendants were Bat Lady and a Faerie.

When we were planning our wedding several months earlier, Sean and I took our minister Patricia, who is also a longtime friend, for a walk through a cold driving rain to our bridge so we could show her what we envisioned for our ceremony. Patricia isn't usually a minister. She became ordained just to officiate at our wedding through a helpful website called Universal Ministries. Usually she is a Jungian analyst and a sensible person. So she asked, clutching her plastic rain hood beneath her chin as the wind threatened to whip it from her hands, if we had an alternate site for the ceremony in case of inclement weather on the day of our wedding.

"Oh, it's not going to rain on our wedding," I said with the superb confidence of a completely addled bride-to-be.

The morning of our wedding, I was alone at home. Sean had spent the night at his parents' house. We had decided to be playful about this, even though we'd been living together for several months, since we bought this house just off the bayou. I took Lance for his walk and found the weather to be damp. My heart thickened with dread. This could not be true. But no, Lance's coat was definitely getting wet. I held my hand out to the sky and peered into the wafting sheets of mist to see if . . . if . . . yes, it was resolving itself into actual droplets. Big, fat, wet droplets. This was no *mist*! This was now certifiable *rain*! I went back home, sat on the edge of the bathtub, and cried—great princessy, melodramatic sobs. I actually heard myself wail, "My wedding is ruined!" I had a full-blown—and for me, uncharacteristic—temper tantrum. It was fun and satisfying, even though no one was there to witness it. I remember that the cool, observing part of my mind said, *Go ahead, indulge yourself. You're the bride. This is the one day of your life that you are allowed to act like an insane person and no one will hold it against you.*

So I did. Lance watched, his forehead wrinkled with concern. Then my hairdresser arrived at the front door, and it was time to get to work.

In a matter of a few hours, the house was filled with my sisters, my mother, and clouds of hair spray. They dressed me. I know every bride believes this, but I really did have the most beautiful wedding dress in the whole world. It was an ivory silk chemise, cut on the bias, with an intricate lace shell over it that had baby's-ear pink inset panels. Tiny crystals dangled from the sleeves and hem. I'm sorry, but it *was* the most amazing dress.

As we got ready, no one dared look outside at the weather. Was the rain pulling back? Had a little sun emerged? I was too tense to make a rational assessment. I may have screamed at a few of my loved ones, but no one has chided me for my behavior that day, so maybe I wasn't quite the freaky Bridezilla that I recall. A friend of mind did force a glass of champagne on me, hoping it might untangle my rat's nest of anxious anticipation.

By the time we all assembled on the front porch, the weather was back to misting again. Not perfect, but workable. I could live with mist. I didn't cry. And I didn't raise my voice. The Panorama Jazz Band arrived to escort me and my large crowd of attendants, all in various states of fanciful costume. We were afloat in feathers, sequined magic wands, gossamer wings, and more than a few tiaras. Lance wore a blue-and-red plaid bow tie. We headed out toward the bayou, the band tootling funky Klezmer music ahead of us. To my ears, Ben Schenck on the clarinet will forever be the sound of stepping over the matrimonial threshold.

We walked into the shifting, cloudy dreamscape that this odd weather had blanketed over the bayou. The pale sunlight, filtered through the mist, cast my surroundings as if in a black-and-white photo, simplified into their archetypal forms and held in time. Shadows were gone. My mother held an umbrella over my head, but we still didn't have rain yet. The air swirled around us in a near watery form, dancing on the light breeze. Not rain, but hovering in that delicate, indeterminate range, pulled back just enough to balance on a point between the two elements. Air and water wafted up and around together in beautiful defiance of the customary rules of physics, where rain falls down and air is invisible. What a strange, overturned scene had appeared for us that day. This was how I walked to our wedding on the bayou—through a soft wash of airy water, as if passing into a new world.

At the Magnolia Bridge, they all went ahead of me and blended in with the guests already assembled there. During the short walk from our house to the bayou, my nervousness had left me. Now, I was here, at the edge of the bridge, waiting for my life to begin. Often I have trouble remembering who came to our wedding. I couldn't see much in that moment. The vision I have in my mind's eye when I recall that day is a tunnel of vague shapes, and then Sean waiting for me at the other side of the bridge. He was wearing the blue suit and the red tie I had helped him pick out. He was smiling. We waved at each other and laughed.

After waiting a moment for our guests and the band to settle, it was quiet, the most quiet I have ever witnessed. Everyone was looking at me as if I were responsible for all this. For a second I didn't know what was supposed to happen next. Then Ben wiggled his eyebrows at me: the signal for us to begin. I wiggled my eyebrows at my future husband on the other side of the bridge, and with that, Sean and I began walking toward each other, serenaded by the lovely voice of the clarinet. The haunting gypsy song rose into the gray, low-hanging clouds over the bayou. A thready, untamed sound, trembling near the edge of a howl that held us all in a hushed spell, the music pulled me and Sean closer together and brought us to our meeting at the center of the bridge.

Brides should never be held accountable for remembering the details of their own wedding ceremonies, because, as I have documented here, they are not in their right minds. I was certain that Sean and I got married, but only because I had the certificate to prove it. Honestly, I couldn't remember how it happened. I knew we met in the middle of the bridge, and we kissed. There was some lighting of candles. We walked three times in a circle. Did we jump over a broom? No, that was something else. There was a lot of laughing and cheering. At Patricia's invitation, our guests shouted, "Yes!" in unison three times to show their approval of the whole thing. One vivid image was our photographer Tom (another good friend of ours), as he climbed onto the bridge railing to get a wider overhead shot of us and nearly fell backwards into the bayou. Our vows? I made some wild promises that I would review one day just to see how I did at sticking to them. The part that I carried long after was the memory of Sean holding my hand. The sensation of his warm palm against mine as we walked off the bridge was when I felt truly married.

When it was all over—the ceremony, the parade led by the Panorama Jazz Band in full tilt, the accordion player jitterbugging to his own private muse, all of us dancing over the grassy levee from the bridge to the garden reception nearby, the dinner, the toasts, more dancing—Sean sang an Irish ballad to me. When everyone had gone home full and happy, we began our married life. I stored my wedding dress as if it were sacred raiment. This special costume that I would never wear again would serve one purpose in its lifetime. Having discharged this duty, the dress then retired into layers of tissue paper so that it could be preserved, the magic of our day still clinging within the ivory silk folds.

Of all the icons I preserved from that day—my dress, the bouquet dripping in ribbons, my crown of porcelain rosettes—there were two I had a special fondness for: my shoes. These ridiculously expensive, dyed-to-match slippers nearly gave my mother a heart attack when I told her how much they would cost. I went ahead and bought them anyway, figuring that sooner or later my mother would pick herself up off the floor and remember her own wedding. We both knew I'd wear them just once. What we didn't anticipate was that these silly slippers with the paper-thin soles, pointed toes, and slender sling-backs would be utterly ruined. At the end of their day of service, these once pristine ivory silk beauties wore wide brown swaths of bayou mud. It probably happened when I danced over the levee, or when I danced in the garden. I know I practically danced my feet off that night, and the ground was wet and so . . . oh, it didn't matter how my shoes were ruined. I loved them precisely because they were covered in mud. I loved that I took some of the bayou home with me when Sean and I walked back to our house after the party. Later, when I looked at the shoes in their tissue-paper-lined box, they reminded me of all that our wedding held for me: delicate beauty enriched by the dark, fertile silt that the bayou had pushed onto its banks for us to ground our mysterious transformation.

A BRIEF INTERLUDE
WITH HISTORY, SCIENCE,
WILDLIFE, MYTHOLOGY,
AND CIVIL ENGINEERING

RUMORS CONFIRMED! A LARGE ALLIGATOR WAS APPREHENDED ON the banks of Bayou Saint John. There was a photo in the newspaper. That settled it. Lance would never swim in this bayou. Ever again. Not as long as there was breath in my body.

The situation called for an expert opinion, so I talked to Mark Schexnayder, who was a coastal advisor for the Louisiana State University Agricultural Center. While he was with the AgCenter, Mark also worked with the Louisiana Department of Wildlife and Fisheries on managing the bayou, restocking the fish population, and cultivating vegetation—such as bullrushes, irises, and oyster grass—along the banks to provide nutrition for the fish and also help the ducks find good nesting ground. I figured he ought to know about alligators.

First, Mark wanted to give me the thumbnail version of the bayou's ecology. "What we have here is an unnatural body of water," he said. I was surprised to hear it. It seemed abundantly natural to me. He explained that a natural body would have a free flow of water coming in and water going out. Bayou Saint John hasn't been natural in that way for a long time. In fact, there were a number of agencies devoted to preserving the bayou on life support and keeping it pretty.

"So who's in charge of the bayou? Who owns it?" I asked him. The answer was complicated. The Orleans Levee Board maintains the banks and the structures near the mouth of the bayou at Lake Pontchartrain. City Park lays claim to the central portion between Robert E. Lee Boulevard and the Magnolia Bridge. Since there are drainage outlets from the bayou that lead into the city's pipes, the Sewerage and Water Board presides over the section from Magnolia Bridge to the end at Lafitte Street. Wildlife and Fisheries gets involved whenever a question arises about the animal population. Then Mark (now fisheries oversight director for Wildlife and Fisheries) was also monitoring the water level and quality so the salinity didn't go too far out of whack.

"All these people have to get together in order to get anything done with the bayou," he said. "So it's not a simple thing to pin down who owns the bayou."

It wasn't always so complicated. In its prehistoric years, the bayou was just a geological anomaly, a rift in the ground that became a four-mile-long, narrow, shallow channel, probably a tributary of Bayou Metairie and Bayou Gentilly that drained storm water into Lake Pontchartrain. Back then it was known as "Bayouk Choupic." "Bayou" is a French recasting of the Choctaw word "bayuk," which means "sluggish stream," and Choupic is a fish that thrives in mud. After the Chapitoulas, Acolapissa, and Houma tribes moved out and white Europeans took over, the bayou became the way for barges to bring in goods from the ships that had come into the lake from the Gulf. Rather than take the long way up the river, these barges could unload at the bayou's headwaters, and then it was a short portage downtown to the markets in the French Quarter. In 1931 the city built a lock at the bayou's mouth where it meets Lake Pontchartrain, and in 1962 this was replaced with a dam. Then in 1992 the city put in a sluice gate on the lake side of the dam to exert some flood control. The WPA had cut off the headwaters with a concrete bulkhead, so that now the bayou seems to disappear underground near the post office at Lafitte Street.

The dam and sluice gate near the lake end not only put a stop to large boat traffic on the bayou, but they also do not allow mature fish into these waters because the gate, which was designed to open and close as needed depending on water levels, remains closed all the time, while the dam was never intended to open for anything. Mark is much more concerned with the fish life than barges, which is why he calls the bayou unnatural. Without an inflow of fish with new water, the bayou would languish and stagnate. Fortunately, the fish-restocking program helps maintain the health of Bayou Saint John for the short term. The eventual goal is to remove the old dam and open the gate at the mouth of the bayou. Wildlife and Fisheries has placed monitors in the bayou to collect data for a hydrology report. The data should indicate when it is safe to open the gates all the way and allow the bayou to be restored to a natural state, encompassing a full, self-sustaining life cycle.

Mark did point out that for the time being the only fish that are small enough to slip through the narrow openings on either side of the sluice gate are those in the larval stage. Turns out that the Bayou Saint John of today has been transformed from a hardworking industrial waterway into a nursery. My bayou protects and nurtures tender young life. I wouldn't have it any other way.

It's an estuarine environment with brackish water, mostly fresh but some salt, so it supports both salt- and freshwater fish. There are bluegills, largemouth bass, sheepshead minnows, spotted trout, black drum, several varieties of catfish, and perch. Mark said he'd been catching blue crabs here since he was a kid. There is also an invasive species called a Rio Grande cichlid, which probably got into the bayou when someone emptied an aquarium into it. This cichlid proliferated to the point that it began to threaten the livelihood of the fish that belong in the bayou. Mark reported that restocking the bayou with native species has brought the ecosystem back into balance: "Those largemouth bass have been doing a very good job of eating the cichlid."

I invited Mark to take me on a nature walk along the bayou to show me things I might not recognize on my own. He pointed out the nutria turds. "They're everywhere." Mark also explained the mysterious jumping fish.

"Those are mullet."

"Really? The fish that inspired the hairdo?"

"Yep. Know why they leap out of the water like that?"

"To eat insects?"

"Nope. They're not insect eaters. And it's not because the water is under-oxygenated either."

"Well, that hadn't occurred to me."

"They do it because they're happy. No other explanation."

While we were talking about mullet, a woman walked by with her dog. "There is a huge water moccasin back there," she said. "Close to the bridge. Big fat swollen one."

"You sure it was a water moccasin?" Mark asked.

"Oh, yeah, that's what it was all right." She sounded exhilarated by the discovery.

"I gotta go see this snake for myself," said Mark. So we walked toward the bridge and peered into the tall weeds along the way. We never saw the water moccasin, but we did find a sodden teddy bear tangled in the oyster grass. Mark pulled it out and set it on the bank to dry in case someone wanted it.

I confessed to Mark that I might have seen the Loch Ness Monster in the bayou.

"Really? What did it look like?"

I felt encouraged by the serious tone of his question. So, I told him that I had seen only the fleshy curve of its body, no head or tail. A large, green, slimy hump had risen out of the water and then descended below the surface so quickly I wasn't able to get a good look at it. It had just flashed in my peripheral vision. I thought my account was consistent with other Loch Ness Monster sightings.

"That was probably a gar fish," Mark concluded. "They're an ancient fish, covered in tough green scales. And they can get to be huge, six feet or more. But they won't hurt anyone. Unless you're a baby duck."

This was all very instructive, but I finally had to prod him around to the subject that weighed on my mind—alligators. Mark told me there were plenty of alligators in the bayou, always have been, but that for the most part they were too small and too shy to be a threat to anyone. In the rare instance that one grew up enough to pose a difficulty, then Wildlife and Fisheries would send in a bounty hunter to find it.

"If it's under six feet in size," said Mark, "they relocate it to another bayou where there aren't so many people around. If it's over six feet"—he made a cutting motion across his throat—"then it's gumbo."

When I told Mark that I would not allow Lance to swim in the bayou because of the alligators, he said I was being overprotective. If he had a dog, he'd let him swim here. This is an urban waterway, he reminded me. Scores of people walk here all the time, and if anyone saw anything even remotely like an alligator, they'd start burning up the phone lines to get somebody in there to do something about it. There was no way an alligator of any serious size could live in peace in Bayou Saint John. The human residents wouldn't tolerate it.

"See all those houses along here," said Mark, making a sweep with his hand that encompassed the whole of Moss Street. "The people who live there, they all think this is *their* bayou."

ADRIFT ON THE INVISIBLE

SOME WOULD ARGUE THAT BAYOU SAINT JOHN BELONGS TO MARIE Laveau, the once and future "Voodoo Queen of New Orleans." Legend has it that her spirit inhabited these watery banks not only during her reign but also long after. She made the invisible visible. She plucked prophecy from the rain clouds and summoned truth from the slimy bottom of the bayou. Sometimes I wonder if it was old Marie herself who walked beside me and spoke to me in the dream that brought me to New Orleans. She fit the description: persuasive, mysterious, and alluring.

Though dead for more than a century, Marie Laveau still stands as the quintessential priestess of the faith. The historical documents tell us that there were actually two women named Marie Laveau, a mother and a daughter, both free women of color. Over time, the legends have bound up the two women and blurred their stories so that they have become a single archetype.

This archetypal Marie Laveau was renowned for her beauty, and her social and political influence in New Orleans. She was a hairdresser who lived on Saint Ann Street (or Love Street, depending on the version of the story you prefer), who also traded in the healing arts, dispensing roots and herbs, gris-gris bags, and advice. Many attested that Laveau's powers could bend just about any situation to her will. She is credited with halting public executions and directing the outcomes of court cases. Marie Laveau became so famous that the *New York Times* published her obituary. Laveau, the archetype, may have been a true sorceress, for all we know, or Laveau the actual person(s) could have been a shrewd observer of human foibles. The spiritual truth and the historical truth may overlap in some places and diverge in others. We'll never know for sure because the facts have faded with time and ascended into myth. The point is, everyone believes Marie Laveau was great and powerful, and that's what matters now.

I had read a little about Marie Laveau before coming to my new home, enough to whet my appetite. Later, when I arrived, I made an effort to know more about her and about the practice of Voodoo because it seemed the more interesting stepsister to Catholicism. Since I already knew all I wanted to know about being Catholic, I figured that if I were going to understand this city, I'd have to get a glimpse of this belief system that has taken root so deeply in the spiritual ground here.

One of the first things I learned is not to spell it "Voodoo." That spelling comes from the exploitive Hollywood treatment that has maligned and debased what is, for the initiated, a legitimate and heartfelt spiritual practice. The initiated tend to use "Vodou," or one of the other variant spellings I've encountered, such as "Vodo" and "Voudon." As a spelling-sensitive former copy editor, I am fascinated that this spiritual practice, which is not a "religion of the book," has attracted contemporary followers who are so persnickety about spelling.

I make no claims of authenticity for myself in this religion. I'm not one of the initiated nor a historian. I am only an interested observer of this spiritual practice. In relating my particular experience, I have tried to keep track of how Vodou departs from Voodoo. However, since it is so hard to be pure, as anyone blessed with a Roman Catholic childhood can tell you, I have thrown myself into the semantic swamp and let the variant spellings fall where they may. Sometimes I use "Voodoo" and sometimes I use "Vodou," because I can't be more consistent than the religion I'm writing about.

So for the record: I made an effort to learn about Vodou. First, I went to a couple of the Voodoo stores in the French Quarter, whose creepy atmosphere seemed suspiciously theatrical, like an airport gift shop with bad lighting.

There had to be more to this than black fingernail polish, recipes for causing harm to your neighbors, and yet another show put on for the tourists.

Eventually I arrived at a botanica called Island of Salvation in the Bywater, a neighborhood outside the French Quarter, where I met Vodou priestess Sallie Ann Glassman. The atmosphere of this shop was a far cry from the self-consciously spooky places I had seen. When I walked up to the wide-open entrance to the shop, Sallie Ann's dog, a mountainous Akita named Loa, reclined in a square of sunlight just inside the doorway. Loa lifted her nose and tail from the floor, issued a growl that was more inquiry than warning, decided I was acceptable, and allowed my passage into the botanica by returning to her somnolent meditation in the sun.

The shop had that rare quiet in New Orleans, the no-sound stillness that takes a while to recognize as an absence of air conditioning. The walls along one side of the room were lined with books on Vodou and related topics, an assortment of essential oils, incense, and dried twigs and grasses that ran the gamut from commonplace basil, hyssop, and calendula to the more intriguing mugwort and dragon's blood resin. There were also rows of tall candles in glass canisters that Sallie Ann had painted with swirling images of the Loa, who are like characters in a family epic. The Loa (sometimes spelled Lwa) are the spirits that populate Vodou. They are roughly analogous in form and function to the Catholic saints, with the difference that the Loa are also seen as a manifestation of the numinous divine presence in nature. There is one supreme creator in Vodou called "Bon Dieu" or "Bondye," while the Loa serve as intercessors between the creator and those of us trapped in human form. There is beautiful, dancing Erzulie Freda, who is the spirit of love, and La Sirene with the curving mermaid's tail; she lives on the floor of the sea. I imagined her as the governess of the deep unconscious.

In one corner of Sallie Ann's botanica was an elaborate altar decorated with images of La Sirene and Erzulie Dantor, another aspect of the divine feminine who overlaps with Our Lady of Prompt Succor. Erzulie Dantor holds a child in her lap. She has three long scratches on her cheek, and a dagger pierces her heart. She is the fiery manifestation of the flirtatious lover Erzulie Freda. Erzulie Dantor and Our Lady of Prompt Succor have the job of protecting New Orleans from hurricanes. They do the best they can, given the erosion of the wetlands and global warming. This altar is festooned with offerings of flowers, coins, strings of Mardi Gras beads, bones, pearls, peacock feathers, and other gifts left behind by petitioners. The Vodou spirits require some quid pro quo before they will interact with us humans—a bribe, if you will. The lover Erzulie Freda prefers coconut cakes with white icing and champagne, while La Sirene likes things that are blue and sparkly. Erzulie Dantor wants black coffee and cigarettes.

Sallie Ann sat at the back of the shop and smiled a shy greeting. She invited me to look around the shop, but didn't say much more than that. I wanted to have a conversation with her, but was reticent. I didn't know what I was doing there yet, except that I wanted to learn about Vodou. Blurting that out seemed inappropriate. Sallie Ann's self-containment discouraged direct questions. It appeared that whatever I learned I would have to get by paying attention.

Sallie Ann has distinguished herself in the New Orleans Vodou community by being articulate and organized. She offers lectures, has written a book, *Vodou Visions*, and contributed to two other books on the subject. Sallie Ann also conducts public ceremonies in which she teaches newcomers that Vodou is a life-affirming practice, presenting it in a manner that is open and friendly and therefore reassuring to those who might be wary of Voodoo's lurid stereotype. One of her observations that has stayed with me is, "Vodou's purpose is to heal a broken world."

Another thing I like about Sallie Ann Glassman is her name. It reminds me of girls I knew from my high school in Atlantic City, New Jersey. Maybe that's why she seems so familiar and comforting. Her origins are Jewish and Yankee. What's not to like? Some of the snarky types have called Sallie Ann "the Martha Stewart of Voodoo." This epithet missed the point. Sallie Ann herself hit the mark when she explained her Vodou identity to a journalism student who came to her shop one afternoon to do an interview for a school assignment, while I happened to be there. I studiously looked over the candles and pretended not to be eavesdropping on the interview—I'm a professional, after all. The student asked Sallie Ann if she considered herself the "real Voodoo Queen of New Orleans," a cryptic reference to the competition for Marie Laveau's title. Sallie Ann sidestepped the question.

"No," she replied. "I'm the Vodou American Princess."

Now *that's* cool. A Vodou priestess, in full possession of her powers, deals with the competition by refusing to acknowledge it. Instead, she makes a light joke at her own expense. Genuine or feigned, humility is always persuasive in a leader, the sign of a true monarch. I decided this was a Vodou Queen I could trust.

Thus commenced my brief but illustrative voyage into Vodou with the guidance of this Jewish Yankee priestess or "mambo" (sometimes "manbo"), to use the proper term, who is a vegetarian and so won't do animal sacrifices. Again, a Vodou Queen after my own heart. My journey wasn't long, but I learned a lot.

Vodou presents an interesting challenge to a heady person like me. The basic purpose of the ceremony is to make your body available to be possessed by the spirits invoked in the ritual. True believers say these Loa are disembodied entities that seek physical experience by entering your body and making it move and act in a way the Loa determines. As host for the spirit, you temporarily lose not only your self-control but also your identity. If you are possessed, you generally won't remember any of the experience, because you weren't really there for it. The possessed person becomes the Loa, and observers are supposed to know this is happening when someone suddenly begins to exhibit the specific traits, likes, and dislikes of a certain Loa. Guedeh, who is associated with the dead, will wear sunglasses, smoke a cigar, make dirty jokes, and play pranks, often grabbing people's bottoms and crotches. Erzulie Freda, who embodies the ideal of perfect love and feminine grace, will drape herself in lace, dance, and flirt with the men. Papa Legba, the gatekeeper between the spirit realm and our physical realm, likes rum and cigars and walks bent over as if he needs a cane.

Followers talk of being "mounted" or "ridden" by the Loa, and the possessed person is called a "horse." The sexual connotation here repels some people and attracts others. When your identity goes away for a little while, your inhibitions leave too. So Vodou can attract people who are looking for a way to express their unconscious or disowned desires, and repulse people who prefer to keep their repressed desires firmly repressed. The prospect of spiritual possession, the surrender, the release, the loss of control, puts the ego on alert to the danger of annihilation, just as it also creates a stage for erupting psychodramas from perpetual adolescents who are attracted by the stereotypical exoticism in Voodoo. In any event, possession is a matter of subjective interpretation and so also open to misuse and fakery.

Putting aside for the moment the Voodoo posers who are seeking an excuse to do things they normally wouldn't have the courage to do, and concentrating instead on the true believers in Vodou who walk a sincere path, for me the main question around possession has always been: Why bother? I did not immediately see the value in being possessed. What's the payoff, spiritually speaking?

"Possession doesn't diminish who you are, but expands you beyond your boundaries," Sallie Ann explained. In *Vodou Visions* she wrote, "Vodoun possession is not a descent into darkness but an . . . entrance into the mystery of the Divine that is the Vodoun's most precious gift."

My only brush with possession came one Midsummer's Eve on the Magnolia Bridge. June 24th is the feast day for John the Baptist. Sallie Ann and her fellow Vodou communicants hold a ceremony each year at Bayou Saint John on June 23rd, Saint John's Eve, to honor the Loa and offer gifts, because this celebration of the Catholic saint also stands as an overlay for the Vodou entity known as High John the Conqueror. In the ceremony, the purpose for the humans is to ask for insight from the Loa. The way to get that is through possession. On the night in question, they offered the ceremony on Magnolia Bridge to Marie Laveau, because this is her bayou.

Back in the day, Laveau had hosted her Vodou gatherings on the banks of Bayou Saint John. In the nineteenth century, when the white city fathers of New Orleans attempted to squelch Vodou by outlawing public ceremonies, Bayou Saint John became the secret nighttime meeting place for practitioners. It was an open secret, as nobody wanted Vodou to go away, just out of sight. There are reports that rows of sleek carriages rolled up to the banks of the bayou. Marie Laveau, hairdresser to the city's aristocracy, was a treasured resource for high society. Wealthy white New Orleanians often attended her ceremonies, especially young girls seeking some assistance from the spirit world in managing their love life. When I read this detail, it occurred to me that lots of things change, but girls never do. Ever and ever, we can count on girls to grasp the reins of magic to harness a wild heart.

The custom for most ceremonies is to wear white clothing as a symbol of purity, and to honor the Loa by offering our bodies in a pure state—or something close enough. So I pulled a long, loose white linen dress over my head, slipped into my flip-flops, and ran out the door to the bayou. Dusk was approaching as I neared the Magnolia Bridge. I could hear the sound of drums and see white-clad figures moving back and forth against the setting sun. The pink sky was filled with the reverberating clang of the bells, chiming in the nearby dome of Our Lady of the Rosary. The church made a long shadow, but not long enough to cast a pall on this Vodou gathering. I hurried my step, anxious that they might start without me.

When I got to the bridge, a whole lot of nothing was happening yet. We were on New Orleans time. (Even though I've been living here for more than fifteen years, I still can't shake my Yankee-bred habit of punctuality, or my expectation of the same in others. I am continually disappointed.) There was a crowd of about twenty people, most of them young, tattooed, and standing around smoking. Sallie Ann was there, explaining that she had just returned from the nearby police station, where she had shown the officers that she had the proper permit for this public gathering, in case they became curious about the large crowd of people all wearing white and dancing to wild drums.

"Just wanted to let the guys know we're here and we're okay," Sallie Ann said, laughing. The police are usually pretty decent to the Vodou folks. Having worked enough Mardi Gras detail, their tolerance for oddly dressed people behaving oddly has been stretched and exercised so far that nothing fazes them anymore.

More people arrived from the surrounding area—I recognized a prominent member of the neighborhood association—increasing the crowd to about seventy-five, and so it began. Sallie Ann stood in the center of the bridge near an impromptu altar filled with flickering candles, hibiscus flowers, coins, cakes, statues of Saint John, paintings depicting Marie Laveau, bottles of rum, and cigars. She gave the Vodou primer, describing the basic parts of the ritual. She explained that we would each have an opportunity to approach the altar to leave our gift for Marie Laveau. When we made our offering, we should make a slight curtsy or dip, turning in a circle three times, and draw a cross in the air with the gift before placing it through the center of the "cross" and onto the altar. This gesture opens a space in the veil between the spirit world and our physical world, so that our gift passes through from us in our concrete reality to the Loa in their invisible realm. Then there would be a head washing, where each of us would kneel on the ground, bend over a proffered bowl, and receive an anointment of champagne mixed with a fragrant cologne called Florida Water and a soaked coconut cake covered in white frosting. These ingredients please Marie Laveau. The idea is that this feminine archetype will be lured in through your head if you douse it with sugars and perfumes and sweet bubbly wine.

After that, the drummers would get going, and we would all dance in a circle, waiting and hoping to be chosen by the Loa for possession. Sallie Ann explained that as we danced, we could offer the back of our neck to her, and she would wipe a hand full of cornmeal there. This would be the direct request to the Loa to enter our bodies.

"Just be prepared," Sallie Ann said, her voice taking on a somber, warning tone. "When the Loa choose to come in, anything . . . anything at all can happen."

Sallie Ann began the ritual by opening the door between the worlds, the Loa's and ours. More precisely, she asked Papa Legba to open the door.

"*Papa Legba est a la porte. Ouvrez la porte pour vos enfants, Papa,*" Sallie Ann called as she kneeled before the *veve* she had made of cornmeal on the loose, rain-warped boards of the bridge. Each Loa has his or her own *veve*, an artful rendering of their characteristics that is like a calling card or a graphic invitation to manifest in the human realm.

"*Ayibobo,*" we called in response, the Vodou version of "amen" or "so be it."

As Sallie Ann blessed the space with smoke from a burning stick of incense, a thunderstorm, which earlier in the evening had threatened to descend on our ritual, still hovered close by. The clouds flashed jagged strobes of heat lightning against the darkening sky, but no rain fell. According to the stories, Marie Laveau's power extended to atmospheric conditions, and so she always made sure that the weather was dry for her Saint John's Eve celebrations. Yet, Marie also loved the power of the storms and the cleansing bath of rain. She often led her followers, body and soul, right into the sacred waters of Bayou Saint John.

As I stood with the crowd, I felt my customary split between being and observing. Ever since I can remember, I have felt that I was never completely immersed in an experience, but always watching myself have the experience, because there was always the cool, discerning part of my mind that watches, takes notes, and evaluates. Maybe everyone has this feeling. Maybe it's just the human condition. But I have always suspected that everyone else in the world has sealed this split in consciousness, and that I am the only person doomed to exist with this slight remove created by the part of my mind that likes to observe. It's a real killjoy, as you can imagine.

This observing mind puts a glass bubble around me so that experience can't fully hold me in its grasp—unless a dog is drowning, of course. Then my instincts take over, and I am all action and all animal, fully in the experience, not removed at all by my discernment. Barring dog-related emergencies, however, I have hungered for that ability to slip with gentle ease into pure experience, uncomplicated by my observing mind, which may be why I am drawn to Vodou. This ecstatic spiritual tradition seeks to dissolve the barrier between mind and body by parting the veil between the spirit world and the mundane world. Whether that is just a metaphor for the inner union, or real in the outer supernatural sense doesn't matter. For the true believer, it works either way.

The drummers started drumming around Sallie Ann as she moved through the crowd sprinkling us with water from her bottle. Holy water? Yes, in the sense that all water is holy, as it represents life's beginnings. The gentle bayou water under the bridge below our feet, the rainwater condensing in dark clouds congregating above our heads, the ritual water in Sallie Ann's cork-stopper bottle, the water in our own spit. All of it holy.

We moved to the sound of the drumming, at first just shuffling our feet and bobbing in an awkward search for the beat, but soon the insistent drumming pulled us into itself so that we became graceful without trying. I couldn't take my eyes off one woman who played an African "talking drum," which she hammered with a small, curved wooden wand. I recognized her from around town. She bore ritual scars on her chest, self-inflicted with a razor blade for one of her performance art works. Under even the most ordinary circumstances, this woman looked at the world with freaky eyes that seemed to burn like blue coals from within her forest of midnight dreads. On this night, her pale gaze never left Sallie Ann as she danced and beat her drum in synchrony with the other musicians and dancers. It was starting. They were calling in the Loa.

In twos and threes, we stepped up to the altar to place our offering there. When it was my turn, I was somewhat at a loss. I had forgotten to bring a gift for the Loa. So I reached behind my head and pulled out the tortoise-shell comb that had pinned my hair in a tight knot, and placed the comb on the altar. A fitting tribute to Marie Laveau, the hairdresser and priestess who understood the complex pathways of a woman's power, that she binds and holds so much in the alluring, snaky net of her hair. With my own hair now released and falling in wet ropes down my back, I returned to the circle of dancing.

To be honest, I considered passing on the head washing. The recipe of cake and champagne—there may have been a raw egg in there too—put me off. I balked at the prospect of putting sticky food in my hair, and I can't stand the smell of Florida Water. In the end I went along with it in the spirit of respectful participation. In for a penny, in for a pound. I kneeled before the young, slender blond kid who was assisting Sallie Ann with the head washing. I leaned over and he doused me with the gooey mixture.

"There you go, Doll. You're all set," he said with a darling smile. I lifted my head, and rivulets of champagne and cologne ran down my neck and into the top of my dress. I raised my fingertips to my temples and found a few wet blobs of cake. *Doll? How nice.* No one ever called me Doll. I liked that.

We danced in our own Florida Water–scented clouds, and the night darkened. I watched the people around me and tried not to grow annoyed with the obviously theatrical types. All sorts of "possessions" were starting to happen now. One tall plump guy suddenly went rigid as a surfboard and tipped over backwards into the waiting arms of his friend, who lowered him to the ground. There he writhed and twitched, and his eyes rolled back in his head. I was not buying this. It was all too ostentatious and neatly choreographed.

Then another man, wearing sunglasses, walked through the dancers with a big cigar in his mouth. He was supposed to be possessed by Guedeh, who likes to play dirty tricks on people, grabbing them and pinching them. So this guy was messing with folks. Except that I noticed he only messed with the people he had arrived with, his friends. And so, even as my body danced in a circle with my hair in a sticky coating of champagne and cake, and the strong, loud drums filled my chest and my gut, a doubt surfaced. *Hey, wait a minute! If Guedeh had possessed this guy, he'd mess with any one of us strangers, not just the friends of the guy that Guedeh had possessed. What a phony!*

At this point, I almost went home. I was so irritated with these self-indulgent histrionics, this neurotic demand for attention. It was sacrilegious. I calmed myself by looking at my own feet and listening, just listening to the drums. When I raised my head again, I could see other people in the group who moved to the music in their own way, simply being present to the ritual. Their evident sincerity consoled me. There was a woman who stood out from the other dancers. I hadn't seen her before. It was as though she had dropped from the sky. She was the only African American woman in this gathering, and she was beautiful. She wore a white gown like the rest of us, and her hair was wrapped in a high white turban. She held her head like a tulip, nodding and dipping as she danced. This lovely dark woman, alone among all of us, could have been Marie Laveau made flesh.

"Do you think she might be a princess?" a man whispered to me.

"Yes, I'm sure of it," I answered, grateful that he had spoken because I was worried that perhaps I had imagined her.

The storm rumbled overhead, but still no rain fell. A single cloud had detached itself from the larger mass and drifted closer to our bridge where we danced and drummed. It was unmistakable. A lone cloud, separate from the other clouds, came to us, as if it had a mind of its own, and settled close to the bayou. It hung in the air not far above our heads. It was pink around the edges and deepened toward gray at the center. This cloud seemed to have arrived at our ceremony with its own agenda and its own power source. The cloud suddenly flared from its center, a wild flickering light that illuminated its core. Lightning flashed again and again from this cloud hovering thirty feet above our heads.

I wondered: *Am I the only one seeing this?* It was too supernatural. Clouds didn't do this, I was sure of it. I knew I wasn't drunk, but I might have suddenly gone insane without realizing it. These things happen. Then I heard someone behind me shout, "Jesus Christ!" I realized, okay we were all seeing this cloud, which was so unnaturally close and had chosen to join us for our ceremony to honor Marie Laveau on Bayou Saint John. We couldn't all be crazy, not all at once. So this was actually happening. *What a relief. I'm not insane.*

Then, in the custom of such Vodou things, we all just accepted the cloud in our ritual. Got used to having her there and went about our business, dancing to the relentless drums. I stepped back from the current of dancers. Something had pushed me out of the center. Around me spiraled all sorts of shenanigans, both real and surreal. I closed my eyes and concentrated on shifting my weight back and forth from one foot to the other, just barely moving. Gradually I received the distinct sense that I was not moving my limbs. I was awake in my body, but I was not the one giving orders to my legs and feet. A force not my own, not under my will, lifted my feet from the warped wooden boards and nodded my head back and forth, up and down. I felt like a puppet, and it seemed the drums themselves pulled the strings. I wanted to be close to the drums. If I could crawl inside them, I would. I craved the pulsing sound like a lover.

Without knowing for sure who gave the order, I moved across the bridge to stand in front of the drummers. I forgot everything and every-one, including myself. My surroundings faded into the background. I could sense the candlelight on my skin, while the drumming filled my head and thumped behind my eyes. Everything else, though not com-pletely gone, faded to a distant echo. I hovered in this indistinct realm, something not my own will holding me like invisible hands. After a few moments Sallie Ann drifted over to me and peered into my face. She asked, "Are you okay?"

When I heard her say the word "you," I came back to myself. That sharp pronoun sliced through my cloudy state and reminded me that I am a person who can be addressed as "you," that I am I—or me, rather. The grammar that makes identity also makes separation, loneliness, fear. With one word, my dreamy trance was gone. Her voice cut the strings. I was no longer a puppet, but myself again. Back in my body and back in charge. The scene around me came rushing into focus. Here I was on the Magnolia Bridge. It was Saint John's Eve, and we were all dancing to the drums. A beautiful night. I was ready to go home.

I kept this experience a secret for a couple of years. I didn't want to talk about it, because frankly I have never wanted to be possessed, if indeed that is what happened to me. I realized that even though I have taken part in several Vodou rituals and gone through the motions of offering myself for possession, deep down I don't like the idea of it. I prefer my consciousness just the way it is, without any visitors from the outside. Hypnotism has never worked on me either for the same reason. I can't help but put up psychic barriers to prevent it from happening. Even though I think I'm trying to be open-minded about possession, at my core, I'm not truly open to the experience.

Besides, I was also fed up with all the theatrical histrionics that inevitably muddy the Vodou waters, making it hard for me to see the true spirituality in it. So I avoided the whole scene for a long time. However, this strange experience that happened to me during the ceremony on the bridge continued to pique my curiosity, so eventually I returned to Sallie Ann's botanica to ask her what she thought had happened to me that night. Her shop looked pretty much the same when I returned, perhaps only more crowded with Vodouiana. The main difference was that there was a new Akita sleeping under the desk. Her old dog, Loa, had since left this life and moved on to reunite with all the other Loa.

Sallie Ann listened to my story and told me that I had likely experienced the beginning of a possession. She explained that there are degrees of possession, that it would be possible for me to remember the experience if I had been only partway immersed. Even though it is the Loa who are running things in a ceremony, there are ways to shake yourself out of the beginning of a possession experience if you don't want it to happen. There has to be some cooperation from the horse. She added that if I had chosen to stay with it, rather than go home when I did, she believed that I would have experienced a full immersion.

"So I could be possessed even though I don't want to be?" I asked. "Even though I have put up all these psychic barriers against it?"

"The Loa are not concerned with what you want," Sallie Ann said, laughing. "It's important to remember that the Loa are not just archetypes, but forces of nature. With their own will. The possession is not to benefit the person being possessed, but to serve the community. The Loa possess someone because they want to participate in human life. And because they have some insight or some advice to tell us."

Fair enough, but my question still remained: Why that night and no other night? I have never experienced possession at any of the other Vodou ceremonies I have attended, before or since. There must have been something different about that Saint John's Eve ceremony on the bridge.

During the other Vodou ceremonies, we had gathered on the street or in Sallie Ann's home. We were standing on solid ground for those. For this ceremony, we were standing over the bayou with rain clouds gathering overhead. Now, it seems clear that it was the presence of water below and water above that loosened my usual firm grip on my consciousness. I literally lacked solid ground beneath my feet, and so lost my psychic bearings, cast adrift into the spirit realm and carried on currents that I usually observe. It was the water, with its constant urge to seek a lower level, its oceanic indifference to rigid forms. Only the water and the tricky act of standing suspended with water all around had lured me into the flow of the invisible. It wasn't my doing. I blame it on the bayou.

KICK HIM IN THE BALLS

NEARLY A YEAR LATER, ON THE OCCASION OF ANOTHER PAGAN HOLI-
day, Easter Sunday, I was walking home from that other orgiastic flesh-eating
rite of group hypnosis—morning mass at Our Lady of the Rosary. I occasionally go to mass at this church because it's pretty and it's in my neighborhood.
Each day I wake to the six-o'clock bells, and the sight of the splendid green
dome across the bayou greets me on my walk. I love the look of its curve
against the morning sky, and the small cross at the top pointing upward. It
looks like a Roman cityscape, Mother Church offering her plump breast to
nurse the heavens.

My relationship with the church of my childhood, although cherished,
was strained from the beginning. My mother sent us to catechism school
and to Sunday morning mass to satisfy her father's demands, as well as her
own atavistic suspicion that we might go to hell if we didn't. My mother
herself did not attend mass, even though it was her fault we were Catholic
to start with. My father was Lutheran—not seriously, but enough to cause
him to regard Catholicism as a mildly cleaned-up version of witchcraft. He
never made any secret of the fact that he had been raised to see Catholics as mush-brained and borderline dangerous. Still, he married one. My
mother was raised to see Lutherans as spiritually wooden, unimaginative,
lacking poetry, and finally, simply, not among the elect. My parents have

spent five decades of marriage lobbing religio-ethnic slurs back and forth at each other. (My father is German, and my mother is Italian. Or, as I like to say, I have fascism on both sides of my family.) All in good fun, really. That's how we roll in my tribe. In any case, my mother told me she stopped going to mass because she felt betrayed by her once beloved Church, which in her younger days had so guided and informed her passionate devotion to a life of the spirit—but then relegated the man she loved to second-class status because he declined to convert to Catholicism when they married. So she made her choice and redirected her passion elsewhere. No longer into Him but just a regular him—her husband.

I was not aware of any problem in my parents' choice of each other as mates until I attended catechism school. Sister Ursula introduced my sister and me to the Monsignor one afternoon when he came to visit our class. Dear Sister Ursula, who was blessed with the face of a softening pumpkin and small, black-rimmed teeth that tilted toward the back of her throat, tried to be discreet, but she did feel it necessary to explain to the Monsignor sotto voce, "The Adler girls come from a . . . *mixed* marriage."

At a young age, I loved the ritual, the songs, the magic. I was less captivated by the whole Jesus story than I was by the concept of a Blessed Virgin. Now, *that* was intriguing. When I was seven years old, I walked to Easter mass wearing a cape coat that my grandmother had sewn. The coat had slots in front for my white-gloved hands to appear, while the rest of me was cloaked in yards of fabric that formed a firm triangle from neck to mid-calf. I clasped the prayer book that I had received for my First Holy Communion, a small purse containing change for the collection basket, and a white cotton lace-edged handkerchief to wipe my ladylike nose should the need arise. I also wore a wide, round-brimmed straw hat, special for Easter. On the way to church, the sun was behind me and cast my shadow onto the sidewalk before me. The silhouette achieved by the ensemble effect of cape and hat resembled images I had seen of the Virgin Mary with her long draped garment and halo. It was uncanny. My shadow looked just like the Mother of Christ! I'm sure I appeared awfully pious, with my demure gaze cast downward, but really I was entranced with myself and my resemblance to a supernatural figure.

As a matter of strange fact, my father attended mass more often than my mother. She refused to go at all, whereas he would show up occasionally for midnight mass on Christmas Eve when my sisters and I sang in the choir. I looked for him from my perch in the choir loft. His back was turned to me, and I enjoyed spying on him in the House of the Lord. This was the only time I have seen my father look furtive. He kept checking over his shoulder, as if afraid the Lutheran Police would catch him there. Of course, he refused to kneel when everyone else knelt. He also *lounged* in the pew, his legs nonchalantly crossed at the knee and his arms outstretched along the back, as if enjoying a pleasant afternoon in the cockpit of his sailboat. Everything in his posture was a studied "fuck you."

So I was raised in an atmosphere of skepticism around the Roman Catholic Church that did not immediately penetrate my girlish piety. I held on as long as I could, but then my official break came when I was fifteen years old. I had an epiphany during mass one Sunday morning when I looked at the priest high up on the altar as he preached down to us, and realized that I was tired of men telling me what to do. Tired of all the patriarchal, authoritarian jibber-jabber. Just sick of it. Not to mention, I would never see a woman up on that altar celebrating the Transubstantiation of the Flesh. Of course, I had always been aware of this fact, but something about this day and this priest really put fur on my teeth. I would not remain in a house where my sex denied me and every other woman access to the corridors of power. So I walked out of the church, sat down on the curb, and took off my shoes. It seemed an important gesture of my liberation that I should walk home barefoot.

I held this aloof position for a long time. Yet, despite my adolescent bravado, in my adulthood I found myself stopping by church from time to time. Even though I remain allergic to most priests, I can't seem to stay away from mass. I miss it in spite of myself. The ritual comforts me. The prayers are as familiar as the sound of the bay clapping the bulkhead below my window. Like many outraged feminist Roman Catholics, I live with a perpetual homesickness. And we take the attitude that this is *our* house. Why should *we* leave? They're going to have to make room for us sooner or later. Probably not in my lifetime, but I'm willing to hold an active grudge about it, just to see if that gets us anywhere.

On this Easter morning, I went to mass just for the heck of it and because Father Tarantino was a good guy as priests go. He always struck me as a gentle man, essentially kind, with an open face. Also, he was small and cute, just barely came up to my shoulder, and he offered a jazz mass on Saturday nights. He had been known to dance down the aisle. Mainly what I liked about Father Tarantino was that he opened the church to animals during the Feast of Saint Francis so we could bring our pets for a blessing. Years ago I brought Henry, but he had to receive his blessing in the parking lot because he would have tried to eat the other dogs. I asked Father to give Henry an extra heavy-duty dose because I believed my dog was possessed by Satan. The priest thought I was kidding, but went along with it like a good sport. Later I brought Lance to Father Tarantino and asked him to bathe his face in holy water because Lance has the Devil in his eyes. None of these ministrations improved the behavior of my dogs, but they did make me feel I was trying at least.

One of the indelible bayou scenes I hold in my mind's eye is an image of Father Tarantino leaning on the porch railing of the rectory, next door to the church. He was taking a pause in his priestly duties, enjoying dusk by the water. And he was smoking. His leaning posture and the casual gesture of drawing the cigarette to his mouth made him look tough and sensual. If you didn't know he was a priest, you could mistake him for some hoodlum on the street corner. It gave me pleasure that I caught the parish priest indulging in this unwholesome habit of the flesh. We are all so weak.

This Easter mass was relatively harmless. Father Tarantino didn't say anything to piss me off too much. I considered that a successful Easter. Before walking home, I stopped by the grocery store to pick up some eggs and zucchini that I needed to make brunch. It was about 11:30, a gray March morning, a little chilly. I passed back through the churchyard with my grocery bag in one hand and my purse in the other. As I walked along the bayou heading toward the Magnolia Bridge, I saw a couple of things. A friend of ours, Allen, was walking with his dog Cosmo away from the bridge. Two young men were also walking along the bayou toward the bridge. I waved to Allen and Cosmo. None of these things was remarkable.

I walked across the bridge and headed toward our house. When I got to the other side, I heard rapid footsteps pounding the boards behind me. Someone was coming toward me fast. A sentence formed in my mind: *I'm about to be mugged.*

A split second later, I heard a man shouting, "Give it up! Give it up!" I looked down at my left hand, which held my purse, and I saw another hand reach for the strap and yank on it. "Give it *up!*"

A sudden force whirled me around, and I was face to face with one of the two guys I had just seen walking along the bayou. My grip tightened on my purse strap. I don't know why, but I didn't let go of it when he told me to. I had never been mugged before, so I was a little confused about how this was supposed to go. I didn't want to give up my purse. That was *my* purse, not his. He was not supposed to have it. So I held on, not meaning to be difficult, just unwilling or unable to give it up.

He yanked on his end of the strap with ferocious strength and jerked my whole body in a circle, dragging me off my feet. He yanked so hard that he nearly pulled my arm out of my shoulder joint. It hurt like hell. Still I didn't let go. As this was happening, as the two of us danced this violent waltz, one unwilling partner (me) at the mercy of the other, a raging maniac, my stream of thought, if you can call it thinking, went like this: *Make this scene go away. Change the channel. I want to keep my purse and make this stop. Make it all disappear.*

Go away! I directed my thoughts to the guy yanking me around. *Just evaporate, will you?*

It didn't work. He was still there and still hurting me. Still close to me. He turned his head this way and that—his long, braided hair fanning around his face. Time slowed. It seemed that we danced like this for hours, that I had the luxury of time to take an inventory of his face. He was, I couldn't help but notice, quite pretty. Tall and muscular, he was a young, smooth-faced boy, not yet a man, with wide cheekbones, a pointed chin, and a plush cupid's mouth. His skin was light brown, and his eyes were pale green, like mine. I was terrified, in pain, and yet his beauty was so plainly there between us, I couldn't avoid seeing it.

"Let go of the purse!" he shouted.

"I'm not giving you my purse!" I shouted back, not trying to be defiant, just instinctively so. Although time seemed to have slowed, this all happened in just a few seconds, and if I had taken a moment to think, I would have realized that the smart thing was to give up the purse. But my gut didn't want to! That purse contained the keys to my house and car, my wallet with about two dollars and eighteen cents, and a Viva Glam lipstick, none of which I cared so much about that I was willing to fight for it. I just didn't want to let him have it.

In a situation like this, it would be nice to be possessed by some fierce, protective Loa. Not La Sirene or Erzulie Freda, they're too nice. But it might be exciting to have a sudden visitation from Ogoun, the fiery warrior for just punishments. Or I'd like to be taken over by Kali, the Hindu goddess of death and destruction, who bites off men's heads and wears them in a bloody necklace. How come Kali never showed up when I needed her? No, none of these spirits took possession of me during this Easter-morning mugging. The archetype that came alive within me on this day was Mary Poppins. And boy was she upset!

The mugger was growing impatient with my lack of cooperation. He was tired of dancing with me. "Do you want a punch?" he asked. I understood this to be a rhetorical question, yet I felt compelled to give an answer.

"Do *not* hit me!" I said in the same tone of voice I would use to order Lance off the couch. Mary Poppins was doing the talking now. I think she may have even shaken my finger under this guy's nose. Mary Poppins was certainly not going to tolerate such rudeness. Meanwhile the two of us were still tugging on either end of my purse. This went on forever. In the astral plane somewhere, it's still happening.

During the eternity of time that unrolled after he threatened to punch me and before he took a swing at me, I saw he was standing with his legs spread. I gazed down at his wide-open crotch and had these thoughts: *Okay, now do it. Kick him in the balls. Right now. He's wide open. This is your moment. Right here. Kick him. Now. Do it. Kick him in the balls!*

92

I didn't do it. Mary Poppins simply does not kick people in the balls. My feet were locked in place. I could not connect thought to deed. I was able to envision it. For days and weeks afterward, I replayed the event in my mind, the hot, choking rage rising in my chest. In these imaginary scenes, not only did I kick him in the balls, but I also smashed his pretty face into the concrete. In this crucial moment, however, when I most needed rage and strength, all I had was confusion and paralysis.

Then the guy curled up his hand into a large fist, pulled back his arm, and brought it around in a slow-motion circle, heading toward my face. His mouth twisted in an ugly snarl. I watched his smooth, unblemished knuckles come closer. What a big, clumsy ham of a boy's fist. And then it dawned on me: *I'm about to get punched. This is not worth it.*

I let go of my purse. Since the two of us had been pulling against each other with the purse between us, that sudden change in our dynamic tension put him off balance. His punch wobbled a little off target. I leaned back and watched his knuckles whistle past my nose.

He took my purse and ran back across the bridge where the other guy waited. I watched them drive off. Here's the thing that gets me. They were laughing as they left. They were pleased with themselves. I am pretty sure that I am capable of understanding many of the odd byways in the human psyche. All it takes is a little sympathy and compassion and the willingness to put yourself in someone else's place. But how a person can take satisfaction from frightening and hurting another person lies beyond my scope.

Maybe that was why I had a hard time breathing as I watched them depart. I had encountered something bad and alien. To this day, I remain grateful and amazed that he never actually touched me. No part of his body ever contacted mine. He hurt me, yes, but without touching me. Even so, I stood by the Magnolia Bridge, shocked, disbelieving, clutching my bag of groceries with my shoes strewn at my feet. He had yanked me so hard that I had come out of my shoes. I cried like a baby girl. That was how my neighbors Ivan and Jeanette found me.

They enfolded me in their kindness and tucked me into the front seat of their car—snugging in next to me on either side. Just like that, with all three of us pressed into the front seat, Ivan drove the half-block to their house.

We called the police. An off-duty detective, who had heard the call go out on the radio and happened to be driving close by, showed up first. He went racing around the neighborhood in the hope of finding the muggers before they disappeared. It was too late.

More police arrived. We left my friends, and the officers walked me home. Since my keys were gone, the cops helped me break into my own house (with ease!). Lance's eager, smiling face appeared at the windowsill that the detective was about to haul himself over. "Whoa!" the cop shouted, and dropped back down to the grass. "Does he bite?"

"Lance? He might lick you to death," I said.

"Hey Lance, you eat white meat, right?" shouted another cop who was hanging back, watching the whole thing and laughing at his partner. Oh, my goodness, they were having so much fun.

It took a couple of hours for me to track down Sean. He had turned off his cell phone. I had to hold it together on my own. I waited, imagining that the muggers would get our address from my driver's license and let themselves into the house when I was there alone. I called a locksmith. He couldn't come until the next day. What was I supposed to do? It seemed to me that my sunny sidewalk would soon be thronged with assailants. I was so exposed and vulnerable here. Why didn't I have a real dog? Like a Doberman pinscher or a rottweiler? Lance waggled around my feet, rubbing his forehead on my shins, not knowing anything. When Sean finally got home, I curled up on the bed while he held me. I felt a little bit safer.

Later in the afternoon, I ventured back out to the bayou. I had planned to go for a run. Theoretically, at least, it was important to stick to my plans and not be intimidated out of my routine by what this thug had done. To be honest, I was afraid. For the first time ever, I was afraid to be walking alone on the bayou. In fact, it would take months before I could go anywhere without jumping and turning at the slightest noise. Danger had visited the bayou, and its open, gentle expanse now seemed like a landscape for attack. I saw, or thought I saw, all kinds of threats, just outside my peripheral vision, rushing my back, shouting at me.

Sean had the idea that he would follow me by car while I took my customary jog around the bayou. So I went to the bridge—wearing my blue shorts, a blue T-shirt, running shoes—and I leaned over to stretch my hamstrings, my Achilles tendons. Sean's van idled there, waiting, while I swung my arms around to loosen up my back. My shoulder still hurt, but I was going to do this. I started my run in this rare, dry March air. The late afternoon sun made sharp shadows among the long grasses by the water. I jogged on the soft ground while Sean's van crawled along the road beside me. Other cars, not understanding why Sean was driving at such a slow pace, honked their horns and passed him. Lance sat in the passenger seat and hung his head out the window, his ears and tongue flopping. Thrilled to be included in this interesting new adventure, he watched me with delight.

So in this measured way, we made a circle of the bayou. I looked down at my quick feet, pressing my footprints into the grass. I kicked up the dirt and thought: *Mine. It's mine. This is my bayou. I take it back. You can't have it. I'm not going to let you have it.* With each pounding step along the edge of the water, I squinted against the sun, gulped air into my lungs, and jawed the wind. I took back my bayou with my body's movement along its shores. It's mine because I say so. Because I take care of it. Because I watch it every day. Because I love it. Because I note each turning of its life seasons and see all that is beautiful or ugly here. My bayou, my body. No one may take these.

WORDS THAT FLOAT

THE MAKING OF THE STORY AND THE STORY ITSELF INTERTWINE SO that I can't always tell one from the other. When I began writing my meditation on death-by-water during the winter of early 2005, I didn't consciously anticipate that Hurricane Katrina would come in late summer and drown over a thousand people. During the months leading up to the hurricane, Sallie Ann Glassman made paintings that depicted a hurricane-darkened sky threatening to crush New Orleans. A collage artist friend of mine dreamed about floods and crafted a work that showed a man wearing swim goggles rising from a dark pool of water with the caption overhead: "So where does this leave us?" A sculptor in my neighborhood made ceramic pieces to evoke a massive deluge; she too did this work before the storm. Jimmy, the drunk I shot pool with occasionally, had been walking around muttering, "Water, water everywhere, not a drop to drink." How did any of us know what we were saying with our words and images? We didn't, not in any rational way. Perhaps we smelled her coming. Like good smart dogs, we may have picked up the scent of danger in the distance and then started barking. Or in our cases, ruminating on dark possibilities for reasons we couldn't explain. Dogs don't exactly know why they're barking either. But it's a good idea to pay attention when they do.

Ever since the deluge by water, we here in New Orleans have been deluged by words. So much has been said and written about Katrina and our sad, broken city, and still the stories flow. Just as the tragedy itself has not finished unfolding (as of this writing, eight months after, they have found more bodies in the Ninth Ward and Lakeview), so too the struggle to frame it with words continues. It was nearly a year before I could begin to add my drop to the sea of words. For a long time after the storm, I felt paralyzed, muted by the crushing scenes of loss in the streets and houses around me. From the moment Katrina forced us to leave our home, I felt the grip of a powerful riptide dragging me into deep and unfamiliar water, where it left me to swim or sink into sadness. It took time to pull myself to shore, so that I could lie still, try to breathe, and understand what had just happened to all of us. You can't write about a riptide when you're in it.

There is a story that I clipped from the newspaper that has been curling and yellowing on my desk. It's the obituary for Cecile Dupont Martin, who died in the storm. I can't stop looking at her photo. She wears a pink plaid blouse, has blue eyes and a lopsided smile. She looks like a fairytale grandma you could carry around in your apron pocket. The article came from a series in the *Times-Picayune* titled "Katrina's Lives Lost," a meticulous process of drawing all the lines of every face, every life that ended. The stories are more like mini-profiles than the traditional dry-toned obituaries. The reporters interviewed family members to cull together the telling anecdotes that would make the person's life story more vivid. In addition, each story also attempts to piece together details of the person's death. There is an excruciating tension in these stories, a dogged forcing of the truth, as if the story is daring us to look away, forbidding us to go back to sleep.

Cecile Dupont Martin's life story includes the information that she was born in 1910, grew up on Dumaine Street, and played the piano. She and her sister gave concerts on WDSU radio in the 1930s. She was a diminutive woman, who baked *pfefferneusses*, cultivated roses, and worked as a schoolteacher.

Cecile Dupont Martin's death story includes the information that she and her daughter Judith weathered the storm in their Lakeview home. Judith takes over the story at this point. She tells the reporter that she tried to take her mother into the attic because the water level was rising above their heads. The reporter quotes Judith as saying, "I pulled her up onto the steps. Suddenly, she said quietly, but with determination, 'I give up.' Then she pitched forward into the water." The next morning Judith swam to safety. Searchers found her mother's body in the house over a month later.

The scene that Judith painted of her mother's plunge into the flood pulled me in different directions at once. My immediate reaction was a constriction at the back of my throat that always precedes tears. Then a heavy sensation deep in my chest. Then a feeling of urgency. I wanted to lower my arms into the story and lift the women out of the water.

In my later reaction, the cool writerly section of my brain noticed the story-making apparatus that surrounded the dense emotional core in this image of the woman at the top of the attic stairs. This part of my brain, usually the observer and often the examiner, instinctively seizes on a certain thing to pull it apart, see what it's made of, get to the center of it, understand what it does, discover why it is meaningful. There had to be some reason I clipped this story from the paper among all the other stories. Some reason the reporter chose this quote. Some reason the daughter, Judith, chose to say these words about her mother, Cecile. But why? Where is the true center of this story? How can we know what truly happened, or why it has worked itself into a fold in my imagination, where I return to it, worrying it again and again like a raspberry seed lodged between two molars.

The scene hinges on a quote within a quote, and to those layers of perception that shape the telling and the retelling we must also consider the outer layer of the story, where the reporter herself shapes the telling with her own perception. The arrangement of these elements resembles one of those hollow Russian dolls of painted wood that contains a doll within a doll within a doll and so on, until you reach the tiniest doll at the center. The tiniest doll at last is Cecile, of course, but she isn't alive to give us the story at the center. She is the silent, opaque kernel of truth that we can never reach. So now we have to rely on the outer layers of the story, knowing each is a certain version with its own author, including me.

To begin with, we hear the daughter recalling that her mother spoke "quietly but with determination." There is something so artful about adverbs. Whenever I notice someone has inserted an adverb like "quietly" when relating the details of an event, I sense there is some craft afoot. Then I had to wonder, is this Judith's craft, or did the reporter insert that artful adverb to make the story more vivid in the reader's mind? We don't know, but let's assume the reporter did her job right and quoted Judith accurately. Now the question is, did Cecile speak "quietly but with determination," or is this the way Judith has chosen to remember it? It's possible that Judith has re-created the scene in this way with these qualities of tone for the benefit of her listener, the reporter. Not that she wishes deliberately to mislead anyone, but that in this artful remembering, Judith elevates her mother's death to the level of myth and imbues it with heroism. She characterizes Cecile as facing death with determination, a strong woman who steered the ship of her own destiny to its most terrifying end. How romantic and beautiful, and it may be completely true, for all we know. But if so, I sense that this truth is mythological in nature, a truth we get at through polishing the factual details until they reflect an image we desire.

Certainly it was my sense of Judith's desire to love her mother upward into a beautiful mythological realm by telling her death story in this way that moved me to tears. And if Judith has elevated Cecile's death into a myth, so what? Or rather I should say, why not? This is what we do, we wordy humans. We continually craft stories from the things that happen to us, both great and small. It's the only way we know how to get through this otherwise undifferentiated flow of stuff. Truly the only way to survive the riptide is to tell someone how you did it.

Here is the myth I crafted from the details of Cecile's death story. I telescoped into her decision to pitch forward off the stairs, by saying, "I give up." And then giving in to the water. In my vision, I see a tiny, stalwart woman who had witnessed nearly the entire breadth of a century, and all the ebb and flow of births, friendships, weddings, seasons, first school shoes, economic downturns, gardening chores, scandalous presidents, odd jobs, new frying pans, old houses, arguments, reconciliations, beginnings and endings. Here is a woman who can remember New Orleans and herself when they were both their younger, fresher selves. Here she is at the top of her own stairs, watching as Death comes in her front door and rushes up the steps to meet her.

It's important to the story that Death comes to her as a massive wave of water, a natural force beyond her choice or influence. Clearly if it had been her choice, Cecile would still be among us. By the same token, she and her daughter did make certain choices along the way that led to the two of them being cornered up against the attic—perhaps they might have chosen to evacuate the city before the storm. Not that they had any influence over this, but it bears mentioning that if the Army Corps of Engineers had built the 17th Street Canal properly, that neighborhood wouldn't have flooded. For the myth's sake, however, let's put aside what might have been and focus on the simplicity and the purity of Cecile's decision.

For the myth's sake, I see a woman who has lived nearly a century, who can sit at the top of her stairs and burrow down past all thought, all ego, past all temporal concerns, and find the deep knowledge that now is the time, right now is the end of her long life. Instead of letting the water drag her away, fighting it with fear and repugnance, she embraces it. Instead of hating this water, she finds her calm center and looks into it with honest courage to see it for what it is—the thing that comes next. She returns to the water as if it were home, as an ending that flows inevitably from the beginning. How graceful is Cecile Dupont Martin. How beautiful and brave that she would cherish her death as she had cherished her life.

February 2nd, Candlemas, Groundhog's Day, and Imbolc to honor Saint Brigid. A year after that Lenten season when I accepted my stewardship of the bayou, we returned to the belly of the goddess and celebrated the Feast of the Purification of the Virgin, signifying the moment that hints at distant life to come. This day tells us: Don't be afraid. The world is not as dead as it seems. Spring flickers beneath the dull brown mud.

On that day, they found another body in the bayou. A twenty-four-year-old man named Matt Johnson, who had been missing for a few days. Earlier someone had found his cell phone by the edge of the water. A couple of days later, my neighbor Perry saw the body floating beneath the cypress trees near Moss Street and Carrollton Avenue. It just so happened that Sean's brother was also named Matt Johnson, but he was alive, not dead.

When the dead man's family was looking for him, they posted flyers all around the neighborhood, leaving them in everyone's mailbox. Then, when the news report came out that a Matt Johnson had been found dead, Matt's friends experienced a fright attack of their own, until Sean could assure them this was not their Matt Johnson but someone else's. It felt creepy to see the name of someone you knew, contained in a sentence along with the word "dead." A couple of years ago, a man with the same name as my husband was murdered. It gave me the shakes to read this name with the word "murdered," even though Sean was sitting close by, alive and well. These words, names especially, have a totemic power beyond meaning. They reach beneath our rational radar and grab us in the gut. Perhaps I was superstitious, but I wanted these words to be stricken from the public record. I wanted them not to exist. I was afraid they would open a door that should remain closed.

In a strange footnote to this drowning story, Sean's brother said he had met the other Matt Johnson the night he died. They were both hanging out in the same bar, got to talking, and discovered they had the same name, which they found amusing. The other Matt's roommate had wondered if someone followed his friend when he left the bar and did him some harm. The coroner classified the death as an accidental drowning, and the *Times-Picayune* stated there was no sign of "foul play." (I was irritated that a reporter would still use that hackneyed phrase.) Even so, a police spokesman said the case remains open. In another layer to the story, the drowned man's father had died the previous month, so it's likely he was suffering his own depression on top of the blanket of depression that has muffled all our lives in New Orleans since the storm. This could have been one of the many post-Katrina suicides. Hard to tell.

The cypress tree that stands at the curve of the bayou where this man's body floated to shore bears a small brass plaque inscribed with the word "faith," the quixotic work of one of our neighborhood artists. I have passed this tree on my morning walks nearly every day for several years, and each time I glance up to see that the plaque remains screwed into its bark. Lately, I have noticed that the bark has started to grow around one edge of the plaque, so now it reads, "aith." I'm not sure what I'll do when "faith" disappears entirely.

INNOCENCE COMES TO A CLOSE

FOR MANY OF US, THE STORY OF HURRICANE KATRINA IS DECORATED WITH A string of cheap motels. My version began in the laundry room of a Motel 6 along the interstate in Austin, Texas. That's where we went when we left Bayou Saint John behind in New Orleans to escape the storm. I had propped up my laptop on the washing machine, while our laundry sloshed around inside, and started writing to stay sane. A friend had pointed out that for many women writers, an undeniable facet of their writing lives is that they have had to squeeze their writing into the small portions of time between making life, preserving life, laundry, and dinner. Another writer friend of mine told me that in the early days of Alice Munro's writing career, when she was also raising children, she got her writing done by propping up her typewriter on top of the washing machine. One more reason to love Alice Munro.

So I started writing about my exile from home, and what appeared on CNN to be happening to our home. I was recording my experiences from moment to moment. It was just three days into the catastrophe, and by this time, it had become clear that we were in the midst of a historic moment. It was also clear that we were not going home any time soon. Since there was nothing else for me to do, I bought a laptop and started keeping a record.

I had churned out about 5,000 words—not all of them brilliant, but they were mine. I felt productive. I had been documenting quickly with a lot of shorthand. We had moved on from Austin and made it all the way up to Portsmouth, New Hampshire. Since we couldn't go home to New Orleans, Sean had booked himself a concert tour at yoga studios up and down the East Coast. They were eager to help a New Orleans yoga teacher and to hear Sean's singing. We had suddenly become an itinerant *kirtan* band, while we waited to see what would happen to New Orleans.

One day, I was checking my email, when all of a sudden, in mid-tippy-tapping, my computer started to make odd clicking noises and then froze. Then a flashing question mark appeared on the screen. Then nothing. I couldn't make it do anything at all. It had died. More specifically, I learned, when I finally got an Apple technician on the phone, the hard drive had died. Gone. Swept away. All the words I had written gone with it.

"Data not retrievable," said the technician.

"How could a three-week-old computer just die?"

"Infant mortality," he called it. "Happens sometimes."

Interesting. I plunged into a despairing rage. Sean, absorbed in his *kirtan* tour, could not understand why I was flying around in this aroused state. Oddly this hard-drive crash depressed me more than the hurricane did. Once the reality of it sank in, I felt so defeated. I had worked hard, and now it was all gone. These are the thoughts that I am sure a lot of people were thinking as they stood on the roofs of their crushed, flooded, sodden, stinking, mud-caked homes in New Orleans. It may be true that the loss of a hard drive is small in comparison to the loss of a home, yet it feels similar. I was having a shadow experience of theirs. Not standing in the same place, but hovering in a liminal space around the same thing. This is the space reserved for writers.

There was one other time when I experienced a fatal computer crash. It happened two days after the airplanes brought the World Trade Towers to the ground on September 11th. That occurred on a Tuesday. On Wednesday, the editor of the weekly paper I was freelancing for called and said he was dumping the issue they were about to put out, and instead they were putting together a quick emergency issue. He needed new stories related to the catastrophe in New York. I spent that afternoon at our local blood bank to research a story on the hundreds of people in New Orleans who donated blood for the survivors who we hoped would come out of the wreckage in

Manhattan. On Thursday morning I finished the story, 2,000 words. I hit the send button to email it over to my editor. Then it happened. A sickening weird sound came from my computer, and the screen went blank. This time it was the motherboard that died. Yes, very sad, but no time to mourn. I had to get this story over to the paper. The issue closed in a few hours, and my story was trapped inside my dead computer.

So I jumped in my car, drove to the newspaper's office, borrowed one of their computers, and retyped the whole 2,000-word thing, verbatim, from memory. Quite a neat hat trick, but it didn't work for my second episode of a computer catastrophe mirroring a larger catastrophe in the world.

Hurricane Katrina robbed me of my cognitive skills. And my willpower. I knew I had to start over, but I didn't want to. For weeks, as we traveled on this tour, I carried around a computer with a dead hard drive, like a stillborn fetus. We were moving from city to city, not staying anywhere long enough for me to get the computer fixed or to return it to the manufacturer for a new hard drive. I carried this useless thing around but couldn't look at it. I made handwritten notes, but I was still mourning the death of this laptop. It had signified independence for me. It helped me keep some definition of myself as I got swept along in the juggernaut of Sean's tour. I did not come on this tour by choice. I was along for the ride because I had no place else to go. So I felt trapped and helpless. I didn't realize until my computer was dead how much I was depending on this laptop to keep me connected to the thing that keeps me rooted in myself.

I made one last effort to retrieve the contents of my hard drive during our stay in Philadelphia. A pimply, emaciated kid with blue-black hair who worked at the Apple Store in the King of Prussia Mall—too smart for his own good and not inclined toward sympathy—kept me waiting about four hours before spending three minutes diddling with the keys. He inclined his multi-pierced ear toward the screen to listen more intently to the telltale clicking noise.

"It's hopeless. Sorry," he said in a bored tone that suggested no sorrow at all. I told him we were on the run from Katrina, homeless and desperate. The pimply kid sighed and rolled his eyes. He dug down deep and found a sliver of compassion. He agreed to send it back to those unhelpful people at Apple for me, even though he wasn't supposed to because it wasn't his job.

The laptop went back to the manufacturer and then returned with a new hard drive, its virginity magically restored. Blank, unsullied by use, devoid of words, mine to begin again. I was happy to see it, but still a little angry. Consequently it took me some time to start over.

The *kirtan* tour ended when we went to stay with our friends Jo and Moira in Tennessee for a few days. This was supposed to be a brief rest before our return to New Orleans, and before Sean took his new musical career out to the West Coast for the next leg of his tour. I would not go with him to California, because I just couldn't stand another road trip. Truth be told, I wasn't sorry to see him go without me. I wanted some distance to see my husband more clearly. After so much time on the road, sleeping in a different bed every night, eating bad food, watching the news from New Orleans, in each other's company constantly with little or no privacy, I was pretty much on my last nerve. While I had spent the past several weeks in a state of acute anxiety, trying to imagine what waited for us in New Orleans, Sean had been riding a wave of bliss.

"I really like this," he said one afternoon on Interstate 81 somewhere between Roanoke and Knoxville. "We don't need to go back to New Orleans. We could be on tour like this from now on. Why not?" He smiled at the road before him, the soul of contentment. All images of our house, our street, the trees I had planted, the bridge where we had promised our-selves to each other—all these had vanished from his memory. Now it was the gypsy life for Sean. All that mattered was the next concert and the next round of applause.

"Are you *insane?*" I was coming unglued in the passenger seat as I gripped a map in one hand and cell phone in the other, hard at the task of navigator, while my husband dreamed of the open road and his new, wide fan base. "How can you say you wouldn't go back to New Orleans? We have a whole life back there. A home. You have a business. We can't just walk away from all that. Like it doesn't matter."

The words I didn't say out loud: What about me? And what I want? Aren't there two of us in this car?

Sean assured me that he was just daydreaming out loud. He wasn't really going to abandon our home, and I shouldn't take his words as literal. I wasn't sure what to believe anymore, and wasn't sure who this man was in the seat beside me.

By the time we arrived at our friends' home in Tennessee, we collapsed into their hospitality. This was a safe haven at last, where I could loosen the stays around my troubled heart. I had just spent the past six weeks watching our city fall into ruin, and helping Sean realize a long-cherished dream. I was tired of having my own dream put on hold by this storm and our strained living situation. So, I revived a conversation I'd had with my husband the previous winter. I wanted to have a baby.

Perhaps it was inopportune timing that I chose this period of hurricane-forced exile to bring up having a baby. Yet, I couldn't stop myself. The first time I had spoken to him about it was the previous January, when I took him out to dinner for his birthday. As we looked over the wine list, I gave him what I thought was the most wonderful birthday present ever.

"Well, I think I'm finally ready."

"For what?" he asked, flipping through the menu.

"To have a baby." I leaned across the table. My heart thumped. I was a little breathless. It had taken me weeks to work up the courage to say these words. "Sean, I think we should have a child."

"But I don't want a child," Sean said in a mild tone. He wore a quizzical smile, as if surprised I would bring up such an absurd idea. Then he went back to reading the menu with the same neutral air, as if I had said I wanted white wine when he wanted red.

If he had slapped me across the face, I could not have been more stunned. This was not how I imagined the conversation would go. I lifted my fork and then replaced it next to my empty dish. I sipped my water. Coughed. Sean said nothing. I was actually embarrassed to be caught wanting a baby and told "no" by the man who had promised always to say "yes" to me. Had I misunderstood? Shame flooded through me.

For the rest of the evening, I faked my way through his birthday dinner, forced myself to wear a smiling mask, while inside, my vital organs turned to wood. That night in bed I lay awake and stared into the darkness.

There was a weighted mass in my chest. I had to adjust myself around it. I couldn't sleep, and I couldn't believe that Sean had rejected the most precious thing I could offer any man. The man I married couldn't spurn this gift. He adored kids. It didn't make sense. We were in love and best friends. A great couple. Smart, fair-minded, resourceful. We had so much to offer a child. Our lives would be so enriched by a child. Of course we should have a baby. It was the most natural thing in the world. What had just happened? My mind couldn't absorb it. Lower down in my gut, the knowledge waited.

Months later, during our exile from the storm and with our home in peril, I brought up the topic again. I was going to fight for my desire, and I couldn't afford to lose any more time. The familiar touchstones of our shared life were turning to sand and slipping through my fingers. So I took this time, fraught as it was with uncertainty and sorrow, to ask again. To ask my husband to make a bond of love with me through the life of a child.

He said he did not want to be a father. He liked his life the way it was, didn't see any reason to change it. Didn't want to add to his responsibilities. Besides, now that he was becoming a famous *kirtan* musician, he planned to tour the world with his band. A baby didn't fit in with that scenario.

The other topic on the table, for me at least, was that ever since we got married, Sean had become increasingly absent. Not long after we started dating, he opened his own yoga studio rather than teach for someone else. I helped him launch this business. Soon it was as though we were sharing our home with a 3,000-pound gorilla. The studio consumed all of Sean's attention, as well as a great deal of my time and energy. I wanted to contribute to his success, but I also wanted an intimate relationship with my husband. Sean allowed his professional agenda to become so bloated with importance that I had to help him run his studio just to have time with him. This was my pathetic effort to connect more deeply with Sean. Now, I was demanding to have a married life separate from his career.

"Don't you get it? I am trying to tell you that I miss you!" I cried in exasperation. "How am I going to get pregnant if you're never around?" Sean had no answer. He was honestly dumbfounded by the question. He didn't see that there was a problem.

I tried reasoning with him. I believed that if I just found the right words, he'd come around. In the past, I had always been able to appeal to his good sense. I could always count on Sean's love and that he wanted me to be happy. But Sean was deaf to my words and distracted. He couldn't see or hear how devastated I was by his refusal to have a child. Or by his absence. He could only look hungrily to the future, where there were more audiences waiting to hear him sing. It would take time to understand the full extent to which Sean was becoming dazzled with himself and a stranger to me.

The topic of having a baby was swept aside by Katrina, and by Sean's rush to get to the next gig. There wasn't time to talk in depth or come to any conclusions. There were too many other pressing details to take care of.

"I'll think about it and get back to you," Sean said. That was the best I could get out of him at that point. I knew I wasn't going to put aside my hope for a child, but for the time being I would have to be alone with my thoughts.

The time I spent in Tennessee was a good break for both me and Lance, who got to act more like a dog than ever before in his pampered life. Jo and Moira lived on twenty-five acres of wood and meadow at the edge of Cherokee National Forest. Their two dogs, Danu and Halliday, taught Lance how to bark at coons, run in the stream, and snorfle out dead things buried in wet leaves. Lance was in dog heaven, save for the fact that he had to sleep in the garage with the other dogs. Dogs are loved, but not welcome inside the house. Lance was confused by this rule and didn't understand why he was not allowed to track muddy paw prints all over my bed as he does at home in New Orleans.

Jo and Moira gave me their guest bedroom, which had a wall of windows and a desk that overlooked a forest of changing trees. Each morning, I sat at the desk and looked out onto red-gold leaves and pine needles turning brown as they fell. There was a mirror on the wall next to the desk. I have had a recurring dream for many years that I am sitting at a desk and I am writing. There is a mirror over the desk, so that I look into my own reflection as I write.

So I felt compelled to write the story again of how we escaped the hurricane. I had it before, and it died with the hard drive. I would try to get it back, while understanding it wouldn't be the same. When I began again, I was writing from a different time and perspective, a greater distance. It was less confusing by then. From this vantage point, it had already begun fading into myth, the sharper details softening with time. Well, anyway, here's the story.

When I looked at the newspaper on Thursday, August 25, 2005, I saw a map of our region showing that a hurricane was heading into the Gulf. The tracking line showed that the storm would veer east toward Florida. *Oh, poor Florida, not again.* It was a heartfelt thought but brief. Though I have enjoyed vacationing there, let's face it, Florida is not my home, so I am not deeply stirred with fear at the news of a hurricane heading that way. So I went about my life as if things were normal.

On Friday, I invited my friend Michele to go to a wine tasting at the Pitot House, which is just across Bayou Saint John from my home. They were calling it "Vino on the Bayou." In the early evening, nearing dusk, with the August air hanging heavy as a fur cloak, Michele and I walked the two blocks and over the Magnolia Bridge. The Pitot House, which also happens to be where Sean and I had our wedding reception, is one of the city's original plantations. Built in 1799, it was the home of the first elected mayor of New Orleans. It's a spare, open French colonial house with green shutters, a wide gallery on the second floor, and a garden fenced in with old gray weathered boards. Now it's a museum and a great place for parties.

We ran into another friend of mine, Anne, at the wine tasting. I remember we enjoyed a nice Pinot Noir. Anne mentioned that she had heard a hurricane was supposed to be turning toward New Orleans. This news inspired only mild interest. We walked outside to the cobbled courtyard overlooking the gardens, the flowers making their customary display of sexual readiness, the fleshy petals pushing through dense thickets of green, winding tangles of vines reaching ever farther along the fence for more light, more rain. Nature can be *so* vulgar, but I loved this garden and its gorgeous, shameless excess that is utterly New Orleans. Anything worth doing is worth overdoing. That has always been the guiding theme of our city's life.

Not enough has been said or written about the weather in New Orleans. More specifically about late summer in New Orleans. No mere weather pattern, August in this city is a presence of such density that it qualifies as its own entity. It's not enough to say that it's hot here in August. Having lived through many of these seasons, I can attest that it would be more accurate to describe August as a stalker. Not the skinny, furtive kind that knocks on your door and runs away. No, August is the big, slow, obvious type of stalker, who is too dumb to realize you don't want him around. He breathes hot dirt down your neck and wraps his meaty arms around you, pulling you into his fat gut, slick with sweat. And you're pinned there, helpless to escape. August follows you everywhere and could drive you crazy. Even when you're sitting in your air-conditioned house, you know he's out there waiting for you. If you open your door, August will descend on you and fill your nose and ears and eyes. The air can actually push into your skin like a dull punch that you can't punch back. It's too big and too thick and everywhere all at once.

Michele and I stood outside the Pitot House, enveloped in August's suffocating embrace. We talked about the creative-writing program at the University of New Orleans that Michele had just started. Her face gleamed with happy anticipation and sweat. We were dripping just standing still in this woolen air. The sweat rolled down my thighs in streams into my shoes. Whenever I think about the New Orleans that existed before Katrina, this image comes back to me. The two of us standing there, surrounded by fragrant flowers, and completely at the mercy of the weather. We could have taken refuge inside the Pitot House, where an elderly, asthmatic air conditioner offered small respite. It was my idea to stand outside with August. Even when it is awful, there is something tempting about the weather in New Orleans. Occasionally I feel the urge to give myself over to it, that obscene stalker. Sometimes I want to stop resisting it and let it roll over me, just for the sensation of being immersed in a humbling natural force beyond my control.

Of course, I didn't know what I was thinking that Friday evening in August. I didn't know anything about natural forces or the weather. We all went to our homes that night and thought about what we'd do on Saturday. We made dinner plans and talked about the farmer's market. Normal things.

On Saturday morning I checked the weather again, and all those computer-modeled multicolored tracking lines were running right through

New Orleans on the map. The weatherman said contraflow would soon begin on the I-10. The phone started ringing. It was my friend Anne from the previous evening, now a white-nerve case over news of the storm. She tends to become loud and demanding when she is upset. She wanted us to make simultaneous motel reservations so we could all escape the hurricane together. I got us rooms in Memphis, which is where we had waited out that big nonevent from the previous summer, Hurricane Ivan. (I would later change this reservation to a motel in Austin, Texas, when it became apparent that the storm was going to pass right over Memphis.) Then I had to hang up on Anne because she was screaming at me, "I can't deal with this!" I had an appointment to meet a writer friend of mine to discuss the latest chapters of his novel-in-progress. We sat in a coffee shop on Magazine Street and did not talk about the weather.

After that, I went to Sean's yoga studio. We had a tense discussion that went more or less like this:

Me: We have to get out of town immediately. There is a hurricane coming.

Him: Bruce says it's not coming here. It's going to Florida. (Bruce is Sean's father.)

Me: We have to get out of town immediately. There is a hurricane coming.

Him: Sweetie, but what if it misses us again, like Ivan last year?

Me: Then we'll be wrong. Then we'll take an unnecessary trip to Memphis. So what? Who cares? We have to get out of town immediately. There is a hurricane coming.

Him: I can't leave while Bruce is working on the renovation. (Just a few weeks earlier, Sean had begun the expansion of one of the yoga rooms that involved knocking through a wall. His father was doing much of the work. While the rest of the city scrambled to safeguard their homes and flee for their lives from a category 5 hurricane, Bruce was sanding the edge of a new door because it had exhibited a vexing drag against the frame.)

Me: You have to put plywood on the studio windows and then come home and cover the windows of our house. We have to get out of town immediately. There is a hurricane coming.

Him: But I'm not sure yet that I'll cancel classes for tomorrow. What if students show up and we're not open?

Me (*in a shrill voice*): The governor has declared a state of emergency! No one is coming to class tomorrow! They are all putting plywood on their windows and leaving! Do you understand what is happening? We have to get out of town immediately! There is a hurricane coming!

FLIGHT FROM THE BAYOU

A FEW YEARS AGO, SIX MONTHS INTO MY RELATIONSHIP WITH SEAN, a tropical storm headed toward New Orleans. It looked as though it might turn into a hurricane by the time it reached us. Naturally I assumed that when I shared this information with Sean, he and I would leave town to avoid being in the path of a dangerous weather system.

"We never leave for hurricanes," he said coolly. He uttered these words as a manifest article of faith. It came from a fixed family ethic that emanated from the patriarch, Bruce. Sean, his mother, and his brothers adopted the family ethic without question. Simply put: You're a pussy if you leave town for a hurricane. This ethic is not unique to my husband's family, for as we know, many people in New Orleans think this way. The thinking follows the basic line that you earn your right to call yourself a local if you stay for hurricanes. You also earn the right to sneer at the pussies who *do* leave—which is quite gratifying, I gather.

I have to believe there is something more complex than mere idiocy driving this train of thought. The way I parse it is that the people inclined to stay through a hurricane have a strong attachment not only to the actual house they live in, but also to the larger home of the city. There is a familial devotion to New Orleans that grows stronger in the face of an extreme threat like a hurricane. It is precisely because they could be wiped out by a storm that the devout locals cling even more tightly to their city. They show contempt for the leavers because they believe if you loved New Orleans as she deserves to be loved, you would never leave her.

Many New Orleanians are also frankly exhilarated by the prospect of a hurricane. One local legend centers on that lover of pelicans, the painter Walter Anderson, who is rumored to have tied himself to a tree during Hurricane Betsy in 1965. In Anderson's journal *The Horn Island Log*, he included one brief entry on Betsy, where it appears he weathered the storm on Horn Island by hiding under his overturned rowboat. "Never has there been a hurricane more respectable," he wrote. Some New Orleanians prefer the story of Walter tied to a tree with Betsy's wind and rain right up against his skin. In any event, he lived to tell the tale.

Sometimes missing from the story is the fact that Walter spent time as a patient in a psychiatric hospital. This fact alone is not an indictment of his character. I'm sure he was a fine man, and charming too. However it does lead me to think it might not be prudent to hold his choices as a measuring stick for those of a less antic disposition. Nonetheless, Walter is a hero in some quarters. He was not afraid of Betsy, or if he was, he didn't let that stop him from accepting her full embrace.

One of my dog-walking bayou buddies, Nancy—mother to a lanky white and tan mutt named Renny, whose tail curls exactly like that swirling hurricane symbol they put on the TV weather maps—told me later that she and her partner Bill had stayed in their home through Katrina, but would never do it again. The storm itself, they didn't mind so much. Bill had put on his motorcycle helmet and gone out into the wind just to feel it. It was the long stretch of time they were stranded in their own house by the floodwaters that wore them down. Without electrical power, running water, or a way out, the plain bodily discomfort of the situation quickly grew unacceptable. Poor Renny had no place to conduct his own bowel and bladder evacuation. Nancy spread some newspapers on the porch for him, but Renny didn't know what to do with the papers. He needed a patch of grass to conduct his business—that's what he was accustomed to before the flood. So Bill urinated on the newspapers in the hope that this would inspire Renny to do likewise. Nope, that didn't work either. It was days before

Renny was able to release his own discomfort. Then food and water started to run low. This was all a little too much nature.

"Yeah, hurricanes always excited me in the past," said Nancy. "But not anymore. I'm over it."

Clearly many of the people who stayed behind in New Orleans during Katrina did so because they did not have the financial means to leave. Most of the folks who went to the Convention Center and the Superdome didn't have cars to drive out of town or a credit card to pay for a Motel 6. Many others, elderly people, stayed in New Orleans because they were physically and mentally unable to move. There is a certain age of inertia that folks reach when they tend to think that however bad the storm, it couldn't be worse than a long car trip to Houston. Better to take their chances at home.

Still there remains a portion of folks in New Orleans, able both in body and bank account, who are nonetheless possessed with a perverse curiosity to know up close just how bad the hurricane could be. My hunch is that there is an unspoken desire for sensual contact with nature that goes beyond any ordinary encounter. A lot of us probably don't get to feel enough of the natural world—or the part that we can feel doesn't feel like enough.

One friend, who had evacuated for Katrina, said later that if another hurricane came to New Orleans, she'd stay. "I want to be somehow . . . stronger than the storm," she said, and punched her soft fist into her palm. I wonder if now that she has an infant daughter, she would still make that choice.

Mixed into this messy nest of motives among those who could leave but don't is a streak of vanity that drives the decision to stay and greet the hurricane in person. There is an undeniable desire for bragging rights. Or put another way, to have a good story to tell. It's incredible what some people are willing to risk just to have a good story to tell. Although I would never stay for a hurricane, I can see the allure. Our placement on the continent makes New Orleans a unique funnel for this amazing story. Few will ever know firsthand what it's like to hear the wind like a freight train running through your house. (This is the most repeated image that survivors of Betsy use to describe the sound of the hurricane's wind.) And there is no substitute for a story that comes from direct experience.

Hurricanes excite us because these storms bring a disruption into lives that are too orderly and boring, although no one will admit this. The hurricane stirs things up, and loosens the blocks that have been clogging up our lives. I imagine that a lot of us will be living differently and choosing differently as an outcome of Katrina. The hurricane's enormous power to change attracts people who feel stuck. What makes it even more attractive is the awareness, lurking at the edge of conscious thought, that this power could bring the end of your life. The attraction grows with the threat of death because if you can be immersed in this power and *not* die, well then your orderly life becomes something quite remarkable.

What makes this even nicer for folks is that they don't have to seek out this threat of death—like bungee jumpers, for example. Now *there's* a stupid hobby, and you have to buy all that equipment. New Orleanians don't have to go to any trouble or expense for the gift of danger. They can just stand on their porches and wait for the storm. Staying in your house through a hurricane is a rare chance to do something, without looking like you're trying, that could be interpreted as pretty ballsy. Who could pass that up?

Of course, the whole thing hinges on living to tell the tale. Dead or alive, we are still idiots. But the ones who live to tell the story at least get to hold the enchanted status of the wise fool.

Therein lies the Katrina conundrum. She made fools of us all. And the worst fools were the ones wielding their bragging rights. It just wasn't so cute anymore when over fourteen hundred people died, thousands more were homeless, and the city was crippled. I'm the fool who wants to take back the story. I won't allow it to be a story about how cool it is to be stupid. This is a different story.

By the time we finished our tense conversation in his office, I had convinced Sean to take this hurricane seriously and leave town with me. So I went out to secure provisions for our trip: a few gallons of water, dried banana chips, organic raisins, power bars. The usual fare that we take with us on long car trips across America, because America is hell for eating, especially if you are vegetarians and not inclined to eat foods fried in corn oil. This seemed important to me at the time, making sure we got wholesome food in our bellies.

I watched the news on TV, switching channels every few minutes—first

Bob Breck on Channel 8, the merry elf of our local weather news, and then the announcers on the two other channels we get. (We were not a cable family.) In the few hours since I had last checked the news, the situation had grown worse. The tracking lines now pointed to New Orleans as a bull's-eye for this storm. And the wind speed had increased to a category 5 level. I didn't need Bob Breck or his toupee to tell me that it doesn't get any worse than that. In the segue between each newsflash, Channel 8 ran a continuous loop of an old piece of video from some other storm years ago where Bob Breck says, "We're not going to leave you alone with this storm."

"Thanks Bob!" I wanted to yell at the TV. "Will you come to my house and hold my hand? Because I am getting a little nervous."

Then there was Mayor Ray Nagin, talking in that sleepy stoner, hipster way that he has—he always sounds like he just woke up from a nap—bobbing and weaving around an interview with Norm Robinson on Channel 6. Nagin hinted that he *wanted* to order a mandatory evacuation, but had been prevented from doing so by some legal technicality. Had everyone gone insane? Where were the grownups?

TV was making me feel worse, not better, so I returned to the studio to find that Bruce and Sean had not yet gone out to get plywood to cover the windows. The day was slipping away. It was getting dark. No one around here seemed to share my sense of urgency. Sean was dithering in his office. Bruce was muttering snide comments about pussies who leave town for hurricanes. I tried to convince Sean's mother, Mary, that she and Bruce should get out of town with us. She seemed embarrassed by the suggestion.

I went home to put away everything in our yard that might be picked up by the wind and turned into a missile. I tried to imagine what a category 5 hurricane with wind speeds of 175 miles per hour could do to a city made of wood and mud. Well, it could toss it around like a panther clubbing a sparrow. Yet, it seemed a sensible task to put away our flowerpots, trashcans, seashells, and every other little thing that we had scattered around our yard. These I stuffed into our shed and piled up cinder blocks against the door to hold it closed. Bear in mind that our shed was a splintering wreck. It held itself together with rust. If this thing survived a hurricane, then I would have it dipped in gold.

At around ten o'clock that night, I went back to the studio to help put plywood over the studio windows. The team consisted of Sean, his parents, and me. Bruce did most of the work, while we held the ladder for him and handed him tools. Bruce cussed the entire time, frequently addressing his own power drill as "You cocksucker!" Bruce's everyday conversational style is filthy, a style he has cultivated with pride. He uses the word "fuck" as a comma. On this night, as his exhaustion grew, his manners wore especially thin. Just to complicate things more, he was wearing a patch over one eye because he had just gotten a splinter in his cornea while helping the guy across the street with *his* plywood. So now Bruce was reduced to driving screws into the wood while looking with one eye. Try that sometime. It would probably make you cuss, too.

We finished the studio at about one o'clock in the morning. Sean asked his parents to leave the city with us.

"We got through Betsy," Mary said in a tentative voice. She was wavering. Bruce put an end to the discussion. "We are not going anywhere," he said. "It's just a big storm."

Sean and I went home to secure our own house with plywood. Unlike his father, Sean didn't cuss much. Years of yoga practice had granted him a considerable well of personal reserve. He did sigh deeply, and that was a sign he had reached the end of his not quite infinite patience. I dreaded those deep sighs. It was also true that my husband—although a great yoga teacher and a great musician—never did bother to learn how to wield a power drill. He could fold his ankles behind his neck and sing like a lion, but he couldn't put up plywood for anything. Neither could I, for that matter, but I am the girl. It was not supposed to be my job to know how to wield a power drill. So the two of us struggled with the drill and the plywood and the ladder and the screws and the drill bits that kept getting worn out—for hours. During this time, our marriage passed a new test of commitment. Every couple should have to cover their windows with plywood in the middle of the night in August while a deadly storm bears down on them, just once, to make sure they have what it takes to stay married.

At one point Sean fell off the ladder. It was my fault, of course, because I was supposed to be holding the ladder. Luckily he landed on his feet like a cat. Those years of yoga training saved the day once more. He did have to stop at that point, though, and close his eyes and breathe. When he opened his eyes, he did not yell, for which I was grateful. He did say that it would be bad for both of us if I accidentally killed him.

To get the full picture of this adventure, you must know that the temperature was about 90 degrees. Even at night, August in New Orleans doesn't give you a break from the heat. Most people retreat into the cool air of their homes at Easter and stay there until Thanksgiving because the climate is not fit for any kind of vigorous outdoor activity. Consequently, I was sweating more than I have ever sweated in my entire life. My clothing felt as though it had been painted onto my body. And we still had to pack.

I hard-boiled some eggs to take on the road with us. I was still fretting about how we would eat. I stuffed a bag with some dog food, Lance's blanket, and a few of his squeaky toys. Only then did I think to attend to my own packing. You can tell a lot about a person by what they take when fleeing a category 5 hurricane. Hours later, when we were halfway to Houston, I would call my parents to tell them we were on the run from Katrina, and my mother would ask, "Did you take the silver?" She was referring to her own wedding silverware, a Reed and Barton rose pattern that she had never liked in the first place because her mother had chosen it for her, which is why the silverware came to live with me at my house. No, I told her, I did not bring the silver.

I did pack a few changes of clothing, enough for three days, which is how long I assumed we'd be gone. I pawed through my stuff and assessed things according to that standard. *Eyebrow tweezers? Nah, I can go three days without those.* I did take some books and magazines, our house deed, our homeowner's insurance policy, an Art Deco garnet ring I had inherited from my grandmother, the negatives of our wedding photos, a bathing suit, my diaphragm, and a wine-bottle opener. (I never travel anywhere without a bathing suit.) I also took a quilt and a soft down pillow from our bed because I couldn't stand those rocky Motel 6 pillows and coverlets that feel like they're made of some industrial byproduct. Whenever we evacuated for a hurricane, we stayed at a Motel 6 because they allowed dogs, but I tried to mitigate the experience by bringing a few comforts from home. At the last minute, I grabbed a folder from my files that contained our marriage license, my birth certificate, and copies of my graduate school transcripts. Interestingly, I neglected to take our passports or our checkbooks. But I sure am glad I remembered those graduate school transcripts. They would prove so useful in the coming months.

Sean had a much simpler approach to the situation. He took a yoga mat, his favorite harmonium, and a box full of lyrics, poems, and mantras—songs he meant to sing. And then he was ready. (I had already packed his bathing suit for him.)

As we headed out the door, it was about four o'clock in the morning. The sky was dark. It was still sleeping time. Yet, our street was alive with activity. All our neighbors were hurrying about the same tasks as ours. The darkness was filled with the whine of power drills and the dull slamming of plywood against window frames. In tacit deference to the darkness, our neighbors spoke in hushed voices, as if they didn't want to wake the sleepers, when in fact we were all awake and walking around outside in this upside-down hour of the morning. We should have been safe in our beds, but instead we were running for our lives, although we still didn't know how true that was.

The man who delivered our newspaper came by and threw the fat rolled Sunday edition onto our driveway. I realized that I had never seen the man who brings our paper each day, because I had never been standing in our yard this early.

I opened the newspaper and saw the shrieking headline: "KATRINA TAKES AIM." *This document will have historical significance. I should archive it.* The last thing I did before we locked up the house was to leave the newspaper on the couch. Two months later I would find it again and hate the sight of that headline so much that I would throw the paper in the trash. *Fuck historical significance. I hate this bitch Katrina.* Even later, I would be sorry that I threw it out. When I calmed down, I understood that it's good to hold onto those documents, even when you feel personally attacked by them.

We paused on the sidewalk in front of our boarded-up house to take one last look before leaving. We stood there, gripping our bags, while Lance danced at the end of his leash. He was happy. He thought we were going on vacation. Our house didn't look like itself anymore. With the plywood over the windows and doors, now it looked like a corpse, lying in state with coins covering its dead eyes. Waiting for a hurricane to come wash it away. We might never see our home again. This could be it. The last look. And our garden too. The jasmine I had planted to climb over the chain-link fence, sometimes called a "hurricane fence," that I had always thought ugly and hoped would soon be covered by the twining, fragrant vines. The young gardenia that all spring and summer had struggled for life beneath my loving ministrations, fishmeal fertilizing tea, and iron supplements before finally rewarding me with three blossoms. The sweet olive trees, the sweet viburnum, the sweet basil. Did I overdo it by planting so much "sweet"? I wanted to give our home sweetness, put this quality into the ground where we stood. This is the house we had come home to from our wedding. After our guests had gone, Sean and I had walked from the bridge where we had said our vows. It was a theatrical stroll beneath the massive arching limbs of the ancient oak trees that lined the street. These giant trees and the exaggerated height of the doors and windows of New Orleans houses make the streets look like a stage set. Then we had tucked ourselves into bed in this honeymoon cottage, where now the climbing jasmine vine curled one tendril in a "come hither" gesture, innocent of any knowledge that a ferocious storm was on her way.

It was time to go. There was no more time to stand and look and remember. Luxuriating in the languid flow of thoughts, my customary state of being, was a habit I couldn't indulge in now. We had to act, right now. We had to leave the house and the garden to fend for themselves. That phrase "safe at home" sounded bittersweet. We had to take care of ourselves. We had to hustle down the sidewalk, stuff Lance and the bags into the back of the van, and get going. I felt my heart pulling from my chest as we drove away from the curb. I had left large chunks of myself back at our house, and I didn't know if I'd ever get them back again.

We drove through the dark city and headed toward Interstate 10 West. The streets were filled with other cars, people who had hoped, as we had, that we'd miss the worst of the traffic if we left before dawn. Our van eased into the stream of cars that stretched ahead on the highway on-ramp. Sealed in air-conditioned darkness, we joined the slow, silent line of red brake lights that blinked with each tiny movement forward. We all drove west, where we thought we'd be safe from the storm. They say the future lies in the west. I had always thought of it as the place the sun goes to die each day. That's where we headed, not knowing, just going.

HONORED GUESTS

ABOUT A HUNDRED MILES LATER, AS WE CRAWLED ALONG I-10 WEST, past the prairies around Lafayette, I checked in with my friend Michele. She had tried to follow us west, but by the time she got onto the interstate, traffic was at a standstill. So she had looped around onto the east-going side, where she gunned it toward her mother's house in Florida, at one point dipping into the country roads to sneak around the state troopers who were redirecting the traffic north.

We were listening to the radio, and the news was getting worse. Mayor Nagin finally announced a mandatory evacuation order. It would surely be a direct hit on New Orleans, and the on-air personality told everyone, "It's time to get the heck out of Dodge." *Oh God, how corny.* Then I looked over at Sean, who was crying. "Our home is going to be destroyed," he said. "There won't be anything left." He kept driving, his cheeks wet and his tired eyes now more red and strained.

We had until now been holding onto the hope that Katrina might veer east before making landfall. In the selfish mental calculus that drives pre-storm thinking, you find yourself hoping the hurricane will, at the last minute, shift just enough to spare your home. Unfortunately, with hurricanes it's impossible to hope for a reprieve for yourself without also by extension wishing the disaster on someone else. If we got our wish and the storm veered just a few miles east, that would take the brunt of it off New Orleans but put the worst of it onto Mississippi. I felt guilty. Yet, I couldn't help wanting and hoping for a reprieve. It had happened that way so many times before.

Every July, Sallie Ann Glassman conducts a public Vodou ceremony calling on Erzuli Dantor to protect New Orleans from hurricanes, as she did this summer as well. Later Sallie Ann would tell an interviewer that the Loa had been giving prophecy for years to warn us about global warming, coastal erosion, and the weak levees. So she had done the best she could. It seems that even Vodou practitioners acknowledge some helplessness in the face of hurricanes and governmental incompetence. Even with the spirits on your side, you can't stop the storm. The best you can hope is to save your own soul, which is what we all were doing out there on I-10 West.

Sean called his parents to tell them we had just heard the mayor had issued the mandatory evacuation order. Bruce said, "We'll take that under consideration," and hung up the phone. It was ten o'clock in the morning, and they still had not decided if they would leave the city. Part of the problem was that Sean's ninety-three-year-old Grandma had declared she was not budging out of her apartment. The previous summer, her son had taken her on a long and pointless trip to Houston for Hurricane Ivan, which never came, and so she asserted this so-called Katrina was not going to push her out of her comfortable home. Grandma hated long car trips. This left the rest of the family, Sean's parents, his two brothers Jeremy and Matt, and his aunt and uncle, standing around waiting for Grandma to understand that this storm was a serious threat and she had to go. Sean's uncle Danny finally went over to Grandma's apartment and forced her into the car and took her to her sister's home in Houston.

Sean checked with his parents later. The threat from the mayor that the police were authorized to arrest anyone they found still residing in the city in defiance of the mandatory evacuation order had convinced them it was time to move. They got out of the house at about noon and were driving east on I-10, toward Florida, caravanning with Jeremy, who had Matt with him. Mary had shoved a Benadryl down their dog Rocky's throat to make him sleep in the car. Like Grandma, Rocky also hates long car trips. Their plan was to outrun the storm, go as far east as they could in one day, hunker down in a motel for three days, and then come back home. That was the last we heard from them for a long time.

We continued our slow pace along the highway, accompanied by thousands of other cars. Our fellow travelers' cars were jammed to the rims with stuff packed in haste—boxes of photo albums, and grocery bags of clothing, baby blankets, toys, and pillows. Dogs panted in the back, while kids knotted themselves into tangled quarrels in the middle seats. Mothers leaned over the seat to toss snacks at the cranky children, while dads hunched over their steering wheels with grim faces. These passing car scenes did not carry the holiday air of families on vacation, but the urgency of fearful retreat.

"This is like a middle-class *Grapes of Wrath*," Sean observed.

At some point in this journey, I got a phone call from a broadcast news producer in New York. He had tracked down a story I had done a couple of years ago on survivors of Hurricane Betsy, and he wanted to know if he could borrow some of the photos.

"I would love to help you out," I said. "But all my clips are in a box in a closet in my house in New Orleans. Right now I am driving *away* from New Orleans. There is a hurricane coming!" He wished me well and hung up the phone. He was a busy man.

The traffic remained thick well toward Lake Charles. A distance that should have taken us three hours to drive took eight. My nerves popping with impatience, I got behind the wheel and took us off the interstate onto the back roads. We passed through little prairie towns, yellow in this midday sun. It was a picturesque detour with lots of stoplights. But the roads were clear, and we could go faster than ten miles an hour, which made us at least feel like we were getting somewhere.

As we got closer to Houston, it was nearing late afternoon. We hadn't slept in thirty-six hours. My eyes blurred the road in front of me. I pinched my own earlobe from time to time to shock myself awake. It was agony not to sleep. I could tell when I was about to nod off when my hearing became muffled, and then I'd feel my head snap as I fell onto the wheel. Sean traded with me, but then I had to stay awake to make sure he was staying awake. I caught him nodding in the driver's seat too. We were becoming a danger to ourselves.

Our original plan was to get to Austin, because we figured, hey, if you have to be stuck someplace for three days, it might as well be someplace fun like Austin. But as we got closer to Houston, we realized that if we tried to push all the way through to Austin, we might kill ourselves by driving off the road. So I started calling all the Motel 6s in Houston. I finally found a motel with one vacancy, but it was a smoking room. I hesitated. Neither of us wanted to sleep with the smell of cigarettes. The man on the phone said, "Lady, I promise you, this is the last motel room in Houston. I think you should take it." We took it.

Hurricane Katrina has transformed me into a connoisseur of Motel 6s. They have few distinguishing characteristics and so blur together, which gives me comfort. I always know what to expect. For instance, the rooms all seem to have the same damp rug and odor of mildew. Yet none of these was so welcome to me as this, the last room in Houston. Finally we could stop driving. I unbent my creaky legs, and we threw our bags onto the floor. I forced myself to walk Lance so he could relieve himself on the small patch of grass in the parking lot, with the roar of interstate traffic rushing by. Poor dog. Loves vacations. Hates long car rides. The parking lot was packed, every space taken up by cars loaded to the roof, and young guys cranked up their car stereos to achieve that bone-shaking bass line. The motel manager walked through the parking lot and pressed his index finger to his pursed lips. Shhh, he said, could they please turn down the volume? Refugees were sleeping. The guys said, okay.

We watched the news. What a luxury. CNN and everything else. For us non-cable people, this was sensory blast, but all the information was useless because nothing had happened yet. There were scenes of New Orleans just waiting. Long lines of people looking bored and irritated as they trailed into the Superdome. Stray revelers enjoying one last cocktail on Bourbon Street. A man who had refused to leave his shrimp boat.

The national weather news had grown even more hyper since the morning. It seemed the whole world was crackling with awareness of New Orleans. The spooky strain of music that CNN played on every segue of its Katrina coverage still haunts my head. It was actually kind of exciting to see Wolf Blitzer (former Pentagon reporter during the first Gulf War!) paying so much attention to my little town. The previous year when Hurricane Ivan had passed us by without so much as a ruffle, I had come home from that evacuation and watered the garden because it hadn't even drizzled while Florida got slammed. Back then, we sat in a Motel 6 in Memphis and listened to Wolf Blitzer fret in a kind but, at the time, irrelevant way about what might happen to "New Orleans, that beautiful city" if there were ever a direct hit to her. The CNN reporter, who was filing his Hurricane Ivan story from the French Quarter, replied that it was only a matter of time before New Orleans was submerged under fifteen feet of water. I know I heard that.

While Wolf manned the Hurricane Katrina CNN "Situation Room," I called the editor of the paper I wrote for and found him in the checkout line at a Wal-Mart in Lafayette with his kids. We talked about photos for a story I had just submitted that was scheduled for September. Then he asked me to keep an eye out for hurricane evacuation stories.

"If this thing does hit us, we'll do a special issue when we come back to the city," he said.

"But what if the city doesn't exist?" I asked.

"Well, the city will exist in some fashion," he answered, in the tone of voice one uses to explain something obvious to a slow child. We talked a little longer about the future as if it were real.

At this point there was nothing for Sean and me to do but eat hard-boiled eggs, watch the news, and go to sleep. We crashed onto the scratchy coverlet of the bed.

We napped for a couple of hours, and then we woke up and made love. It seemed like the right and sporting thing to do. After all, here we were in a motel room with nothing but time stretching before us. What else does one do? Play card games? Sean hates card games. In retrospect, it's curious that we felt inspired to choose that particular moment, given that mildew-smelling motel rooms do not typically have an aphrodisiac effect on us. For all we knew, our home and our world was on the brink of falling to pieces behind us. Who could think about sex at a time like this? I hesitate to make too much of this as a life-affirming gesture in the face of devastation. We did not yet know for sure that New Orleans would be devastated. Maybe it was just an effort to forget what might be happening at home. Perhaps it was a simple benediction that whatever happened, we would at least condition our present lives with this act of love. That seems good enough.

After blessing our shabby room with optimistic sex, we slept for real. Or Sean did. That man can sleep like a stone at the bottom of the ocean, no matter what. Nothing interferes with his night's rest. As for me, I dozed and woke all night, drifting up and down the scale of consciousness from deep dreaming to foggy wakefulness. In my sleep, I had murky visions of New Orleans wiped out by a hurricane, flooded and knocked to splinters. Then I'd rise to the surface again, lift my head from the pillow, and think: *Oh thank god it was just a dream. For a second I thought New Orleans had been destroyed by a hurricane.* A moment later, I'd remember where I was and why. *I'm in a motel in Houston because a hurricane is sweeping over my city. It really is happening. It's not just a bad dream.*

After a few hours of shallow rest, I couldn't stand my own dreams any longer. I got out of bed. Sean was still sleeping, so I couldn't turn on the news. The early morning sun had just begun to turn the sky gray. I took Lance for a stroll around the crowded parking lot—not quite our customary morning ritual of circling the bayou, but it would have to do. The atmosphere had quieted down since our arrival the previous afternoon. Only the windy rush of traffic on the nearby overpass. Each car belonged to New Orleanians on the run. We were all in the same ark, pressing for hours toward this safe haven, stretched to the last remnants of our strength. Here all of us had collapsed beneath identical scratchy coverlets by the side of the highway, too bleary-eyed to think about what lay behind us, while our dusty, silent cars waited in the parking lot.

Lance nosed around until he found some scrubby weeds that he decided would be a good place to poop. Mindful that I was "an honored guest," as the mayor of Houston referred to the New Orleans refugees holed up in the Astrodome, I used a plastic bag to clean up after Lance. There was no place for him to run, so I kept him on the leash and we walked around the parking lot, trying as much as possible to find grass under our feet. That seemed important. Excessive contact with concrete and blacktop made Lance and me both feel heavy, anxious, imprisoned. I found it hard to breathe. We were also a long way from the water and felt the lack of it in this strange dry air.

We wandered past the back end of a pickup truck that contained three metal cages. Lance and I stood there for a couple of minutes, wondering why the owners of the truck had driven four hundred miles with these empty cages in the back. Lance gave his signal that he had grown impatient, a babyish whine that starts in his sinuses and then rolls from his throat in a rocky growl of annoyance that means, "Let's get going!" He knew something I didn't know.

Then I heard gentle scraping from the bottom of the truck, and a breathy sound like whispering broke the morning quiet. Three enormous dog heads appeared above the edge of the truck's tailgate. I hadn't seen them at first because they were lying on the floors of their cages, below my sight line. I took a step back, startled to see signs of life in this gray morning air. A huge German shepherd and two Dobermans, each in a separate cage, rose onto their shaky legs. They raised themselves with aching slowness, unbending their stiff limbs, as if waking from a hundred years' sleep. They stood with difficulty because their cages were too small, so they couldn't turn around or stretch out the kinks in their backs or lift their heads up all the way. All they could do in their small space was shake the slumber from their ears a bit and work the hinge in their jaws, an abbreviated waking ritual for dogs. They looked like circus giants who had come to visit the dwarfs at home and gotten accidentally locked in. With their great heads hanging low, the dogs appeared sheepish, as if ashamed to be caught in these dumb cages. Yet they wagged their tails at me, in happy anticipation that I would let them out. The dogs started yipping a soft cry for release. They looked at me as if I was the one they'd been waiting for all night. The dogs' cries grew more insistent. Soon they'd be barking their heads off.

I pulled Lance away to avoid a scene. He wanted to stay and investigate these dogs, or even better, spring them from jail. It took me a minute to work this out, but I figured that the motel, although it permitted dogs, probably had a limit on the number of dogs you could keep in your room. Fair enough, and this was an emergency situation. Even so, I was disturbed by the sight of the dogs in their too-small cages, locked in for hundreds of miles. Disturbed that their human slept in a comfortable bed while his dogs struggled to find a new way to fold their paws. I didn't understand how a person could do that and not feel the bars of the cage closing in on him too. *Jeez, some people treat their dogs like animals.*

We walked over to the next patch of scrubby grass, and I considered my own silly dog. Lance with his mismatched ears, slender ankles, and fairy feet. I can't imagine who or what mated to deliver the combination of physical characteristics that is Lance. Perhaps a Border collie and a flying reindeer. Little about his body makes sense, his head being too small for his torso. Yet the parts do add up to make a dog, of sorts.

Lance was displaying his essential dogness to me just at this moment. My mind was a fertile jungle of fear, sprouting thick vines that stretched miles back to New Orleans, back to our honeymoon cottage on the bayou, where I twined my impotent thoughts around these images, trying to know something I couldn't yet know. These vines wound around my eyes so that I could barely see the ground before me right now.

For his part, Lance was just looking for the right spot to pee. He had accepted without difficulty that he was not in New Orleans any longer. Now he was here in this parking lot where there were some interesting new smells and other dogs. If he considered the future at all, it was to anticipate that he would get breakfast in a little while, because the woman who always gave him breakfast was close by. As long as she remained in his sight, it was a good bet food would soon appear. He knew enough about the past to remember that his blanket lay on the motel-room floor along with a squeaky toy. Given all that mattered to him was in place, Lance was the soul of equanimity.

How could I reach his state of calm balance? Would I have to allow someone to put a leash around my neck, and let that person be responsible for my welfare? Give it all up to a "higher power," as Lance has given up his power to me? There are lots of times that I have wished to be a dog. What relief to lead a simple life possessed of a simple mind. Let someone else do all the worrying, thinking, planning, anticipating, avoiding, and controlling. Of course the hitch is that if I were a dog, I'd also wish to be cared for by a person like me, otherwise it might not be so pleasant. I might end up in a cage in the back of a truck. No, I'm not willing to chance that, not willing to give over the power and responsibility for my care to someone else.

So, I'll never achieve Lance's perfect bliss of dogness, because I will always be the God-in-charge. If being that means I live with anxiety, then so be it. I am cursed with an uncaged mind that surges backward and forward and side-to-side all the time, a mind that believes in its own power to shape reality with thought. Such a mind may be shocked to encounter forces of nature beyond thought, such as a hurricane. One of the many things I learned on our escape from Katrina was how to acclimate my fertile mind to that mindless force. She schooled me in the art of accommodation—or marriage, if you will.

When I got back to the room, Sean had turned on the news. We sat on the corner of the bed and let the pictures of New Orleans flicker over our faces. It was not as bad as we had feared. At the last moment, Katrina had turned one tick to the east. She first made landfall by passing over Buras, Louisiana, on a long, skinny piece of dirt that stuck out into the Gulf and was home to numerous fishing camps and shrimp boat captains. Then she came fully ashore at the border with Mississippi. This path left New Orleans on the western side of the storm—the "good side," as they say. The winds that sweep counterclockwise from north to south are less intense than the winds whipping back around from south to north. We had been spared the eye.

"Yes! Thank you!" Sean shouted. He jumped off the bed and raised his arms in joy. He landed back on the bed and clasped both my hands in his. We couldn't believe our ears. It was too good to be true.

Still there was a lot to get through. We didn't know what had happened to Sean's family. He tried to call his brother's cell phone, but the signal was gone. The cell towers must have been damaged from the storm. A little while later, Sean's phone started buzzing and clicking, sounds we had never heard before. (Not only were we a non-cable household, but we were not cell-phone savvy either. We did gardening and yoga, not much into technology.) It was a text message. We had never received such a thing before. For some reason during this broken time and space, even though cell-phone service stopped working, text messages could get through. Sean stared at his phone for a little bit and pushed a few buttons just to see what would happen. Eventually the message came up. It was from his brother Jeremy, saying the family had gotten to a motel in Hattiesburg, Mississippi, and was weathering the storm there. They were okay.

Sean, who is not only quick on his feet but quick-witted as well, figured out how to create a text message and sent our whereabouts back to his brother. I resumed my vigil by the television.

The news showed scenes of trees bent over sideways, and street signs downtown whipping and twirling like crazy. One reporter, a small woman, stepped away from the sheltering brick building where she was reporting her story, and the wind knocked her off her feet. The cameraman had to run out, grab her, and drag her back. Some yahoo was larking about in the middle of the street with his arms outspread, making like Superman, his windbreaker plastered against his body, while roofing material flew past his head. The guy leaned into the wind as if it were a giant, invisible hand and let the hurricane support his weight.

Governor Kathleen Blanco gave a news conference and told those of us who had evacuated not to come home for at least three days, because it would take that long to get the electrical power back on and attend to other civic housekeeping duties. A little while later, Blanco came back on and said, on second thought we should stay away for at least one week.

"A whole week!" I said. "What are we supposed to do for a week?" I had not brought enough clean underwear for a week. We decided to drive to Austin, where another Motel 6 waited for us. In the past, we had vacationed in Austin and knew we could find a good independent bookstore there, a fresh cold creek for swimming, and a vegetarian restaurant, three necessary items for us to pass the empty week before us. Houston didn't seem to hold such promise for our comfort. Sean text-messaged his brother, letting him know we were moving to Austin, and we packed the van.

When we stopped to get gas before going back on the interstate, a man pulled up his car next to ours and noted our Louisiana license plate. "I'm glad you're here," he said. "But I wish it were under better circumstances."

With this cordial welcome, we set off on the Texas highway again, innocents abroad.

AWASH IN GRIEF

IN THE UNSPOKEN NEGOTIATION THAT OCCURS IN ALL RELATION-
ships, Sean and I established, somewhere along the line between our first
meeting in the yoga studio to our evacuation from Katrina on I-10 West,
that on long car trips he would do the driving and I'd be in charge of reading
maps. I'd spell him on the driving when he got tired, but mostly my job was
to scan the unfamiliar landscape; recognize something that corresponded
to information on the map; quickly divine if we were heading east, west,
north, or south; and tell Sean to take either a left, right, or complete U-turn.
I hate to brag, but I am good at this. I am a natural-born navigator with
an extraordinary sense of direction to start with. But our exile from New
Orleans refined my skill as a map reader to such an exquisite point that I
am confident you could set me down anywhere in the world—the Sahara
Desert; Cleveland, Ohio—and I'd be able to find a visitor's center or a gas
station, get my hands on a map, and tell someone which turns to make.

My duties as the map reader expanded to include anything that required
written or specific information, such as an address or a telephone number,
as well as the preservation of creature comforts. It was my job to find places
to eat and sleep. These tasks fell under the general heading of "gathering,"
while Sean maintained authority over anything that involved the driving
force of the engine: getting us there, filling the tank, checking the oil and

tire pressure, following my directions. You might see these duties under the "hunting" rubric. It was a crude separation of powers, but it worked for us.

So on the way to Austin, I worked the phone while Sean drove. I found rooms for us at an extended-stay Motel 6. These rooms were a notch above regular Motel 6 rooms in that they lacked mildew but included a kitchenette. If we were going to be stuck in Austin for a week, we might as well have a fridge to keep the beer cold. We drove around the city, looking for a coffee shop with WiFi access, and wondered when we could go home.

The truth of what was happening at home came to us piece by piece, in the same way the chunks of the floodwalls fell into those waiting backyards in Lakeview. The problem was that no one in New Orleans could see what was happening. It took a while for the winds to subside before anyone could go out and look. The only people who knew were the people whom the rising water had pushed into their attics, and who were hacking through their roofs with axes.

We spent a day thinking it was not good, but not the worst either. But then on Tuesday morning, Wolf Blitzer only had bad news for us. New Orleans East was flooded, and the water was creeping into other neighborhoods. The governor begged us not to return to the city. We stayed in our room and watched the news, looking for streets we could recognize.

"There's Claiborne!" I shouted.

Water lapped halfway up a street sign near the Mother-in-Law Lounge, Ernie K-Doe's bar. I had witnessed one of his unique performances there. It's the kind of thing you need to do at least once, if only to confirm that the stories you had heard about his singing and his long curly wig were true. "I'm cocky, but I'm good," Ernie would announce to his audience. In 1961, Ernie had recorded a hit called "Mother-in-Law"—written by Allen Toussaint, who wrote everything—hence the name of Ernie's bar. (In a few months, Allen Toussaint would report from his flooded Gentilly home that the next time, he was going to put his piano on the second floor.) Ernie, who often reminded people he was a "Charity Hospital baby," coasted on that song and his own chutzpah for the rest of his life. In The Mother-in-Law Lounge, there was a life-sized mannequin of Ernie, which he had commissioned himself, dressed in the purple raiment of royalty. He had anointed himself "Emperor of the World." Really, Ernie was famous for being Ernie—or infamous, rather—and was a beloved icon of New Orleans peculiarity. He died a few years ago, but death did not stop him from running for mayor in the election that fall. Now it seemed Ernie's landmark club might be gone too. This made me sad because when Sean and I first started courting, one of our early dates was to dance in the second line that followed Ernie's jazz funeral. Within the context of New Orleans, it makes perfect sense to attend a funeral on a date. Just like the bumper sticker says: "New Orleans. We put the fun in funeral."

While I watched bad things on TV, Sean text-messaged his brother, telling them it was impossible to return to New Orleans. Since his family was in a motel that lay in the path of the storm after it came ashore, they had no power and therefore no news. Sean sent them directions to the motel; we had gotten rooms for them too. His parents and brothers left Hattiesburg as soon as the winds died down and drove sixteen hours to Austin. When they pulled into the parking lot late Tuesday, Jeremy peered out his car window. He looked glass-eyed right at us but didn't recognize us.

We celebrated their arrival with a bottle of wine, and cheese and crackers—evacuee food. Lance was overjoyed to see his pal Rocky again. They wrestled in the corner of Mary and Bruce's room. Then Rocky, who is a yard dog and so has never had the need for good indoor manners, peed on the corner of the bedspread to let Lance know that this was *his* room and not to get any ideas. Poor Rocky spent the rest of his extended stay at this Motel 6, when he was not out for walks, housed in the bathroom.

Our mood over the next few days flew like a boomerang between stunned exhaustion and heightened alert as bad news from New Orleans washed over us. The images got worse by the hour. We walked around like zombies, but then some new frightening scene on the TV would yank us out of that sleepy state. This was a "breaking story," as the journalists like to call it. And it shattered us to watch our city, our home, breaking apart.

On Wednesday morning, I ran into Jeremy in the parking lot. "The 17th Street Canal was breached. The whole city is under water!" The stricken expression on his face spoke the rest. The 17th Street Canal is close to their parents' house.

I rushed back to our room, and there it was on CNN, a great wide-open gap in the floodwall, and a vista of the Lakeview neighborhood where Sean grew up that now appeared as a sea, glinting in the sunlight with just the roofs of houses showing above the water. Then we saw more flooding in the neighborhood around Jeremy's house. We got all of this mediated for us through a TV screen, which typically leaves me with a sense of emotional distance and dislocation. Yet I have never felt so pulled into anything before in my life. This was no mere news story. We sat for hours and watched our city die. Although far away, we lived it and felt the water on our skin too.

After a while, the disintegration and all its details grew too overwhelming to absorb at the rational level. My tired brain transformed it into an impressionistic series of images that carry such emotional and psychic weight, when I summon them from memory even now, I sink into wordless grief: The body of a dead woman at the Convention Center, slumped over in her wheelchair and pushed against a wall, her face covered with a blanket. The teenagers standing guard over an old man on a rooftop where they had chalked out the words: "Help! Diabetic! Needs meds." The kids shouted and jumped and waved their arms at the passing helicopter. The near catatonic expression on the face of the man whom rescuers pulled from a tiny window in his attic. As they settled him roughly onto a seat in the rescue boat, one rescuer offered to shake the man's hand and asked, "How're you doing?" The man was incapable of answering and could not even clasp his own trembling fingers around the hand of his rescuer. A stately old home across the street from Notre Dame Seminary, consumed in flames and black smoke as firefighters stood in the street up to their knees in water. They could only watch because nothing worked. No pumps, no water pressure. There was nothing they could use to put out the fire. *Water, water everywhere and not a drop to drink.*

A quick glimpse of Bayou Saint John flashed by now and then. The bayou had swollen up over its banks. It looked like a huge lake stretching from a house porch on one side to the house porch opposite, with none of the usual landmarks in between. Our street had flooded too, but it was impossible to tell if the water had risen high enough to come up through our floorboards. I studied the aerial photographs on the Internet and was able to make out our roof, our trees, and blue-green water all around our house. That was pretty. This lovely bird's eye view of our home told me nothing of what I wanted to know. Had my rugs and books been soaked? Would we come home to creeping mold in our walls? Was our honeymoon cottage destroyed?

CNN brought Bayou Saint John back again, this time to show that a helicopter had crashed next to it. There was a thin strip of grass along the bayou that was still above water, and an assortment of rowboats and pirogues were bringing people from all around the neighborhood to stand there and wait for another helicopter to come down and take them to the I-10 overpass, where presumably someone else would take them somewhere else. Maybe the airport? Or Baton Rouge? No one knew for sure where they were going. The people stood up to their ankles in water and held a few belongings. Later I learned that many of these people spent the night there, sleeping on the wet, narrow strip of grass, until morning when the helicopters could fly again. Even later than that, on the first anniversary of the storm, an artist would construct a wooden raft to spell out the word "HELP" in large letters, and float the raft on the bayou near the site where these people had waited.

Soon the news shocked me again, this time with a pleasant surprise. In the middle of the Paula Zahn show, I heard the voice of Jack Fine coming at me from the TV. Jack is a cornet player I have chatted with from time to time. At age seventy-eight, Jack enjoys the cachet of having roots in the old days of jazz. He played with Eddie Condon and Danny Barker, and to hear Jack tell it, all the greats. Nowadays Jack hacks around town, playing wherever he can, sometimes sitting in with the Jazz Vipers when they let him. Jack has the habit of showing up uninvited to a club where a band is playing. Then, in the middle of a song that he likes and thinks should have a cornet solo, he'll pull out his horn and start blaring into their gig from the back of the room. It's pretty dramatic. He gets away with it on sheer moxie. I like Jack. He's a genial wiseacre and a happy drinker. Now here he was on the phone, talking to Paula Zahn from his home on Algiers Point, just across the river from the French Quarter. Due to some odd twist in the wiring, Jack Fine had what was probably the last working telephone in New

Orleans. He used it to speak up for the musicians and voice his fear that New Orleans culture would be lost. Paula steered him around to report on the state of the city at that moment.

"I'm alone here, all alone. There is nothing, no light. Just silence," he said. "It's ghostly. The silence, the blackness."

"What are you doing there by yourself?" Paula asked.

"Well, I have a bottle of gin," Jack answered. "And I haven't lost my sense of humor. I can practice at will now, because I will not upset my neighbors."

There was an unforgettable interview with New Orleans police officer Lawrence Dupree, who had been working with the Coast Guard, helping take people off the roofs of their houses by helicopter. Dupree reported that some of the people they tried to rescue at first resisted getting into the helicopter. They thought they had to pay for a ride in a helicopter, which they believed would be expensive, like a ride in a limousine. They said they didn't have enough money to buy a ticket. It took some doing, but the rescuers convinced the people that no payment was expected.

This small misunderstanding pointed to a vast, hidden cavity of societal failure. My heart still constricts when I think of it. That there are people in this world who have grown so accustomed to being passed over—no, I'm sorry, but the accurate phrase is "fucked over"—that they don't realize they are entitled to expect help, simply because they exist. They have been conditioned to accept that it must be their poor luck to be stranded on their roof under the baking sun, and they would just have to wait for the water to go down. That only wealthy people who can buy a ticket for a ride in a helicopter can get help. That if you don't have money, your life just isn't worth much. This is New Orleans's shadow and our shame. Katrina exposed it and rubbed our noses in it.

The scenes of destruction reached an apex for me when the cameras found a submerged house with water up to the roofline. A gas line in the street had broken and ignited. A spectacular yellow-orange fireball boiled up through the water. The explosive fuel that flared from the gas pipe fed the ravenous fire, making it so hot that even its natural enemy—the water—could not kill it. Fire burning undiminished beneath water brought to a fine point the understanding that everything had gone wrong. The natural order had been perverted. In its place, an apocalyptic war had erupted between the elements—so much water, so much fire. Left to their own, these heedless forces only take and conquer. Each tried to dominate the other and then eat New Orleans. We could do nothing but watch while fire and water fought for their share of our sweet city, so pretty.

STRUGGLE FOR THE SHORE

WE LIVED IN THIS LIMBO FOR TEN DAYS AND MET OTHER DISPLACED New Orleanians in the coffee shops. Austin continued its regular comings and goings around us, while we felt like a separate species, torn from our normal lives and dropped in this place that, although pleasant, was not home. So when we saw folks from New Orleans, we fell on each other with amazement, grateful to touch someone from the same alienated soup. One morning we met a guy Sean's parents knew, Jim Fitzmorris, who is a playwright in New Orleans. They discussed the onslaught of New Orleanians in Austin, and Jim observed, "Ya know that bumper sticker they have around here, 'Keep Austin Weird'? Well I think we just *guaranteed* it."

Later Sean ran into one of his students in Whole Foods. She put him in touch with her friends in Austin who happened to have a spare house, fully furnished, which they offered to Mary and Bruce (and Rocky) to live in rent-free for a couple of months until they figured out what they'd do next. There was magic in the air, along with all the grief.

When I go back over my calendar from that time, those ten days look like nothing, and I can't believe we experienced and accomplished as much as we did. We had to make a lot of decisions and arrangements about our lives in that compressed time. We couldn't just sit and absorb the shocking words and pictures that came at us from the news. We were jamming the

Internet with e-mails flying back and forth, trying to find the people we knew in New Orleans to make sure they had gotten out safely, and also writing back to all the people we knew elsewhere in the country who were trying to find us to make sure *we* were safe. We also had to figure out how to fill the gap in our lives left by this storm.

When it was clear that there was no New Orleans to go back to, at least not for several months, we all assembled for lunch one afternoon. Sean's parents, his brothers, Sean, and I lined either side of a long table at a diner and waited for our sandwiches. Mary was having one of her giddy phases that interspersed the gloom, when she laughed at everything. She was especially amused this afternoon that she and Bruce had left New Orleans with nothing but the clothing they were wearing. She kept grabbing the collar of her shirt and saying, "This is it!"

Jeremy leaned forward and announced that he thought we should circle the wagons, so to speak, like a pioneer family on the dusty, inhospitable frontier. He wanted us to get organized, get jobs, and pull ourselves together.

"Okay, we have six people at this table," he said. "I think we should start assigning tasks."

Matt rolled his eyes and poured himself a beer from the pitcher in the middle of the table. Bruce looked into the middle distance and hunched over his plate. He wore a dazed half-smile, as if he still couldn't believe where he was or what was happening to him.

"I know I'm supposed to be a strong leader and take care of things, but all I want to do is get drunk," said Bruce.

I ordered a margarita and went into the bathroom to write notes.

After lunch, we drove Jeremy to the University of Texas campus, where he knew someone who might offer him a job. Within a week, Jeremy had two or three job offers, one of them as a physical trainer in the University of Texas recreational center. Even before Katrina, Jeremy always worked several jobs at once, seeming to operate out of the fear that his entire livelihood could be wiped out at any moment, and so one job was never enough for him. According to Jeremy, spare time was just time that you're not making a living.

When we left Jeremy at the door to his job interview, I poked him in the arm and kidded him. "Good luck in there, Jeremy. You know you're going to have to support all of us, now." He laughed to be polite, but I could tell he didn't think it was so funny.

Sean went to work planning his *kirtan* tour. He had a gig already in New York that had been booked for mid-September since before the storm, and so he started booking other gigs around that. Our plan was to start driving to New York from Austin by the end of the week. Sean made his temporary office at the bookstore next to Whole Foods, called Book People. It was open late and had free WiFi access in their coffee shop. Yoga studios around the country had tracked Sean through his studio's website and were offering to host his *kirtan* concerts. The yoga community was rallying around Sean, and he jumped on this trend to create a new career boost for himself.

As for me, I worked the phones, my usual job, to get hold of our insurance company, our mortgage company, our bank, our accountant (who'd had the presence of mind to collect the receipts and the studio's checkbook before she left town with her 95-pound Labrador named Buddha). I had to find the other yoga teachers from Sean's studio to make sure we paid them for the month of August. I learned that the publisher of the newspaper I wrote for had declared himself no longer in business. The offices had been flooded. He had told his staff to find other jobs. A couple of months later, the paper would rise from its coffin and resume publishing, but for these early weeks it was presumed dead. And I couldn't get an answer on whether I'd be paid for the story I had just handed in. Poof! Gone. Onward. There were so many survival-mode details to cope with that taking the time for normal human reactions was a luxury we couldn't afford. Yet, these would not allow themselves to be banished, so, often, as I attended to necessary life tasks, I would have to pause, stricken by nameless emotions that came pouring over me without warning.

I was shocked and a little disgusted with myself to discover that my emotional containment broke open when I was on the phone with my mother. All my life I have kept up a strong fortress of sarcasm against feeling my feelings in the presence of my mother. But damn if Katrina didn't change that too. I learned this when I was walking down the street, heading back to Book People. I had just gotten a cell phone for myself (Sean and

145

I were not going to survive this if we had to share a phone), and I tried it out by calling my mother. I thought I was holding myself together, keeping cool, taking care of business. Then I heard my mother's faint voice on the line asking, "Are you all right? What's happening?" And then, oh horrors, it started. I was crying.

I had to sit down on the curb of this busy downtown Austin street. I was tired of handling things. I wanted someone else to do this. Something in my mother's voice gave me permission to forget for a few minutes that I was a competent adult, doing my best to manage daily life through a crisis. Despite my effort to hold this volatile and untrustworthy woman at bay, the sound of her voice resonated in a primitive chamber of my native self. I dissolved into my hope for safety there.

My mother wanted to know if I had learned what had happened to our house yet. "I don't know. I don't know. I don't know." I hugged my knees and rocked.

When I finished the call to my mother, I stood up from the curb to continue walking back to the bookstore and saw a woman standing there on the sidewalk, watching me. She had been listening to my conversation and my tears. She pulled me into her arms and embraced me.

"Honey, I want you to know that I am so sorry for you and for your city," she said. "We, all of us in Austin, we just want to help you."

I thanked her and thought that her generous offer had done well to counterbalance the exchange I had witnessed earlier in the day at Whole Foods. I had been sitting at my laptop, scouring the bulletin boards for some sliver of information about how high *exactly* the water had risen in the vicinity of Bayou Saint John, when I couldn't help but overhear the conversation among four Austinites at the table next to me. I wasn't eavesdropping. They were offering loud opinions as they rattled their Sunday edition of the *New York Times*.

"I don't see why we should pay for these people to rebuild their houses," the woman said, pointing to photos in the *Times* of submerged homes in Saint Bernard Parish. "I mean those are our taxes right there. They shouldn't be living there in the first place. We shouldn't have to pay for that, just so they can be wiped out again." The other people at the table agreed at high volume and some length.

My jaw stiffened with rage. It was starting already, the corpse not yet cold in the grave. I stared unseeing at my computer screen and thought, *Okay what do I do now? Do I take a stand, here? Or just let these fools drivel down their shirtfronts?* I wanted to stand up and yell, "Hey! Just want to let you know that I'm sitting right next to you, and that's my New Orleans you're pissing all over. By the way, we pay taxes too. And those are not just houses in those photographs, they're homes. People celebrated birthdays and high school graduations in those houses. Children were conceived there. Some people just sat in those houses and read the newspaper and drank coffee. Those are reasons enough for my taxes and your taxes and everyone else's taxes to help rebuild them!"

I wanted to go nose to nose with the woman who started it and say to her, "I hope you never need help. I hope you're never in trouble and that you never feel vulnerable and shocked. I hope you never lose your home and never have to depend on the kindness of strangers. *Because you're probably not going to get any!* What goes around comes around, sister."

(When I told the story to a friend later, she observed that if they were truly natives of Austin, they would not have been reading the *New York Times*, so I should not take their remarks as representative of that fine city.)

I am still mad at myself for not having the guts to tell those idiots off. In retrospect, given my fragile state at the time, I would have melted into girly tears anyway, which would have been humiliating. So it's for the best that I kept my mouth shut. I'm never as thrilling in person as I am in my imaginary conversations afterward.

Most of the time I was able to hold myself in a contained state because it also fell to me, as usual, to secure our creature comforts. Lance needed his monthly heartworm-prevention medication, as well as a certain fancy brand of dog food that only organically inclined feed shops carry, because he has sensitive skin and would have a flaky reaction to regular dog food. Sean and I would need warm socks and sweaters since we were driving to New England for the fall. There were all kinds of things we needed or thought we needed. *Middle-class Grapes of Wrath indeed*, I thought as I purchased a replacement for my Oil of Olay Foaming Face Wash that I had left behind at home. This became my mantra as I sat on line for three hours to receive benefits from the Red Cross. What a bracing experience that was. Previously I had envisioned the Red Cross as those good people who go into war-torn countries to bring bowls of gruel to starving children. Well, now we were the starving children. We were grateful for the help, but this fact was hard to swallow.

It was Mary who sat her family down in the motel room one afternoon and read them the riot act in her own gentle way. "I know you don't like it," she said, "but we have no choice. We have to accept charity now."

She was speaking mainly to Bruce. Care packages and money had been arriving from their extended family members outside of Louisiana, and Bruce was having a hard time receiving these. With the exception of his own wife and children, Bruce could do without family—or anyone else, for that matter. Now, Katrina had knocked everything out from under him. It was certain that the 17th Street Canal breach had engulfed Mary and Bruce's home in at least ten feet of water. The customers for their housecleaning business were mainly in the flooded neighborhoods, so their livelihood was also destroyed. They had literally nothing left. Katrina had slammed Bruce into a vulnerable position, forcing him to soften his defense against other people. Now he had to accept help from family and strangers—even as he readily admitted that if the situation were reversed, he would never offer the same help to someone in trouble. He needed his wife to show him how to swallow this bitter pill.

I was learning so much about husbands and wives and the distribution of strengths and skills between them. That marriage is not only a composition of two individuals, but it is also a discrete organism with its own movement and boundaries.

Take Sean and me, for example. It was no accident that while I sat around wiping my nose, the infinitely sure-footed Sean had wasted not a minute churning this dross into gold. Like Lance, he seemed to have forgotten what we had left behind in New Orleans. Or at least he had exerted such mastery over his mind and emotions that he could for the time being choose not to dwell on it. He made that choice because he would not be able to function effectively in this situation if he allowed his emotions full rein. His survival depended on staying light and bright. He had to keep his energy high in order to manifest his long-dreamed-of concert tour.

So, he didn't have any room in his schedule for the dark paralysis that afflicts those who are immersed in their emotions. He had to stay moving to stay alive, and that left no time for the prolonged stasis of feeling.

Since we were not just two people but also an organism, it naturally fell to me to take over the feeling part of our shared body. The stuff he didn't have time for all came washing over to me, so I became the container for everything watery and formless and frightening associated with our experience. As the container for our shared emotional life, it was also my job to figure out what we explored, to understand what we experienced. And take notes. So I'd be able to identify the terrain should we pass this way again. This was consistent with our usual distribution of labor. Sean drove, while I navigated. Sean carried us forward, while I carried the shadow.

The time came for us to begin the next leg of our journey. Sean's brother Matt, who had brought his guitar and saxophone from New Orleans, would come with us on the *kirtan* tour, as he was a member of the band. (We would stop in Asheville, North Carolina, to pick up a New Orleans refugee drummer.) Bruce would stay in Austin, while Mary would go to Houston to help take care of Grandma, who was staying with her baby sister Aunt Agnes. Jeremy would work.

Mary knocked on our door while Sean and I packed. She had Rocky with her and had stopped by to see if Lance wanted to join him for a play date on the patch of grass beyond the parking lot. Instead, all three of us sat on the bed while Mary's face crumpled into tears. She had been thinking about all the family photos she'd had on the first floor of their house. There had been perhaps thousands of pictures that she had collected over the years, most of them images of her three sons, documenting nearly every moment of their lives. At each Christmas she demanded that they pose in front of the Christmas tree with their arms around each other—Sean, the eldest, in the middle, hugging his two brothers. In most of these photos, all three of them glowered at their mother and her camera, trying to make this annual portrait look like a mug shot. She didn't mind at all and loved any photo she could get of her boys. All these, all the Christmas trees, and all the boys were gone. Mary poured her self into our hands that afternoon in the Motel 6 while Rocky yanked on the leash.

Through her sobs, Mary told us she had just spoken with her brother Danny by phone. "He said we're going to have to be like the Irish when they came here a hundred years ago. They didn't have anything. All they brought were their songs and stories. Now everything's gone, we'll just have to sing our songs and tell our stories. That's all we have."

The family said goodbye in the parking lot. More and more the atmosphere resembled a scene from a Steinbeck novel. Mary and Bruce had probably not spent more than a night apart from each other in thirty-six years of marriage, and it would be weeks before they saw each other again. Mary clung to each of her sons, all of them flying off to the horizon to seek their fortunes. Bruce would have no one but Rocky to talk to for some time. We stood in a circle with our arms around each other.

"Okay, Christmas in New Orleans," said Jeremy, trembling and red-eyed.

"Thanksgiving!" I countered. He thought I was nuts, but it turned out I was right. We were home for Thanksgiving after Katrina. But we had many miles to go before then.

MY CONVERSATION WITH DEATH

When November came again, more than a year after Katrina, the pelicans showed up too. It was their time to visit us here in Bayou Saint John. I was relieved to see them. Each year it seems as if they might not come again. When they do, it feels like grace. In truth, the pelicans' arrival represents a turn in the wheel that draws us into the darkest phase of the year. When the pelicans come, the sun has just moved into Scorpio, and we enter the season of death. They are a harbinger of a realm beyond this muddy trickle.

According to the Medieval Bestiary, a compendium of animal myths, the pelican is a symbol for Christ. She got that reputation because the mother pelican supposedly feeds her young by pecking open a wound in her own breast and offering her blood to the waiting mouths of her hungry children. One version of the story says her blood offering revives her young, who have been dead three days. She had pecked them to death because they had pecked too fiercely at her beak, demanding food. There is some fact driving this myth. A pelican stores the bloody remains of animals she has caught in her pouch. Then when she brings up the red mash to feed her children, it might appear she is offering her own blood. Thanks to this myth and the bird's own cooperation in keeping the story going, the Pelican-Christ has come to grace the state flag of this Roman Catholic outpost, Louisiana.

I have always enjoyed that such a clownish bird should represent the greatest clown of all, Jesus Christ. This image of Christ-the-clown may have its roots in Paul's exhortation in 1 Corinthians that "we are fools for Christ's sake." God knows what he meant by that. But the line has inspired a number of artists to see this strange teacher, the wandering revolutionary, this silly rabbi, as an intriguing, opaque literary device. Fellini created my favorite Christ-the-clown in *La Strada*. As a character, Christ is at once appealing and difficult to read, persistent in his power to move us. A seemingly simple puzzle that only deepens the more we attempt to solve it. He left us with crazy instructions. *Love your enemies? Bless them that curse you?* I don't think so. Like a clown, he allowed people to ridicule him, laugh at him, and still he never wavered from his message of unconditional love that, in the bitter context of this hell we humans have made, sounds absurd. Most ridiculous of all, he knew exactly when and where he was going to die, and he went along with it anyway. What a fool.

The Fool card in the Tarot deck, like a magickal child, roams a dangerous landscape, protected by his innocence and trust. His naive belief in a benevolent universe appears foolish in a broken world of raging egos and suspicion. This enchanted idiot looks ever upward to Heaven and utters simplistic observations that don't make sense. Throughout our ancient stories, the archetypal Wise Fool has spoken prophecy in absurd riddles. He knows more than he thinks he knows. His words say more than they seem.

Recently I went back to my King James to dive more deeply into the Sermon on the Mount, and found that it is the origin for some of the most hackneyed expressions. It struck me that a lot of people who would be disinclined to quote Scripture are quoting Christ all the time without realizing it. There is the line about hiding your light under a bushel, beware of wolves in sheep's clothing, never let your left hand know what your right hand is doing, no man can serve two masters, salt of the earth, the city on a hill. There was some bad advice: "If thy right eye offend thee, pluck it out." Some good advice: "Judge not, that ye be not judged."

When I got to the last lines of the sermon, I was startled out of my critical literary review.

"And every one that heareth these sayings of mine, and doeth them not, shall be likened unto a foolish man, which built his house upon the sand.

"And the rain descended, and the floods came, and the winds blew, and beat upon that house; and it fell: and great was the fall of it."

There he goes again. Score one more for J.C., who saw it coming and tried to warn us. I don't know how he did it. That's fine. I don't need an explanation of how the pelicans glide on air, either. Enough to love their shapely flourish against the sky like grace notes scattered on sheet music. Despite their foolishness, both the pelicans and Christ hold us in their thrall, as they float beyond our reach, always mysterious.

In fall of 2006, this season of the pelicans' return began with the death of Father Tarantino. He had a heart attack in the rectory of Our Lady of the Rosary. He was sixty years old. On the following Sunday evening there was a vigil at the church where he had served as pastor for eleven years, and had attended as a child. The vigil happened to fall on the last night of Voodoo Fest, the headbanger alternative to Jazz Fest that takes place in City Park, right at the edge of Bayou Saint John, a few blocks from the church. They schedule this event around Halloween, which is why it's called Voodoo Fest, not because it has anything to do with the ancient spiritual practice. Tossing the word "Voodoo" in there, regardless of its meaning, sells lots of tickets to the twenty-somethings.

The concert kids ambled along the bayou and then down Esplanade Avenue, littered with empty cardboard Bud Light packs, past Our Lady of the Rosary. They were half-drunk and mostly baked, wearing cut-offs and sweatshirts. Chatty and slight, they flip-flopped past the subdued mourners in somber garb who gathered on the steps of the church and seemed dumbfounded by this noisy parade of kids. It's hard to hold a funeral face when there's a party streaming past. The warped, booming chords from The Flaming Lips floated over the treetops from the concert in the nearby park, while white strobe lights crisscrossed the night sky. The hearse idled at the curb. Father T. was getting a festive send-off, whether he liked it or not.

I stood on the steps with the mourners and remembered that the last time I'd seen Father Tarantino was on these very steps, just a few weeks earlier, for the Feast of Saint Francis. I had brought Lance for his annual bath of holy water. Father had stood on the top step in his long white and gold robes and gazed over the assembly of dogs, who were sniffing each other's assholes, as they waited for God's blessing. Father Tarantino had laughed. He stood there for several minutes, his face filled with joy, shaking his head and laughing. The rude absurdity of the dogs did not diminish the sanctity of ritual.

Father Tarantino and I had our differences, but I will always appreciate this priest for his kindness to the dogs. Certainly not too many other priests would have the patience or the imagination to see that ministering to the spiritual life of a human community would be unfinished business without attending to the animals that fulfill a spiritual connection for the humans. We are only slightly glorified dogs ourselves, and in our relationships with our pets, we discover an innocence and trust that God intended for us to have in our spiritual life. It takes a priest with depth and sensitivity, a true parish priest who ministers to people in the earthbound way they truly are, to understand all that. This is the sort of priest Father Tarantino was. I'd miss him.

The church was filling up with people. Two men stood to the side and waited, slumped in sadness. They had the distinct air of guys from the old neighborhood. Thick-necked, gravel-voiced, possessed of what in New Jersey we'd call a *faccia brut*, I could imagine they'd known Father T. since they had all served as altar boys together.

"He was great guy," said the first guy. He pressed his hand to the center of his chest, where his belly pooched out. "Little, but strong."

"Eh?" said the second guy, who leaned heavily on a cane and appeared hard of hearing.

"Father. He was little, but tough."

"Hunh," replied his friend. It sounded like agreement.

A tall robed priest stood at the door to Our Lady of the Rosary. At a funeral for a priest, there are bound to be lots of priests. This particular priest seemed to be running things.

"Okay, let's get moving, so we can get the body inside," he barked in an officious voice. "Pall bearers, please!" He sounded like he was in a hurry to get this over with so he could go home and watch the ballgame. I knew that voice. I had heard it before. I recognized that abrupt condescension, the cold distaste for all the messy stuff of being human—the deep feeling, the spiritual hunger. He spoke in a tone that sneered at the soft animal part of us. The hair on the back of my neck went up. I knew this guy from some time ago. *Jeez*, what was he doing in my face again?

A few years back, the Carmelite order in France who steward the earthly remains of Saint Thérèse of Lisieux, also known as the Little Flower, brought her reliquary to the United States so the devout here could have some close contact with the saint. I called it the Saint Thérèse World Tour. She drew a bigger crowd than the Rolling Stones.

This is the part I love about Catholicism, where it gets so gothic and morbid and pagan and deliciously magical—this obsession among otherwise rational people with the dead bodies of saints. I am fascinated that a religion so rife with intellectualism also perpetuates this fantastical belief that the physical matter, the actual molecules that make up a sainted person's flesh and bones, carries a supernatural power to bestow miraculous healing on the person who touches it. In this belief, the saints are an elevated species compared to us ordinary people. They stand between us and God. Yet, they are enough like us in that they have physical bodies; they eat, sleep, drink, and die. But if we believe that their bodies can defy the usual laws of physics, then we can believe in that God who is remote, unseen, and unfelt. The saint's flesh and its powers are the physical proof we need in order to accept this theoretical concept of God.

This hunger for miraculous touch is what I find so delicious. Why? Because it is raw and literal-minded. Forgive me, but I *do* mean this in the best sense of the word—it's so *dog*-like. We require touch to accept that something is real. Just like Lance. He believes in a benevolent universe because my loving touch makes it so. Catholics' passion for their saints springs from their craving for a palpable, lived experience of God. It just isn't enough to read about Him or think about Him. The veneration of the saints is where the fairy tale comes to life in the physical plane. We love the literal magic that usurps the intellect. We need something that defies rational explanation. Without immediate contact with mystery, we are just bored to death. This is not some quaint custom of an earlier era when we were a bunch of tree worshippers. No, the Saint Thérèse World Tour came through New Orleans in 1999. We humans will never be more than we are.

Saint Thérèse's visit to New Orleans made the front page of the newspaper three days in a row. The traffic in the normally quiet neighborhood around Saint Dominic's, where the Carmelites offered a viewing of her relics to the public, required a large police presence to maintain crowd control. Thousands of New Orleanians came to the church to view her reliquary, which resembled a little castle and rested inside a protective bubble of glass, probably bulletproof.

When I got to Saint Dominic's, a group of monks, who wore thick beards, long brown robes, and sandals, had formed two lines facing each other, making a protective channel leading to the door of the church. Saint Thérèse was late, naturally. You know how those rock stars can be. She arrived in a carriage drawn by white horses, and then the priests carried her reliquary through the phalanx of monks into the church. All around them, the huge crowd of people milled, straining for a glimpse of the saint as she passed over the rough brown shoulders of the monks. Like Mick Jagger's bodyguards, the monks were doing everything in their power to separate Saint Thérèse from her fans. The difference between the two is that Mick Jagger is alive and Saint Thérèse is dead, but that distinction does not mean much in New Orleans.

Above the tumult I could hear that priest whose sharp voice carried so well at the vigil for Father Tarantino. Let's call him Father Nasty. "Come now, this isn't a circus!" he shouted to the assembled petitioners. I'm not sure if anyone else heard him. The people surged forward, quickly filling the church. They wanted their Saint Thérèse, and they weren't going to let any priest stand in their way. I slipped inside just moments before they slammed shut the church doors, leaving most of the crowd to wait outside on the flagstones.

Inside was near mayhem. People pressed against each other to stand on the long line in the center aisle, waiting their turn to be close to the reliquary, which rested on the altar. The line moved slowly because once someone actually got to Saint Thérèse, that person tended to linger before her. This was a once-in-a-lifetime audience with the remains of a miracle worker. No one was going to squander it. So people knelt at the reliquary and prayed and begged Saint Thérèse to give them some relief from their troubles. Who knows? She might come through for one of us. Certainly there are plenty of stories about the Little Flower bestowing miraculous cures on those who asked. It never hurts to ask.

This was where I felt a tender stirring within me toward this religion of my childhood, because I saw it as a moment of deep humility for Catholics, when they turned themselves inside out and simply asked for help. They asked the Little Flower because they were willing to be vulnerable and place their trust in the saint, who they believed would look with compassion upon their pain. And *do* something about it. They didn't want any more nice words and interesting concepts about God's love. They wanted their mother's liver cancer to go away.

"No prayers!" a priest shouted into a microphone at the altar. "Please, keep the line moving." It didn't work. The people were determined to pray.

Off to the side of the church, Father Nasty moved through the pews. He held a small oval medallion with a glass cover high above his head. "Only for the sick! Only for the sick," he said as he pressed through the crowd.

A woman standing next to me whispered, "You know what he has in there, don't you? It's a chip from her bone. Or maybe even—" Here she stroked the base of her own neck. "It may be some . . . you know . . . of her flesh." It was another reliquary of Saint Thérèse, travel-sized. Parts of her were all over the place apparently.

As soon as people realized there was a small piece of Saint Thérèse nearby, they closed in on Father Nasty. One by one, with vivid need in their eyes, these men and women of ordinary lives and means moved closer to the priest and lifted their faces so he could press the medallion to their foreheads. Everyone wanted that touch. This was the magic they had come for. As he moved from face to face, their gaze followed the arc in the air he made with the little reliquary as he blessed each one. A murmuring wave moved through the crowd as in one pew after the next people realized what was happening. The tide turned toward Father Nasty, who was growing irritated. "Only for the *sick!*" he insisted. With a thin, sarcastic smile, he added, "I had no idea there were so many sick people."

The priest held the reliquary above their heads and watched them jump for it like hungry dogs. Then he mocked them for their yearning. Well *done*, Father Nasty.

It occurred to me later as I was driving home that this priest was probably jealous of Saint Thérèse. I could well imagine that it irked him to see that the Little Flower, a *girl* for God's sake, who also happens to be *dead*, could inspire such an enormous devotion. It's a good bet the church never filled up with a crowd of passionate thousands when Father Nasty came to say mass. I'm sure the whole day made him feel irrelevant and annoyed that Thérèse had the magic, not him. So he had to piss on everyone's enthusiasm to give himself some comfort.

There is a good reason Father Nasty felt irrelevant, which is that he was irrelevant. None of the faithful seemed to care that he mocked them. Everyone in the church was too drunk with love for Saint Thérèse to notice his vain twittering. I paid attention because I maintain an active shit list for priests, and it's my job to notice things. Interestingly, the truly devout Catholics are not terribly bothered by their priests. The tail doesn't wag the dog around here. Those who came to venerate Saint Thérèse got what they wanted because their passion and their imagination demanded it—an unmediated apprehension of the Divine.

How I love Catholicism in this swampy New Orleans, I thought as I stopped at a red light. People take their religion right down into the mud where they live. It's not an idea. It's in the direct material of their everyday lives, where the priests are just along for the ride. While I waited for the light to change, I looked with idle interest over my shoulder at the strip mall by the side of the road. It was one of many such ordinary clusters of shops in New Orleans. Like a beacon, directed by some unseen force, my gaze fell on precisely the gift I needed to complete my adventure that day. There was a large sign over a plate-glass storefront.

"Beatitudes Hair Design," it said in flickering light.

All Saints Day, November 1st, came a couple of days after Father Tarantino's funeral. Catholics clean the cemeteries on this day, which is a nice thing to do for your ancestors. The first day of November is also the Day of the Dead, when the Vodou community goes to town.

Sallie Ann Glassman announced her annual ritual to honor the ancestors. In the e-mail she sent around, she noted that she had been holding a

Day of the Dead ceremony in New Orleans for at least twenty-six years, but she wasn't sure of the exact number because she had lost count. This year, we met in the peristyle (or temple) she had built across the alleyway from her home. Her neighborhood is just across the canal from an area that was wrecked by Katrina, the Lower Ninth Ward. In the peristyle, there was an altar covered with photos of people who had died as a result of the hurricane.

This Day of the Dead ceremony, like all those before it, would call on the Loa who embodies death. His name is Gede or Guedeh. The characteristics of Gede developed among Haitian people who do not have the same antiseptic relationship with death that Americans do. Throughout their history and well into the present, Haitians have lived with death right in their faces. While we Americans have this strange tendency to treat death as if it were something embarrassing to be pushed out of sight, like evacuating our bowels, people in Haiti embrace Death as their constant companion and have made him into a vivid character.

Thus, Gede is a merciless prankster who dances like a wild animal. His purpose is to undercut our pomposities and remind us that we're all worm's meat in the end. He is also a sex maniac. No crotch is safe when he's around. He smokes cigars, drinks peppered rum, and wears sunglasses with one lens popped out. He also likes to wear a big black top hat decorated with dark purple ribbons and black cock feathers. He's seedy, greedy, and charming.

"Gede is also the Loa of absolute truth," said Sallie Ann to the people who had assembled for the ceremony. "So if you have a question and think you can handle the truth, ask him."

For this ceremony, we all dressed in black and wore purple headscarves. I had brought a heart-shaped stone as an offering. I found it on the beach years ago and kept it in the back of a drawer. Tonight it seemed to fit my mood in this season of death. My mind was dwelling on loss and all the farewells.

I was also seeing connections between this Vodou ritual and the Roman Catholic ritual I had witnessed two nights before. At the vigil for Father Tarantino, the priest who said the homily (not Father Nasty but another, nicer priest) gave all of the usual talk of "leaving this sinful body." He led us in singing the prayer from Saint Francis, "Lord make me an instrument for thy peace," a sentimental favorite, and it sure sounded like possession to me.

Then the priest reminded us, "Life and death are part of God's plan for us. We have the great promise given by the Resurrection that we will never die. At the beginning of his life, Father Tarantino received a baptism into death."

How creepy. Catholicism is a morbid cult. I envisioned all the babies this priest has baptized. Is he mindful of their coming deaths in that moment he pours holy water over their downy heads? Maybe so.

It struck me that both these belief systems profess a victory over death. Supposedly, Christ promises us immortality and showed it by walking out of that cave. Vodou promises, with possession by the Loa, that the spirits of the dead may return through the office of our living bodies. Both seek to reassure us that death is not the banishment we fear. I'm not sure I believe either one, but I'm willing to listen. I marvel at this human need, surfacing in nearly all the spiritual vocabularies, to conquer death. The difference I see is that Christianity claims to vanquish death with tricky semantics: "Through death we have eternal life." While Vodou says: "Dance with Death. You might as well."

While we waited for the Vodou ceremony to begin, a guy named George came up to me and touched my wrist. "I know you from somewhere, don't I?" he said.

We had never met before, I was pretty sure, but I made up an innocuous answer. Perhaps we had met at Sallie Ann's in the past. Something about George made me uncomfortable. Threw me off balance. There was some chaos unleashed in him. He wasn't housebroken. The warning sensors in my nose tingled.

The ceremony lasted for several hours. There is a core group of folks, George among them, who have made a commitment to this spiritual practice. They have learned the traditional songs from Haiti and sang them in the Kreyòl language. I hummed along mostly, and sang where I recognized a few French-sounding words and names of Catholic saints that have gotten mixed in with the Loa. The music went on, and the air filled with smoke and incense. Soon simple exhaustion itself became intoxicating. So that when it came time to dance in a circle around the altar to Gede, I was getting punch drunk. We danced and swayed as the drummer kept time. Bits of singsong phrases assembled in my mind around the rhythm of my body in the dance. I was getting my Emily Dickinson mishmashed with my Robert Louis Stevenson.

"Because I could not stop for Death, He kindly stopped for me."

This line kept running through my head as we danced for Gede. Then, inexplicably, my loopy brain inserted a line from Stevenson's "My Shadow."

"And what can be the use of him is more than I can see."

My mother had required me to memorize the Stevenson poem as a child and then recite it at a Christmas party for her friends. Funny how the rhymes you memorize at a young age are the ones you can never shake. That poem, which begins, "I have a little shadow that goes in and out with me," has been dogging me my whole life.

Not surprisingly, George began to stagger and stumble. Gede appeared to be making an entrance through him. George snaked his way over to stand by the drummers. His eyes were closed, and he danced sway-backed with his arms close to his side, elbows crooked, and hands waving spastically, the unbuttoned cuffs of his shirtsleeves flapping. He seemed to have a greasy hinge at the base of his spine and waggled his butt as he spun in circles. Yep, this looked like a real possession. George seemed to have gone somewhere else. Or maybe it was that George's own essential inner "Gede" was coming out. Either way, something was happening.

Sallie Ann came to him with a black top hat decorated with feathers that she keeps around for Gede to wear, and sunglasses, too. Someone else handed him a bottle of rum and a cigar. He grabbed these gifts and dressed himself. Then he strutted around the altar, sucking on the cigar and blowing clouds of smoke. His cock-of-the-walk posture said it loud: "Ain't I fine?"

Because I could not stop for Death, He kindly stopped for me. Gede was just about the last thing I wanted in my life right now. *And what could be the use of him is more than I can see.* I didn't want him near me. I didn't want to talk to him. I didn't want to hear what he had to say. Every muscle in my body told me to get away from him. The floor of my stomach fell out. The sight of him made me want to run like hell. Instead of running, I danced around the altar, always careful to keep George/Gede on the other side of the room from me. I was going to get through this. I would. But I would not have any contact with this character.

161

George/Gede paused in his strutting to bend into a slight spread-kneed squat, and delivered a loud, slow fart. "Ahhhh, releasing the spirit," he said. Cute, but I was still not gonna play. I was not afraid of the phenomenon of possession itself. There had been other Loa in the past that I was happy to meet. I'd had a nice chat with Legba once. And La Sirene was always welcome to me. I have done what I've done and gone where I've gone in my life as a journalist because I always knew I could talk to anybody. I've never avoided asking a question. Never backed off from a new experience. But for this guy, this Death, my natural curiosity had evaporated.

Sallie Ann was delighted to have Gede as a guest. She was the first to speak to him. Gede leaned into her ear and whispered something that made her laugh. They were having a big time. I weaved to the drumming and tried to make my mind blank. As I slithered on by Sallie Ann and Gede, hoping to dance past them without getting caught, Sallie Ann touched me on the arm and said, "Would you like to talk to Gede? Ask him something?"

I supposed I could have said, "No thank you." That would have been fine. But something clicked. I knew immediately what it was. I have never been able to turn down a dare, a weakness that has lured a fair amount of trouble across my path. I am afraid of some things, but I am more afraid that people will know I'm afraid, which is how I have gotten tangled in the treetops a few times. So, to my ears Sallie Ann's invitation sounded like a dare, even though she probably didn't mean it that way. I was going to have to talk to Gede.

"*Bonsoir, bonsoir*," he said without making eye contact with me. Instead his gaze shifted about the room. Was Gede shy? Or was he just keeping an eye out for the next victim? Not sure. I did know that something was expected of me.

"Thank you for coming to visit," I said. I am nothing if not polite, even when faced with Death. In the hope of deflecting his attention away from me, I decided to go with a general open-ended question. "Gede, what have you come to tell us this evening?"

"Stop thinking so much," Gede said, and turned to face me, looking me right in the eyes. He took a long pull on his bottle of rum and wiped his sweaty face with his sleeve. "Move into your heart instead. Live by the light

162

of your heart. When you sing a song, sing it with all your heart. If you don't know the words, hum it with all your heart." He cackled and waved his cigar in a wide gesture, as if to take in the whole room and all the dancers.

This was good advice, something I've heard often. I mean the part about thinking less, not the humming. The advice does irritate me a little bit, though. Telling a person like me not to think so much is like telling a champion figure skater to get off the ice and take up bowling instead because that will make her happier and give her more of a social life. All true, but what about those magnificent double axels she can do?

Gede wanted to say more. He leaned close to me. I could smell him. He was stinky. Gede spoke in a near whisper. "Beware the thief of your desires. We all have a thief inside us. You can't get rid of the thief, but when you see him, slap him on the wrist. Don't let him steal your desires. You have a destiny to live out. Don't let anything distract you."

Then he leaned back, swiveling on his oily hips, and concluded his prophecy with a roar. "If you do all this, the Loa will sweep in behind you and carry you forward!"

With that, Gede released me from our conversation, and I resumed the dance around the altar. The drumming guided me until, tired and empty, I rested on the floor. Gede's words ferried me home.

Beware the thief of your desires. I cogitated on that for days. There were so many thieves. Television. Vodka. Obsessive ruminations on various injustices. Where should I begin? There was going to be an awful lot of wrist-slapping around here. I was exhausted just thinking about it. Sorry. No more thinking.

My conversation with Death actually began a long time ago. I had requested his presence the first time when I was fourteen years old, as I lay in my childhood bedroom in New Jersey. It was the first night I had to sleep in my back brace. This brace was essentially a cage, custom designed and fitted to imprison me. It held my head and neck in a metal collar that was connected with metal bars to a heavy plastic girdle that encased my pelvis. It locked me in with metal screws at the back and held me in a stiff posture so that I could not bend at the waist or turn my head from side to side or up and down.

163

I was permitted to remove it for one hour a day so that I could bathe. The final effect of the brace was akin to a medieval instrument of torture. It was hideous, and I was hideous in it.

People have asked me why my parents put me through this. I still don't have a good answer. The best I can offer is that my mother and father possess what I call "a pathology mindset." He is a doctor and she a speech therapist. They believe in sickness and worship medicine. Doctors are the priests of their religion. So when my father, a thoracic surgeon (the alpha male in the medical social hierarchy), asked the orthopedist to make a back brace for his daughter, naturally they all agreed to it. Because Doctor Knows Best. All these decisions took place over my head. No one talked to me about it or explained what was happening or the reason for the brace. No one, least of all my parents, gave any consideration to how this would affect me, the soft little girl inside the brace. They couldn't pause for that consideration because that might undermine the authority of the priest-doctors. The pathology mindset treats everyone like a specimen. The whole person and all her feelings are of no concern in such thinking.

During the course of fitting me for this brace at the clinic, one of the doctors took photographs of me wearing nothing but my underpants. They wanted to see how I stood on my own without anything in the way. My mother had smiled and waved me off. She held a Styrofoam cup of coffee decorated with a coral crescent of lipstick. The camera flash blinded me. I kept my gaze on the sun-filled windows. Maybe if I did not look the man in the face then he wouldn't be able to see me. He showed me the photos afterward. I glanced quickly, not wanting to see what had been recorded. I couldn't avoid taking away an image. Two purplish bruises in the center—those must have been my breasts. Above was an ugly clenched fist of despair that I was shocked to recognize as my own face.

In the photos, naturally I stood with my shoulders curved forward. I was trying to shield my breasts from view. Wouldn't you, if you were a fourteen-year-old girl, naked and alone in a room with a strange man and his camera?

In the car on the way home, the enormity of what lay before me finally sank in. I felt the cage door closing over me, and I was powerless to save my own life. I turned my face away from my mother and allowed tears to roll down my cheeks. Protest was useless. I was alone with my fate. I tried not to make a sound. Without moving her gaze from the road ahead, my mother snapped, "What are *you* crying about?"

My parents had to harden themselves against my suffering or they'd never be able to do what they did. They regarded compassion as weakness, because they weren't strong enough to feel that and still function as parents. Instead they made up a story that would help to make their behavior possible. My parents decided that my poor posture was disobedience. They had threatened me with a back brace if I didn't stand straighter, and so they had to follow through on that threat or look weak. The brace was their punishment for what they saw as my crime of disrespect.

The truth is that I was unaware of my slouching. I lived in my dreamy thoughts and didn't pay attention to correct posture. So I didn't even know what they were talking about most of the time. I had other things on my mind.

Once they had seized on "power struggle" as the story line, my parents warmed to their theme. When I was actually locked into the brace, they treated my terrified misery as a full-blown adolescent rebellion that they must put down. My father became angry over some sassy comment I had made. He came after me, swinging his long, rope-muscled arms, his hands as big as steam shovels. He grabbed the metal rod that ran down the front of my body and shook it, rattled my cage with me tossing inside. He spit in my face and smiled as he taunted me in my trap.

After the first three months, my mother brought me back to the clinic to have the brace adjusted. There was a pad underneath the metal rod down the front that pressed hard into the center of my chest. Over time, the pad made a pressure sore that ballooned into a festering, pus-filled wound about the size of a silver dollar. At the clinic they took photographs of it. They had never seen anything quite this spectacular. I was an interesting specimen, well documented.

Before taking me to have this wound tended, my mother had peeled my T-shirt away from the sticky hole in my chest to display it to my father, expecting him to call the clinic. "We can't bother the doctors with every little thing," he shouted. Later he accused me of intentionally wounding myself as an attempt to get out of the brace.

It was true that I didn't want to wear the brace. Who would? I am surprised it didn't occur to my parents that I was exhibiting normal, healthy instincts. No smart dog goes willingly into a cage.

Let us pause here for a little historical perspective, the backstory behind the back-brace story. Indeed, how *did* my relationship with my parents reach such a shocking low point? It wasn't always this way.

My father taught me many useful things. He gave me my first Swiss Army knife and showed me how to use it without cutting myself. From him I also learned how to tie a bowline and how to take the luff out of my sail: "Fall off! Away from the wind!" I learned to sew by repairing sails down in the dank cabin of his boat, while it wintered out of the water. To this day, whenever I fix a dropped hem, my stitches remain seaworthy and possess none of the delicacy one expects in such a domestic art. My dad showed me the proper splinting of the broken wing of a wild goose, should I ever encounter a wounded bird on the marsh road along the causeway between the mainland and the island. (These things do happen from time to time, and a goose convalesced in our garage for several weeks before my father released it back into the wild.) Once he woke me up before dawn—his customary waking hour to begin rounds or get to surgery at the hospital—and made me sit on the back porch with him, listening to the shore birds sing their morning chorus. I curled up on a lawn chair. He stood with a coffee cup in one hand and stared at the blue-black horizon, where a cacophony of squawks floated across the bay from the distant marshes. "If you never got up this early, you'd never know about this," he pointed out. The surly child in me wanted to say, "Yeah? Big deal." Despite that, I got it: *Pay attention.*

When I was thirteen years old, he taught me how to drive a stick shift, the idea being that in the event of a catastrophe (atomic bomb, Allied invasion, you never know) I might be called to take the wheel of his red convertible VW Beetle if he were wounded in the crossfire. He also taught me how to keep my knife sharp and clean in case I had to perform an emergency tracheostomy. My father, who grew up in the shadow of the Third Reich, also advised me at a very young age that I must always keep my passport current, "because you never know when you might have to leave the country in a hurry."

When I review the things I learned from my father—knife skills, intricate knot-tying, the precise moment to release the clutch—I realize that he was training me to be his son. He did eventually receive an actual son, but my brother, born eight years after me, arrived relatively late in the family history. By that time, my father, who was impatient to begin training a son, had already chosen me to be indoctrinated as his replacement in the world.

I didn't mind. What did I know? Captain Daddy (whom my sister had also dubbed "The Pacemaker King of South Jersey") knew everything. Plus, I was pretty sure he was the biggest and strongest man in the world. I'd follow him anywhere to absorb his expertise, even if it meant pretending for his sake that I was not a girl. This was an easy masquerade. My mother kept my hair clipped in a short pixie fuzz all over my skull, and my body resembled a bundle of dry sticks strung together with piano wire.

My father resembled a larger bundle of dry sticks. We were nearly twins, and I raced after him on the ski slopes, so intent on keeping up that I almost didn't notice I was going faster, faster, faster. Snowplowing was for girls, sissy skiing. I learned how to wield my skis like a scalpel, slicing with swift, fearless precision from one mogul to the next, shifting my weight without thought or plan. Letting gravity and instinct take me, gliding in and out of the mountain's shapely turns. Skiing was a combination of surgery and dance, which was probably how the two of us found common ground out there. I loved the windy speed. No time to think. I'd throw myself off the top of the slope and go!

My father, always in front by many yards, would occasionally stop and look around to diagnose my form and scream instructions. "Heels together, God *damn* it! Lean *into* the turn! You've got to attack the mountain!"

I didn't want to attack anything. I wanted to revel in my own grace. (My inward cry: *I'm a girl!*) But I found my aggression. For his sake.

It should be noted here that when I was twelve years old, I fractured my lower tibia while attacking a slope called "The Wall." I also want the record to reflect that I had already skied "The Wall" with perfection in the past, and on this occasion (last run of the day, warming weather, light rain, sludgy snow) I had gotten almost all the way through it before crashing at the bottom. Furthermore, I was not going to allow this spectacular crash to stop me from finishing the run. I shoved my heel back in my boot, snapped on my bindings, and continued skiing for another two hundred yards. It took a while, but eventually I recognized a persistent sharp jab in one foot whenever I made a left turn and concluded I could not go on with right turns alone. Only after first attempting to finish the run on a broken leg did I decide (with *extreme* reluctance and embarrassment) to sit down and wait for my sister to fetch the ski patrol to bring me off the mountain. I wasn't showing off for my father with this display of stoicism. He wasn't there when I broke my leg. He didn't have to be. By then the fix was in. I had been programmed not to notice pain. Never complain. And never, *ever* ask for help.

My mother's contribution to my development was to bathe me in words. Words, words, more words, and stories upon stories. She almost couldn't buy books fast enough to keep up with my appetite. She fed my hungry eyes with an intrepid Girl Detective, a red-headed orphan girl wreaking havoc on Prince Edward Island, a magnificent black stallion, a young witch of Cornwall and Blackbird Pond too. She introduced me to our librarian, who became one of my dearest friends. My mother taught me how to use my imagination when I couldn't sleep at night. "Pretend you're a tree," she advised. "Let all your branches and roots grow out and up and down." She was standing in the bathroom in her nightgown, smiling with her arms outstretched, demonstrating how she pretends to be a tree sometimes when she has trouble sleeping. *Oh, I see. I make a picture in my head, and it changes the way I feel . . . Cool.*

My mother gave me the keys to the kingdom. Sure, knife skills are handy, but the room inside my head was vast and infinitely more absorbing, once she showed me the way in.

What I didn't know at the time and would only understand much later was that there was an unspoken contract in this exchange. My mother would show me the power that lay within my mind through imagery and words, but only if I agreed to remain in this dry, theoretical space between my ears. If my awareness traveled south of my cerebral cortex, there'd be hell to pay.

On my mother's watch, I was to be a big brain only, and my body regarded as a dangerous afterthought, better to be ignored.

I have to believe she meant well and thought she was doing right by me. For instance, one day I walked in the house, and my mother met me at the door. She wore an impish gleam and leaned toward me as though she might burst with a secret. For a second I thought we might have a new puppy. No, she led me into the living room and showed me the surprise. There, standing alone in the middle of the rug, was the Compact Edition of the *Oxford English Dictionary*. A gift! For me! It consisted of two volumes, bound in blue with gilt lettering, and stood nearly two feet off the floor. Its traveling cabinet had a little drawer in the top, replete with magnifying glass for ease of reading "The Complete Text Reproduced Micrographically." In these pages lay all the words in the world. My mother had signed up for a membership in the Book-of-the-Month Club in order to buy this gift. I appreciated the sacrifice because I knew she considered BOMC awfully middlebrow, and she never wanted anyone to tell her what to read. She went along with it just to acquire this rare treat for me. This was the only time I can recall my mother seeing into the depths of who I am, and letting me know that was good.

I took my new *OED* upstairs to my room. I opened one of the volumes and leaned down into the pages to smell them. They carried the clean scent of brilliance. I pulled out the magnifying glass and read the first word my eyes located: "Eveish, *a. nonce-wd.* [f. *Eve* the first woman + ISH.] Like Eve; curious. 1754 RICHARDSON *Grandison* vi. 210 (D.), I saw it was a long letter; I felt very Eveish, my dear."

Wow. This would keep me busy for a long time.

Then I actually hugged the books. How many girls do you know who do this? I put my arms around these weighty volumes, held them to my chest, and thought, *All the words in the world. Now I am invincible.*

The event that changed everything occurred when I hit early adolescence. Nature transformed me from a bundle of dry sticks strung together with piano wire, into a bundle of dry sticks adorned with two apricots. (I was thrilled: I *am* a girl!) My father treated this change as a profound betrayal. He never forgave me. And he never stopped punishing me.

He didn't have anything else to teach me then. It was as though I had spoiled everything by being, in an obvious way, a girl. He seemed to view the physical facts of my sex as not only a grave breach of contract, but also vulgar and embarrassing. Captain Daddy turned away from me, my education finished.

My father didn't even know about the blood that appeared in the crotch of my underpants. I showed that to my mother early one morning. "Look!" I whispered. I had woken her from deep slumber to confront her with this evidence. My father was still sleeping. "This is it! It's really happening." She opened one eye, looked at my underwear, and groaned, "Oh noooo." As if the world had come to an end. I knew this was the start of an exciting new chapter in my life story. The beginning of the world. I knew this better than anything. Nothing, not my mother's dread, nor my father's disgust, could dampen my joy. I held it like a secret treasure.

Still, this business of growing and changing presented some problems. My father found me vulgar. And my mother was frankly terrified that I'd get knocked up before I was sixteen years old. I don't know why she thought this would happen, but I know she was convinced of it. Neither of them could stop the changes in my body. I was becoming too alarming, unfettered, and on my own, just being . . . you know . . . a *girl.*

So, there was nothing for it but to put me in a cage. I believe that decision made sense to them at the time.

My friend Judy came by our house to visit me the first night I wore the back brace. We were in Creative Writing Club together, and her mom had tutored us in the Great Books Program. For these reasons, I allowed my friend to see me. Judy was quiet. I stood there, frightfully erect and dressed in my floor-length bathrobe. I didn't have clothing yet that would fit over the brace. I remained silent because when I opened my mouth to speak, my chin bumped against the metal collar that held my head in place. It was also hard to swallow. I couldn't see my own feet. Couldn't look at a plate of food in front of me, had to guess at what I might be eating. It would take time to acclimate to this loss of my body's simple freedoms. At the moment, when I faced my friend Judy, it still felt like a fresh violation. Plus, my form was drastically changed. The slim, supple girl I had

170

been before the brace had been replaced by a monstrous, bulky thing. The pointed metal pieces of the brace made hard, ugly lumps through the fabric of my robe. No doubt my face was a grim study, while Judy's face showed something unreadable. Finally she spoke. "You kinda look like Queen Victoria."

We both laughed. She had a twisted sense of humor, which was why she was my friend. That evening, we played cards and talked about stuff two fourteen-year-old girls would find interesting. Once she got past the shock, Judy treated me like me. Somehow she was able to see her soft friend in the cage and let me feel normal. I never had a chance to tell Judy how I cherished her compassion. Her gift sustained me. Sometimes I lost track of it. Then I'd stumble across it in the dark, surprised to remember that yes, I had a friend, who could see me and cared for me. Even with this grain of normal, I still had to face the night alone.

My parents decided the best approach would be to leave me to myself on the first night I had to sleep in the brace, and let me scream until the fight went out of me. Until I had submitted to the cage.

In my bed, I prayed for death. The darkness broke a spell. It released something that I had been holding at bay. With the light gone, I understood that I wanted to exit my body. I could not live another minute, let alone sleep in this thing. I clawed at the metal collar around my neck because it was choking me, and I screamed uncontrollably for hours. I begged to be released from my body and this cage.

"God, kill me! Bring death to me, now! I don't want to live. Kill me, please! I want to die!" I howled like a trapped animal until my voice was in shreds.

God wasn't listening. I did live. No one else appeared to be listening either. My younger sister, who shared a bedroom with me, had fled to my parents' room when she heard me. Later she told me that my older sister was there too, and they had huddled around my mother in her bed, terrified by the sounds I was making on the other side of the house. No one came for me.

I screamed until drained of energy, but could not sleep. The brace did not permit me to curl up, nose to knees, which was how I liked to sleep. It forced me to lie stiff as a corpse on a plank. So, I committed one of the few brave acts of my childhood. I got up from my bed and removed the back brace. Only then could I sleep. I didn't have the words for it, but that night drilled a lesson into me about who I could trust. I knew it like the taste of my own spit. The next morning I woke up and stepped back into my cage like a good, obedient girl. My brief rebellion wilted in the daylight. For the next year, I wore the brace as prescribed, and went about my business as though I were the living dead. The girl I was went underground. "*Silence, exile, cunning.*"

When I wore the brace to school, I could see the other kids were disturbed by my appearance. Many thought I had been in a horrible car accident. Their pity burned like acid on my skin. I also saw disgust in their faces. Even worse, some of them looked away quickly, as if embarrassed by the sight of my suffering. It made me feel like a splayed frog, pinned and gutted for dissection in the biology lab. I would change that. So, I walked the hallways and practiced shooting my death-ray eyes at the kids who dared look at me. My gaze was a weapon. Since I had seen the expression demonstrated for me on the faces of my parents, I was skilled at making my own face into an impenetrable mask of contempt and rage.

One day my older sister told me that her friends at our school had asked what was wrong with me. Why did I look angry all the time? The kids had said they were afraid of me. I absorbed the information with deep satisfaction.

I stopped speaking and numbed myself with silent loathing, sure that no one would ever come for me. That was how I survived until I could wake myself up again. I posed as a girl, but truly I was sleepwalking like a zombie with jagged eyes.

Over many years, the pain of numbness gradually became greater than the pain of feeling. I woke up in my body, which continues to be a pleasure, even though being alive and awake means speaking the unspeakable. Still, I hope it goes on that way. I prefer life. There have been many moments along the way when I can forget the time in the back brace. Life has improved a lot since then, and I know I'll never be fourteen years old again. My old bedroom in New Jersey is far away in space and time, yet I carry a scar on my chest, left behind from the weeping wound the brace inflicted. At times I can sense a ghostly image of the cage still weighing on my body.

One method I have tried to make the ghostly brace go away is creative visualization, deploying my greatest weapon, imagination, to liberate myself. I summoned a shark to drag it down to the bottom of the ocean. I transformed the brace into golden light and let it dissipate into the sky. None of these visualizations worked for long. The brace always reappeared like a bad dream to clasp me in a rigid lock from jaw to hips, so my words choked off, and the snake in my spine could not bend and twist as it desired.

On this Day of the Dead, after I had such an interesting chat with Gede, I came home from the Vodou ritual and took Lance for a walk around the bayou. Sean was out of town on one of his concert tours. The night was cool and windless. The water was a black mirror, reflecting nothing. I was looking for more from my brush with Death. The bayou seemed to be saying, "Go home."

When we got back to the house, I settled onto my meditation cushion. Still caught in the smoky trance of the Vodou ritual, I closed my eyes. A vision began to unfold. It started with a memory, clear and sharp. In my mind's eye, I returned to that old scene in my childhood home. I saw myself lying on my back in my nighttime bedroom with the pink shag rug and the floral print curtains that matched the bedspread. Of course there it was; quick as a wink, my old cage came back to me and held me close in the dark.

This time in the childhood scene of my visualization, I looked to the side and saw that Death had appeared in the doorway to my bedroom. Interesting that God didn't answer me when I called out, but Death did. One more reason to believe that Death is real, while God remains a dubious proposition. In this vision, Death was a large moving shadow without a face, palpable but indistinct.

"What are you doing here?" I asked Death.

"You called for me."

"I changed my mind. I don't want you."

"You should be careful what you ask for. Now I'm here. You have to talk to me." Death came over to my bed and sat next to me. This was creeping me out. I did not want him anywhere near me.

I yelled at Death. "I was just a kid, for God's sake! Fourteen years old. I didn't know what I was saying."

"You were a pretty complex fourteen-year-old. You had wise thoughts, and you said more than you knew. Now I'm here." Death leaned closer to my face, as if to lie beside me like a lover.

"No! I do not want you as my lover!" I yelled and kicked and pushed him away. I moved without restraint now, free of the brace. Death stood up and went to the end of my bed, where he held my feet in a light grasp that from anyone else but Death would have felt comforting. His touch was warmer than I expected.

"Can't we just be friends?" Death asked. He sounded aggrieved. I sensed I might be gaining the upper hand.

I stood up on the bed and lunged at him, waving my arms in a menacing gesture. I bared my teeth and stuck out my tongue and made snarling noises from deep in my throat, like a mad dog. I made myself as hideous as I know I can be. Death didn't flinch. "I'm not afraid of you," he said in a mild voice. "I'm not afraid of anything."

I lay down in my bed again and pulled the covers up to my chin. "We are not going any further in this relationship until I see a face. Something. I need to know who I'm talking to here."

Death came out of the shadows for a moment and showed me his face. He was handsome, but in the most conventional sort of way. He looked like a blond pampered frat boy with smug cheekbones.

"You do have a certain bland good looks." I was trying to hurt his feelings.

"Yes, it's true. I am quite beautiful." He wasn't listening. Or he was impervious to insult. Death has a bulletproof ego, it seemed.

"Let's get serious," I said. "I want to know why you're here with me. Right now. For real. And don't give me any of the usual clichés about living every day as if it were your last . . . yadda yadda, yadda, yadda."

Death waited before he answered.

"I'm the period at the end of the sentence. You like that. You like things to be completed. You hate it when something is left unresolved. I am part of what you sign on for when you come into life. I am one of the steps. Nothing to be afraid of. I'm just the thing that comes next. Without me, life is an unfinished work of art."

Now he had my attention. I listened. Death talked.

"I am here to liberate you from fear, to remind you that Death is ever near. So nothing matters and everything matters. It's the paradox you live with. But you don't have to be afraid of anything. I've got your back."

"Death, you're so funny. I am enjoying myself. But I am going back to sleep, if you don't mind."

"You're going to write about this later, aren't you?" he said.

"Yes, of course. Throughout this entire conversation, I've been humming at the back of my mind: *How can I use this?*"

"That's okay. I give you permission to write about me."

"Thanks, but I don't need your permission." I rolled onto my side and closed my eyes.

"Think what you like," said Death.

KATRINA LITTER

DURING OUR EXILE FROM NEW ORLEANS, WE DROVE FROM CITY TO city, yoga studio to yoga studio, where our hosts welcomed us refugees with warmth and generosity. They gave us places to sleep, meals, and a lot of unsolicited advice.

"Don't go back," they said, more or less uniform in their assertion that New Orleans was a lost cause and should be left to decompose on her own. "Better to cut your losses and run," these kind people said to us.

One afternoon I sat in the Connecticut living room belonging to our hostess for that weekend's concert. It was a large, comfortable home with a rolling expanse of lawn, littered with children's toys and shaded by elm trees in a neighborhood where people came and went without anything heavier on their minds than getting to yoga class on time. I sat on a soft white couch in this sunny, peaceful house and watched the news of New Orleans with tears streaming down my face. There was report on the Hot 8 Brass Band playing with donated instruments to get a little second line going for the refugees in a shelter. They had been forced to evacuate without their own instruments, which surely now had been destroyed. The musicians' faces stretched wide with the joy of making music. And the people danced behind them as if it was just another great Saturday afternoon. The woman who hosted us passed through the back of the room and saw my hot, wet face.

"Stop torturing yourself!" She made a move to turn off the TV. I begged her to leave it on.

Usually I fumed in silence. It was so easy for them. None of them had any real stake in the outcome of this thing. Even though I understood they had good intentions, I was still astonished at their abrupt dismissal of an entire city that I loved.

These people had based their advice on the news. It portrayed our home as a diseased and depraved place, where children were being raped and murdered in the Superdome. Cholera would soon proliferate, killing thousands in a biblical epidemic. One e-mail making the rounds disseminated the apocryphal claim that an eight-foot alligator was swimming down Tulane Avenue. Most of the worst stories of violence turned out to be untrue. There was wild talk of an armed mob marching up Saint Charles Avenue—some called it a "Zulu nation"—bent on killing white people. Some wealthy Uptowners hired a private army detail to protect themselves. The soldiers landed by helicopter in Audubon Park. The mob scenario never materialized. There were unconfirmed reports that a nurse at Charity Hospital had locked herself into a ward with her patients because addicts roamed the halls and smashed open drug cabinets in search of a fix. The infamous account of a seven-year-old whose throat had been cut in the Convention Center was never proven; the police never found a body.

Some of the reports of crime were true. People were looting stores on Canal Street and running off with big TVs, not just food and drinking water. The Jefferson Parish sheriffs fired shots at innocent people as they tried to cross the bridge from New Orleans to Gretna, where they believed they would be saved. The New Orleans police killed a mentally disabled man, shooting him in the back as he ran with a small dog cradled in his arms. Those early days were so fraught with chaos that too often the hysteria screamed louder than common sense. Overlooked were the many stories of people who acted with calm decency and helped each other.

I made the mistake of telling my mother about the poisonous snakes that, according to one alarmist report, had come boiling up out of the ground with the floodwaters.

"She says there are poisonous snakes all around her house," my mother said, turning away from the phone to convey this information to my father. I could hear him muttering in the background.

"Yes, of course," he said, as if he had known all along.

The dire predictions of sickness from the tainted environment also turned out to be exaggerated. We had the "Katrina cough," probably from the dust clouds rising over the houses that were being gutted, but there has been no sign of the plague. At the time, back when it was a fresh shock, everyone thought New Orleans was a hopeless waste pit that had collapsed in on herself. No one could imagine life there again.

I could imagine it. Many times over, I could see us living there. It was easy, because New Orleans is our home. We belong to this city, and she belongs to us. You don't just abandon someone because she's in trouble. On the contrary, it was precisely because New Orleans had been brought to her knees by this storm that made our return even more necessary. Even though all the physical evidence suggested we should do otherwise, I couldn't still my urge to go back as soon as possible, to see it with my own eyes. I wouldn't be able to integrate fully what had transpired in my home, until my feet touched the old ground there and my nose took in the odor of the air. Nothing less would satisfy me. My desire for New Orleans, our honeymoon cottage, my bayou, springs from a deep, atavistic well. It might not look sensible beneath the rational scrutiny of those who don't make their home in New Orleans, yet the heart of this desire beats stronger than their sensible advice. And so while these good people were busy telling Sean and me what to do with our lives, all I could reply was, "I want to go home."

In October, about seven weeks after the storm, I got my wish. The mayor had lifted the ban on residents returning to their houses. We started the drive home. As we took Interstate 59 South, the highway was crowded with FEMA trucks carrying trailers, and huge flatbeds loaded with new lumber, all of us headed to the same destination. As we got closer to the city, the landscape changed from the fresh green forests of the north to the blasted, brown, and twisted scenes of the south. Gradually it came to match up with what we had seen in the news. I thought I was prepared for what I would see, but I was wrong. It looked like some other planet. Mile after mile of houses showed that telltale horizontal dark mud streak, ten or fourteen feet up the wall, where the water had come to rest. Windows punched out like blind eyes, cars nosed up and pinned to the tops of fences, angry trees slammed onto crushed roofs. The trees that remained standing appeared to overlook the wreckage with their bare dry arms lifted in frozen madness, shrieking at the sky.

We pulled off the interstate onto Orleans Avenue and headed toward Bayou Saint John. We drove slowly, pausing at each intersection because the stoplights were out, and the street was littered with piles of torn sheetrock, broken glass, chunks of battered stoves and reeking refrigerators, and rusty nails, lots of those everywhere. We would replace the tires on our car many times in the next several months. On the way home, we passed a dead rott-weiler in the gutter, his large black-and-tan body bloated in the heat, his stiff legs pointing up. I drove past it several more times over the next month before someone took it away. The police and the National Guard were still looking for human bodies. The dead dogs would have to wait.

Our street had been transformed into a smoky heap. There was just a narrow path in the center. On either side stood tall piles of stinking junk, broken furniture, moldy shoes and shirts, sheetrock, and stained floor planks that our neighbors had pulled from their houses and dragged to the curb. Some people had already returned to begin cleaning and gutting their flooded homes. Our car crunched over the compressed gray stuff on the ground, while thick clouds of gritty dust swirled through the yellow bars of late afternoon sunlight that came through the tree branches. Soon, and on a daily basis, I would discover brown gunk in the Kleenex into which I had just blown my nose. This was the air Katrina had left us to breathe. Since we didn't have a choice about breathing, we learned to live with brown gunk.

We parked near a refrigerator, one of many, that its previous owner had placed on the curb. People had thrown them out, not because the refrig-erators didn't work, but because no one could face the maggots that had proliferated in the rotting food during the long absence of electricity. Some-one had written on the side of this refrigerator, "Bush sucks!" Someone else had added below, "Even their first CD?" It was nice to be home.

On the sidewalk to our house, my feet crunched on the dead leaves and ripples of dark chalky stuff that I realized was mud that had dried in a rivulet pattern, an imprint left behind by the hand of the water. It was as though I was walking on the bottom of the bay after the tide had gone out. Our house, still wearing plywood over the windows, looked sad and drab. The porch screens hung loose from their tacking, and branches littered the dry, crackling lawn.

Liberated at last from the confines of the car, Lance skipped ahead of us. He stretched his legs in a merry dash up the walk. He was so glad not to be curled up on the floor of the front seat of the car that he didn't seem to care how different everything looked since the night we had left weeks earlier.

A brown pall hung over our home and yard. The sweet olive trees had died, and the Japanese magnolia that grew by our kitchen door and gave us a shower of pink blossoms every April was dead. The fig tree dead, and all her figs as well. Normally, I'd get a second harvest out of her this time of year before she went dormant. The sweet viburnum stood brown and desiccated, drowned in the salt water like the others. First there was flood, then a drought, famine for the garden. Only the jasmine lived and curled itself around our front fence, still green and flirting. *What cheek.* I brushed her leaves with my fingertips.

The waterline across the front of our house came just below the floorboards of our porch. Sean and I had painted the porch floor a deep blue called "Lakefront" and painted the trim a lighter blue called "Bayou." My habit is to choose paint colors as much for their names as the actual color. This stems from my belief in the power of naming—that we invest our home with the qualities suggested by the words used to identify the color. At the time, these paint colors and their names were romantic choices. Now, it seemed that I might have called the water right to our front door.

The floodwaters had come up about three feet in our neighborhood and gotten shallower toward the edge of the bayou itself because the ground slopes up slightly at the edge of Bayou Saint John, where it has a natural levee that has built up over the centuries as the flowing water pushed silt to the sides. Our house is raised off the ground a few feet and sits on brick piers. This is a sensible house design, popular in New Orleans throughout most of its building history until the practice of placing houses on concrete slab foundations poured directly onto the ground took precedence in the mid-twentieth century. Putting a house above the ground on piers was a good idea for the reason that it permitted air circulation to dry things out, and floodwaters could also flow underneath the house without doing too much damage, assuming the water didn't come up too high. If there was any flooding at all, the houses built later in the century on slabs, flush with the ground, didn't have a prayer. There was a small chance that our 1920s raised house had gotten away without water damage on the interior. From the outside, the house looked to be still intact.

We let ourselves in the back door and walked through the kitchen. The house was dark because the plywood blocked out the sunlight. I got down on my hands and knees and felt around in the dark for our rugs to figure out if they had been soaked. They felt normal. I pulled up one corner of a rug and leaned down to sniff out evidence of mildew. Nothing but old dust, probably been there since long before we evacuated. Except for the mouse droppings in the closets and the bugs swarming in the refrigerator, every-thing was as we had left it.

We hauled a ladder out so Sean could look at the roof, and it seemed to be fine. Then I crawled under the house to see what might have happened to our wiring and plumbing down below. This was another division of labor with us. I couldn't stand going up on a high ladder, and Sean couldn't stand going into the crawlspace beneath our house. This was so like us: He was up there in the clean air where the masculine spirit soars, while I was down in the dirt where the feminine soul abides.

The grassy streak on the floor joists showed that the floodwater had come within a few inches of our floorboards. This small distance was all that lay between us and a ruined home. I wasn't sure whom to thank for this miraculous near miss, so I sat on the damp, shaded ground beneath our house, with mosquitoes buzzing around my bare ankles and my ears, and just breathed a prayer of gratitude to whoever deserved it.

We drove across town to see how the yoga studio had fared. We knew that it had missed the worst because its location happens to be in that slim 20 percent of the city that didn't flood. Even so, we feared the roof might have blown away, or that looters had broken in. We had seen reports that other businesses nearby had been smashed and stripped. We walked all around the building and saw that aside from a single missing board at the edge of the roof, everything was fine. Must have been that bubble of good yoga energy. Someone had written a message on the plywood that covered the studio's front door. "We need yoga! Please open soon."

Not only that, but Sean's office in the building next door was also okay, despite the fact that the roof over the unit next to his was gone. The roofing material had torn away just to the edge of Sean's space, so that his computers and files were dry, while the space next to his was a sodden mess.

This was too much. We were three for three. Home, studio, and office, all more or less intact. It couldn't be real, but it was.

Still there was work. We didn't have much time, because Sean had booked a continuation of his concert tour on the West Coast and would have to begin the long drive to California in a week. I planned to return to our friends in Tennessee for a month until Sean came home because, according to all the good advice I was getting, I wasn't supposed to stay alone in New Orleans. I wanted to stay in our home while Sean was gone, but he asked me not to. My friends begged me not to. They envisioned marauders swarming over our undefended home as soon as night fell.

I had a hard time imagining that happening in our sleepy neighborhood, yet they had something of a point. Although the city was gradually becoming more populated, it was still an inhospitable place with no electrical power in most parts. When we drove across town at night, the streets were in total blackness. If we saw a spray of white light flickering in the distance, we knew it was another car. Driving was a game of chicken with other cars at every intersection because the stoplights didn't work. There was an eight o'clock curfew, so if we got a late dinner at one of the few restaurants open uptown, we had to scoot home along the circuitous route to avoid the cops. They were arresting people on Carrollton Avenue for breaking the curfew. On the way home through one of the hardest-hit neighborhoods, our headlights threw exaggerated spooky shadows on haunted front porches. The houses were empty and broken for block after block. I looked down the side streets. The dark was dense and complete, like a heavy blanket over the city. Not one splinter of life or light showed through.

By some luck we had electricity on our street, but it was sporadic.

Every so often there would be a sudden *thwump* and then dead silence. All the usual humming electrical white noise that fills the air without our noticing it—all snuffed out in a flash. I walked along the bayou during one of these silences and listened for the sounds that would normally be buried beneath the white noise. The birds had not returned yet, nor the crickets. There was nothing. Just the sound of the water lapping at the edge of the levee.

Unfortunately, there was no gas service yet, so we couldn't use the stove to cook for ourselves. Nor could we keep any perishable food at the house, because our poisoned refrigerator had to make a trip out to the sidewalk along with all the other refrigerators. I stocked a cooler with ice just to keep some cream for my coffee. No gas service also meant that our gas-powered hot water heater was unable to provide us with hot water. So bathing was brisk, but we didn't mind the cool showers so much, as the weather was still summery and sweaty. The so-called people in charge had warned us not to allow the water piped into our houses to splash into our mouths as we bathed, because there could be dangerous bacteria. I considered this a ludicrous warning. The tap water in New Orleans was never safe to drink, even before the storm, so a few more germs couldn't possibly kill us.

Our first unpleasant task was to clean out the ruined junk from our shed and all the dead matter from our garden. The shed itself was still standing, another small miracle, but it stood on a slab flush with the ground, so the flood had destroyed everything inside. Our washer and dryer, now brown and stinking, leaned on their sides like a child's unwanted blocks. The hot water heater's machinery was rusted tight, and the air-conditioning condenser was toast. Our lawnmower, my gardening tools, and all the other stuff we had stored in that splintering wreck of a shed was rusted and caked in a thick dry mud. Sean threw himself into the job of clearing the weeds and branches from our lawn. That little patch of lawn had always been his area of expertise—mine was the flowering plants and edible herbs—so he wanted to restore it to a semblance of its former state. I braved the shed.

The smell of the dried mud was something else altogether. I will always associate this smell with Katrina, and I have struggled to find the right words to describe it. Whether in our shed or on the other side of town, the smell was the same. Whenever my nose met that scent, faster than light *Katrina* came alive. The scent summoned an instant visceral distaste, marbled with panic, as if I were being smothered in despair, nailed into a coffin before my time. Katrina smelled like wet dirt and mildew, mixed with human dust that has been cooking in late summer heat, a strangely florid and fertile smell that suggested unwholesome life forms brewing in it. As it filled my nose, I sensed all the things that had died in the water, and the new colony of parasites that flourished and fed on the remains of the dead things. This was an ugly rich creeping odor, the smell of invasion. It was everywhere all at once, in the shed and beyond, everywhere we went—a smell that signaled penetrating decay, sadness, destruction, loss.

Long into the hot day we worked, dragging out moldy chairs, a table, a bookcase, the appliances, things we probably could have cleaned and salvaged. But as we pulled stuff out of the shed, the stink surrounding us, a weird mania took over. I felt all our belongings had been infected by Katrina. I wanted nothing to remain that she had touched. I felt contempt for all of it because this vicious stranger had tainted our belongings with her grotesque uninvited visit. The word "hurricane" comes from the Taino word *huracan*, which some translate as "evil spirit." Such a spirit had invaded us. Our home had been molested. As we worked, I became more angry and disgusted. I wanted all of these muddy things gone, as the rape victim wants to burn her clothing. Then I wanted to scrub our shed, the yard, and everything else in a boiling disinfectant to rid the ground of her vile residue.

The rage was infectious. Bruce came over to help us move our refrigerator to the sidewalk. His face wreathed in savage glee like the Grinch who stole Christmas, Bruce tipped the refrigerator down the back steps, and we all hooted and hollered as it smashed open at the bottom. It was exhilarating. I had egged Bruce on, told him to go ahead, throw the refrigerator down the steps. I wanted to see what would happen when it hit the ground. It's not often you get the chance to destroy a large appliance. No one could pass up this unique opportunity to satisfy an urge to do some damage back. It didn't make sense to attack my own refrigerator because I was mad at Katrina. But it felt good.

Later, my neighbor Ivan told me he was dismayed at the number of perfectly fine, in his opinion, refrigerators that had gone to a landfill. One of the wild sights I saw in New Orleans was a gigantic truck going by with a tower of about thirty refrigerators jiggling on the back. Ivan thought it was wasteful and unkind to the environment to toss out these appliances like used Kleenex. He had cleaned out his own maggoty refrigerator with a bucket of bleach and "good old-fashioned elbow grease," as he phrased it. Ivan owns a majority stockholding in the company that produces elbow grease. And he was quite right. It was wasteful. All of us could have done a better job to salvage our belongings. Although Ivan had staked out the moral high ground here, he missed the larger point of our city's collective disgust and rage. And the release we needed to take in discharging that. It was like shooting a gun into an angry sky.

With the military personnel taking the place of the usual population, New Orleans had been transformed into a cowboy town with ten men for every woman. Children were also noticeably absent, as if the Pied Piper of Hamlin had just tootled through. Imagine a city where there are no children. The first thing that appears wrong is that no one is playing. When I walked in the French Quarter one afternoon, not only was it a sea of men, but also every third man wore a sidearm and carried a rifle. The riverfront was now a large tented village filled with camo-clad soldiers, and the streets teemed with noisy Humvees. That was how our Thanksgiving went. I don't mean with the guns and the Humvees, but that our Thanksgiving dinner party was all male, save for me.

Sean's family had retreated back to Austin for Thanksgiving because they still had that nice borrowed house to live in there, and his parents had taken about all they could handle of the stinking mold in their own house, where the water had gone nearly to the second floor. The structure was still standing, but as a home, it would never be the same again. This had been their safe haven for twenty-seven years, and now all the possessions they had collected and cared for, held and loved—their wedding china, favorite books, family photos, rugs, paintings, couch—all of it was saturated in stinking, muddy water. Mary found pieces of wood caught in the blades of their ceiling fan, and it took several minutes of pondering before she recognized these as the legs from her dining room table. The downstairs looked as though someone had picked up the house and shaken it.

When Mary walked upstairs to the second floor of their house, she found it the same as they had left it on August 29th. No sign of the storm at all. The magazines she had been reading remained undisturbed on the bedside table, the shoes still scattered on the floor where she had left them. Walking upstairs from the wreckage below was like Dorothy stepping over the threshold from the black-and-white tornado-tossed house into the Technicolor Land of Oz, where everything was bright, fresh, clean, and whole. And nothing bad had happened.

During the first few days of their return to New Orleans, Mary would go upstairs, sit on the bed, and look around at her normal room that was so familiar with everything in its place. She would stay there for a long time and pretend that the storm had never happened, that her home was still the same as it ever was. Bruce would have to coax her downstairs when it was time to go. He would stand at the bottom of the stairs and call to her, "Come on, Mary. Come downstairs." She didn't want to go. She wanted to stay upstairs where everything was fine.

They needed a break from the sight of this ruin. They returned to the blessedly functional Austin for Thanksgiving.

So, Sean and I were on our own for the holiday. We had dinner at our friend Patrick's house with about five of his friends. All their wives and children were still residing in the more civilized parts of the world—Maryland, Iowa, and New Jersey—where they had evacuated to for the storm. The women and children were staying put for Thanksgiving because the children had enrolled in new schools for the fall semester, and the mothers didn't want to disrupt their lives yet again. Meanwhile the fathers had returned to New Orleans to clean out the refrigerators, defend their homes from attack, feed the cats, and find out if they still had jobs. The women's lives, interests, jobs would have to go on hold for a time. The primitive nature of the situation had returned these families temporarily to some traditional gender roles. The prevailing and unquestioned notion in New Orleans was that it was not fit for women and children. For me, it was interesting to see how quickly this disaster and its brute necessities could push women into a corner again and limit their mobility, making it their primary job to nurture the children because they are vulnerable and they represent life, the future, the only thing worthwhile. By contrast, the men did their part by getting on the move and returning to the city as soon as it was legally possible. Several had come earlier, sneaking in past the armed soldiers at the checkpoints. The perimeter around New Orleans was by no means tight. It was hard to tell who would cause more difficulty, the looters or the National Guard, so the guys took care of things on their own.

The gentlemen served deep-fried turkey for Thanksgiving dinner that evening, a cooking adventure that Patrick had engineered with a propane tank to boil a large pot of oil in the backyard. Deep-fried turkey is a phenomenon I have encountered only in the South—not even South Jersey, but the true Deep South. Also, it seems that the deep-frying of a turkey only happens when men are left to their own devices for Thanksgiving. If Patrick's wife Nancy had been there, I'm sure the turkey would have been roasted, which is the appropriate way to treat a turkey. Roasting tends to be the woman's choice of cooking a large bird because that method requires a lot of basting and long-term nursing care, while men just love to deep-fry because it's a spectacular and violent thing to do to a turkey. There is also the potential for a grease fire. These elements of drama and danger make this cooking method appealing to men. Furthermore, they know they would not be permitted to do it if their wives were home.

We arrived late to find the guys eating their deep-fried turkey in front of the football game on TV. More spectacular violence! Apparently they had begun to eat dinner at the dining table. They had dutifully set the table with placemats, napkins, silverware, and wine glasses. Everything in its place, as would be expected for Thanksgiving dinner. Then Patrick had stopped, slapped his hand to his forehead, and said, "Wait a minute! We don't have to do this. There is no one to stop us from eating in front of the TV. Come on, this is the only time we'll ever be able to eat Thanksgiving dinner and watch the game at the same time!"

There was a stampede of men from the kitchen to the living room, each carrying a heaping plate of food. That was how we found them, all happily snuggled into the couch and gnawing on bones. Once again I was astonished at how quickly protocols fell away in the wake of this hurricane. The conversation, when they weren't shouting at the TV, consisted of the guys remarking that they missed their wives and children. For some, it had been over two months since they'd seen them. I, too, hoped the women would return home soon. If this testosterone trend continued in New Orleans, we were in big trouble.

For this time at least, I enjoyed that I was the only woman there. They were all nice to me and explained everything the football players were doing. One thing I didn't understand was that I noticed the football players hit each other in the head to express their elation over a good event. But then they also hit each other in the head to express their dismay when something went wrong. So I wondered how one could tell the difference. The other difficulty I had with this Thanksgiving Day game was that it was not a Saints game. And I suffered from a certain strain of "football blindness" in that I couldn't see any other football team except the New Orleans Saints. That was the only team that Sean had ever explained to me, so as far as I was concerned it was the only one that existed.

The guys fed us as well as they could, given that we don't eat meat. Sean and I settled in with plates of mashed potatoes and salad. It was the weirdest and the best Thanksgiving dinner I've ever had. I looked around at my pack of cheerful guys and wanted to scratch their ears. We had so much to be thankful for. We were alive, for one thing. Our homes were in shambles. Our city was crippled. Our futures were uncertain. But we were warm and well-fed and safe, for now.

FINDING THE PULSE

WHEN IT CAME TIME FOR SEAN TO GET IN HIS CAR AND DRIVE TO California, I did something I don't normally do. I broke a promise. Sean had made me agree that I would not stay in New Orleans by myself, that I would leave for Tennessee as soon as he left for California. Instead, I stayed behind on my own for a while. Perhaps the rebellious part of me resented being pushed into a corner. No one had ever told me I couldn't stay or go alone somewhere. It wasn't just Sean that I was rebelling against, but the whole atmosphere of dire restraint. I wasn't buying it. I'd been on my own for a long time and gone into all kinds of strange places by myself before Sean came into my life. I've never taken anyone seriously who tried to tell me I shouldn't do something because my sex made me vulnerable to danger.

The reason beyond my own rebellion was that I wanted to keep New Orleans company a little longer. I wanted to reunite with the bayou in my own way. So I was a little relieved to see Sean go, because I wanted to have some quiet intimate time with this place and feel my way through its troubled story without all the business of getting our house in order and cleaning junk out of the yard. The neighborhood appeared pretty empty, save for a half-dozen intrepid souls. Ivan was there, applying elbow grease wherever necessary. Susan next door hugged me and kissed me and told me I could pirate her Wi-Fi access if I liked. Then beyond our block we were surrounded by vast stretches of emptiness. It looked as though Lance and I could have Bayou Saint John to ourselves. We went for a walk.

The dead grass along the banks was coated in a thick layer of this same stinking dried mud that had covered the stuff in our shed. The water level of the bayou was much lower than normal. A wide portion of the muddy bottom was exposed to the air. I could see what had long been hidden in the past. It was rocks and more mud. That's all. No great mystery.

My feet crunched over the brittle bodies of dead perch scattered on the levee by the flood. There had been large fish kills within a few days because first a wave of water came rushing in bringing large fish from the lake that didn't belong in this bayou. While the bayou was swollen with lake water, it rose a few feet over its banks and allowed all these new fish to swim out into the neighboring streets. When the water level settled down, the fish were stranded on land, where they died on lawns and driveways in the drought that followed the flood.

I headed toward the Magnolia Bridge and noted the detritus that had come to rest there, some brought by the storm, others by people. The sun glinted on the broken windshield glass on the ground. Someone had dragged an old dead car to the bayou, covered it in spray-paint squiggles, smashed all the windows, and then set it on fire. The blackened interior of the car had melted and twisted so that it looked like a lava flow. There was a nearly life-sized statue of a king, one of the Three Kings from a Nativity crèche, standing near a congregation of abandoned refrigerators. Over the next few days, each time I came out to the bayou, someone had come along and moved the king to a different location, as if testing to see where he might fit in best. First I found him tucked inside a refrigerator, then nestled in the low branches of a tree. Finally I saw the king floating face up in the bayou near an empty canoe grounded on a pile of submerged rocks. The king had gone to his final drink. I sensed a performance-art project in progress.

The artistic responses to Katrina flared up around town with vivid speed. There was a broken tree on Nashville Avenue that had snapped in such a way that the tall remaining trunk looked exactly like a giant upraised middle finger. Someone had painted it to reinforce its resemblance to a finger, complete with a red polished fingernail, and added the message: "Yo, Katrina!"

In Arabi, a house that the flood had pushed off its foundation appeared intact and normal, save for the fact that it now stood in the middle of the street. On the side of the house, someone had painted the words "Wicked Witch" and then added an arrow directing curiosity seekers to look beneath the house. Less whimsical, more direct warnings appeared across storefronts: "U Loot U Die." "Looters will be shot. Survivors will be shot twice." A favorite of mine came from the guy who owns a rug shop on Saint Charles Avenue. His plywood offered the following: "Don't try! I am sleeping inside with a big dog, an ugly woman, two shotguns and a claw hammer." Then a few days later he added: "Still here. Woman left Friday. Cooking pot of dog gumbo." Then even later: "Welcome back, y'all. Grin and bear it."

Refrigerators became canvases for public opinion, offering vulgar suggestions to the director of FEMA. More than a few said: "Do not open. Tom Benson inside." Benson, the owner of the Saints, was threatening to remove his team permanently from New Orleans. One friendlier sort had written on the side of her refrigerator: "Namaste Y'all!" Someone else had gone all around town and painted the word "love" on every refrigerator she could find.

The weatherboards of every house bore a big painted X with letters and numbers, left behind by the soldiers who went house to house looking for survivors. The soldiers wrote their own identifying mark on the side of each house to keep track of which division had checked which house, along with the date they had checked it. They also painted the number of the dead, if any, that they found in the house, so the coroner could come through and collect the bodies later. This detail struck me as a perversion of the Exodus story where the Israelites painted their houses with lamb's blood so the Angel of Death would fly overhead but not take them.

There were messages from the people who had come back to town and tried to sort through the mess. Clearly not intended to be waggish, still these formed an artistic document of the city. "Saint Joseph, Pray for us," said one. "The fire next time," said another. The SPCA and other volunteer animal-rescue groups were breaking into houses to save pets that had been left behind. Many people didn't take their dogs and cats with them because they thought they'd be gone only a short time. Thousands of these animals died from starvation or drowned. One garage in my neighborhood bore this note in blood red paint: "Dog dead. Do not remove. Owner will bury."

Our neighborhood was as quiet as the grave most of the time. Every once in a while I heard the loud squawking of a bullhorn. Then a white truck with a big red cross on the side came down the street. A man shouted to the empty streets, "Hot Food! Hot Food!" A lone hungry person sometimes appeared in a doorway. The truck stopped on the grass along the bayou and waited for word to spread. Waited to see if there were any more people among the piles of ruined houses.

Lance and I made our customary circle of the bayou one morning, and we ran into one of our old bayou-walking buddies, Les, and his three dogs, Felix, Max, and Hank. Les and I had gotten to know each other at the 6:30 a.m. gathering of people and dogs that met each morning in the softball field next to Cabrini High School. Lance had made a gradual entry into this society because Max slammed him whenever Lance made a grab for the tennis ball. Les and I took turns throwing the ball, and so I think the dogs were unclear about who was in charge. Max and Lance sorted out their confusion eventually and became good friends. Hank didn't have any objection to Lance, because Hank is only interested in garbage. As for Felix, he only wanted to sit in the grass and squint his eyes against the lingering twilight of his life. For Felix, every moment of the day looked like twilight. He was twelve years old and didn't mind anything.

One of the things I admired in Les was his courage to wear black socks with his sneakers. Few men possess such sartorial aplomb. Our friendship became official on the morning that he told me I have the best throwing arm of any woman he knows. It's true. Not many people know this about me, but I throw like a boy.

"You know just now when I thought about saying that to you, I stopped myself because it occurred to me that it might be a sexist observation," Les had explained. "Then I just decided to go ahead with it."

As we walked our dogs, Les and I engaged in rambling discussions during which we unraveled the knots of a certain idea, each wavelet of cognition deserving our meticulous examination, complete with footnotes and cross-references. One sample morning topic: Why do most people find it nearly impossible to admit when they're wrong? (a minor obsession of mine). And since this is so difficult, may we not then conclude that the ability to do so is the first sign of true maturity?

"'That return of Burke upon himself is one of the finest things in English criticism,'" offered Les, a leash in each hand. "Or at least that's what Matthew Arnold had to say." Hank and Max waited patiently. Perhaps they had heard Les quote his favorite essay before.

On another day, the question at hand was: Who are more realistic? The optimists or the pessimists?

"Don't forget that line from Housman: 'Luck's a chance but trouble's sure.' He had a pretty dour world view, don't you think?" Les's contribution.

"Yes, and haven't you noticed that pessimists always marry optimists?" My contribution.

If you haven't guessed by now, Les is an English literature professor, and I have often been tempted to call him the Hamlet of Bayou Saint John. His days, like mine, have been ever "sicklied o'er with the pale cast of thought." We have that in common, besides our dogs.

Les was the last person I had talked to on the bayou before we evacuated back in August. We had had a discussion, wordy and thorough, looking at all the facets of the question . . . and the question was, would we bother leaving town for this storm?

"I can't stand the thought of having to pack up the dogs and take yet another long drive to Arkansas," said Les, referring to his mother's home where he would wait out the storm. "Then I have to deal with all that plywood . . . What if it's for nothing . . . I don't know." He looked at me as if I was supposed to know.

"This one looks pretty bad," I said.

"I guess you're right." Les trudged home trailing his boys on leashes. Felix trotted in back, bringing up the rear, as always.

Now, seeing each other again two months later after the storm, Les and I picked up the tenor of our conversation as if we had just parted company a day earlier. We walked along the dirty water. Lance dodged and danced around Max, teasing him because Max had to stay on the leash, while Lance was allowed to run loose. I gave Les the bad news that I had heard the

Crystal Hot Sauce factory near the I-10 overpass had been wiped out. Not a single bottle of Crystal Hot Sauce—superior to McIlhenny's by my taste—could be found in any of the grocery stores still open in New Orleans, nor would there be in the foreseeable future.

"That's bad," Les observed. He leaned his tall lanky frame forward and looked at the ground as he walked, seeming to absorb this loss with a heavy heart.

Then I gave him the other bad news I had heard from Karen at Terranova's, the little grocery on Esplanade Avenue. They'd taken water too, but had managed to reopen pretty quickly. Terranova's fed us during these early days. Karen had passed along that she had heard Angelo Brocato's, the gelato parlor and bakery famous for its lemon ice and cannoli, would not open. Brocato's is on Carrollton Avenue and had been swamped in six feet of water. All the confectionary genius that the original Angelo Brocato had brought with him from Palermo a century ago had been ruined. This was a relic of a time long past and impossible to replace.

"It looks like there will be no more Brocato's cannoli," I told Les. This information brought him to a full stop. He turned and stared at me, his jaw dropped.

"Oh, now *that's* bad."

We spent much of the early days of our homecoming to New Orleans in this fashion, trying to figure out what we had left. A year later, Crystal Hot Sauce and Angelo Brocato's Ice Cream Parlor would come back, but at the time all we had to go on was one bit of bad news after the next. As we sifted through what Katrina had left behind, the process pushed us between wild extremes of the sacred and the mundane. Hovering over us always was an awareness of our duty to the dead, attending to their bodies and their memories. It's impossible for anyone to walk the streets in the Lower Ninth Ward and not hear the echoing agony of the people who drowned in their own attics. While carrying this mournful burden, we also searched for the things that were a touchstone for our lives. These seemingly trivial things, hot sauce and cannoli, made life in New Orleans recognizable as our own. So I understood Les's reaction. I shared it. At the bottom of it all, we are simple creatures. We need these comforts as reminders; they give us our sense of place. To lose these familiar pleasures cast us adrift in a sea of frightening uncertainty. We wanted the things we knew. So we could know we were home.

One morning, I made my way over to Fair Grinds Coffeehouse to see who might show up. The shop had taken a few feet of water, and the owners, Robert and Elizabeth, had gutted the interior. This made me sad. It had been a beautiful shop. Local artists had decorated the wooden chairs with picturesque scenes, many coffee-related and emphasizing fair-trade practice, which is the shop owners' article of faith. Above the high wainscoting there was an old restored mural, showing elegant stylized racehorses in action. In an earlier age, the shop had been a saloon for bookies and track junkies who wandered over from the nearby Fair Grounds Race Course, where a few springs ago I won twenty bucks on a horse named Elitist.

These days the espresso maker at Fair Grinds was not working, but Robert and Elizabeth had set up an impromptu coffee station on a card table beneath the side gallery. They were offering free coffee and had turned their shop into an informal community center. There was a bulletin board to post messages and information about FEMA applications, deadlines, and locations for the Small Business Administration offices. There was a table piled high with MREs (meals ready to eat) compliments of the United States Army, the same cuisine enjoyed by soldiers in Iraq. There were boxes of necessities—soap, toothpaste, shampoo, toilet paper—for anyone who needed them. I was so impressed with Robert and Elizabeth's sense of responsibility and generosity. This was truly New Orleans at its weary best. The next morning, I returned with some pints of half-and-half to contribute to the common coffee cause.

When he saw real cream at his table, Robert kissed my hands. "Blessings on you and all your ancestors."

A congenial gathering of pioneers who were resettling the neighborhood met each morning on the benches out front. Smokers and kibitzers reclined on the sunny sidewalk, while Robert fed Lance biscuits, and I listened to the guys shoot the breeze about just how bad things were. The owner of Café Degas had opened his restaurant but was having a terrible time finding anyone, anyone at all, to wait tables. I scribbled down names and numbers of plumbers whenever the subject came up, which was often. Then I met a man named Rosie, who wore a gun in a holster strapped to his belt. He also wore shorts and sandals. I asked him if he had a license to carry a gun. He assured me it was all legal as pie. He was a clean, upstanding citizen, perfectly entitled to pack heat. That long-ago arrest on possession did not result in a conviction. Besides, he was just a kid at the time, the cops simply confiscated his stash, and there had been no hard feelings.

"Why do you need a gun?" I was in a provocative mood.

Rosie snorted through his nose. "You have any trouble ovah atcha house? You just call 911. See what happens."

"Why? What will happen?"

"Nuthin! That's what."

I asked Rosie if I could call *him* if I had any trouble at my house. He said sure, I could call. Gave me his phone number and told me if I needed him, he'd come by with his gun. And do something about the trouble. I walked home feeling more than the usual dread.

Later I ran into Charlie, who told me his Katrina story. He and his German shepherd Daisy had elected to stay behind for the storm. Charlie's wife and daughter happened to be out of town at the time, so he didn't have to worry about them. He didn't want to travel with his big old dog, so the two of them weathered the storm in his home on Moss Street overlooking Bayou Saint John. He had stocked up on water and canned food. He could go without power for a long while and be just fine.

Charlie had a front-row seat to watch this meeting between Bayou Saint John and Katrina. Just like the others who stayed for the storm, Charlie found the hurricane itself to be relatively painless. He and Daisy went out walking afterward in their empty neighborhood, looking for anyone else who might be around. Charlie tacked a sign to the Magnolia Bridge that said: "Bayou Saint John Katrina survivors, meet here every day at 5:00." His plan was to find out who else was still around, to share water and food if necessary, and share information. Since all power and cell-phone service were gone, all communication with the world outside New Orleans was broken. He hoped that if any of his neighbors were leaving the city, they'd be able to get a message to his wife that he was alive. He still planned to stay.

The next morning he went out again and noticed something strange happening to the bayou. The storm was over, the sun was shining, but the water was moving fast and rising.

"Daisy, this can't be right," Charlie had said out loud. Daisy didn't have an explanation either. The bayou wasn't supposed to be doing this, and neither of them had any way of knowing what was happening at the 17th Street Canal and the London Avenue Canal not far away. The water came up over the banks of the bayou. Charlie saw blue crabs scrabbling around in the grass. Then pieces of houses and furniture came drifting by. It was as though Katrina had turned the city's pockets inside out and scattered the linty contents into the bayou.

The water was backing up at the Magnolia Bridge because of the storm debris that floated down from the direction of Lake Pontchartrain. So Charlie climbed down into the low beams of the bridge and pulled some stuff out, clearing the way for the water to push through. "If it's gonna flood, let it flood Uptown too!" he shouted at the water now free to follow its course.

A couple of days later, Charlie ran into Father Tarantino, who was sheltering a group of people at Our Lady of the Rosary. Father had just waded through thigh-deep water down Esplanade Avenue to bless a statue of the Virgin Mother that one of his parishioners had placed in the crotch of a tree near Terranova's. The guy who put her in the tree also placed a ring of pink plastic roses at Her feet, and asked Her to watch over the neighborhood. Father T. then applied the finishing protective magic with his holy water.

Charlie and the priest decided to work together on their next project. Father Tarantino wanted to offer mass, and Charlie wanted to pull together any of the stragglers in the neighborhood. In a matter of days, Charlie had become the Bayou Saint John resident communication specialist. It was his idea to climb into the bell tower of the church with a hammer. Normally the bells rang by means of an electronic mechanism. Since the power was gone, Charlie rang the church bell by whamming it with his hammer to tell everyone within earshot: Come to the church.

It worked. More people from the surrounding neighborhood came to Our Lady of the Rosary. Unfortunately, the bell ringing also alerted the military to their presence. Halfway through mass, soldiers appeared at the back of the church. The officer in charge walked up to the altar, interrupted Father Taran-tino in mid-holy-holy-holy, and announced that they all had fifteen minutes to get ready, and then they were being evacuated. It was not a suggestion. It was not a generous offer of help. It was a command delivered by a man with a gun. Charlie slipped out the side door of the church and ran home to Daisy.

"Not since Vietnam have I been so afraid of the government," he said. "Whenever I saw a helicopter flying overhead, I hid." Charlie and the few other Bayou Saint John residents left behind got to know this officer during these days, as he attempted to flush them from cover. They called him "G.I. Joe" behind his back.

Somehow the military had gotten the idea that they were supposed to treat New Orleans like a city it had captured, rather than a city it had been ordered to save. A flashpoint for many New Orleanians who had stayed in their homes was that the "rescuers" were forcing them to leave their animals behind. The soldiers had decided that pets would not go in the helicopters.

When Lt. General Russel Honoré took over the military command in New Orleans, he tried to change this warped attitude that New Orleans was enemy territory. There is a great news clip of Honoré striding across Con-vention Center Boulevard screaming, "Put that goddamn weapon down!" at a soldier who was pointing his gun at innocent people waiting in line for the bus that would take them out of the city, as if he had single-handedly corralled a pack of criminals. Something tells me that if these soldiers had had to help the residents of Bethesda, Maryland, in a similar situation, they would have minded their manners.

Then Honoré held a press conference to announce that New Orleanians would be permitted to evacuate with their pets, and all military transport would have to make room for the animals. "Some people might not think that's important, but I do," he said. After that announcement, the reporters started calling him Lt. General Russel "Hello Kitty" Honoré.

I wanted to climb through the TV and kiss General Honoré on the lips. It was decent and kind. And it accomplished almost nothing. On the ground, the soldiers operated with their own rogue government. As they always will. A man with a gun is his own country.

G.I. Joe finally caught up with Charlie when he saw him out walking with Daisy.

"You again! What are you doing here? I thought I ordered you out of here." The officer told Charlie he had to leave or he was going to die.

"I am not going to die," Charlie said. "Well, maybe I'm gonna die, but not today."

"Okay, you are no longer my responsibility," G.I. Joe replied. "You are not under our control, and we won't be responsible for you."

"I have never been under your control! In the entire past week! The only reason you found us at all is that I was fool enough to ring that damn church bell!"

They went back and forth like that for a bit. Charlie made a number of good points, but in the end G.I. Joe, who was holding a gun, forced him to leave without his dog. A helicopter brought Charlie to the airport, which was in total mayhem. A soldier informed Charlie that he would be placed onto a plane going to some unspecified city far away. Then Charlie ran into a friend of his who was working ambulance duty at the airport, so he stowed away in the ambulance that was driving to Baton Rouge. There, he borrowed a car from another friend and drove right back to New Orleans. He conned the soldier at the checkpoint to let him through by telling him he had to pick up medical files at his office. Instead he went back to his house, collected Daisy, and returned to Baton Rouge, where he stayed until the city was legally open again. What a man will do for his dog. I was impressed.

"It was fun," said Charlie.

GIVE US THIS DAY

A MORNING CAME THAT I WOKE TO A CHILL IN THE AIR. JUST LIKE that. One minute I was camping without difficulty in my own house, and the next, November had brought a change to New Orleans that would make it uncomfortable to stay without power, heat, or hot water. The gas company let me know it would be at least another couple of months before they could get around to opening the lines to our house. And finding a plumber or electrician? Forget about it. The toilet flushed, but that was about the only thing I could count on. I started to pack my things. I would drive to our friends in Tennessee as promised. I decided that Lance and I would be better off staying elsewhere until Sean came home, and then we could tackle the business of restoring basic comforts to our home together.

Also I had decided that once I dropped off Lance to stay with Jo and Moira in Tennessee, I would fly to Seattle to meet Sean on his tour. Either that or I wouldn't see him for a month. It was my idea to go out there. I had invited myself. Yet I resented that I had to go to such effort in order to spend a few hours with my husband. It was becoming harder and harder to have any time with him. His preoccupation with his studio, his tour, his career, his public image—that had been building up well before the storm— had reached such a consuming level and showed no signs of abating that I wondered how we were ever going to have any kind of family life together.

In the past year, I had grown tired and embarrassed at the frequency with which my friends had to ask, "Where is Sean? Why isn't he with you?" Usually I answered, "Oh you mean my *alleged* husband?" Ha. Funny joke, right? Yet, each time I tried to bring attention to his absence and my desire for a child, Sean broke my heart a little more. He flew away a little more. Still, I wanted to be close to him. I thought he could fix it.

"We'll talk when I get back. I promise." That was one of the last things he said before he left. Later, when I was catching up on e-mails in the only coffee shop in New Orleans that had gotten their Wi-Fi back up and running, I checked Sean's website and saw that he had extended his tour by a couple of weeks without telling me. I had to learn when I would see my husband again by doing research on the Internet.

Before I got on the road, I wanted to craft some gesture of farewell for my bayou. The moment called for a ceremony. Back in August, I had departed in too much of a hurry to say a proper goodbye. My lower back gave me a familiar signal as I walked along the water. My period was about to start. Each month, I experienced the same little drag of disappointment. *There goes another one down the drain.* I would like to say there were three of us out there walking on the bayou. Lance, me, and perhaps a crescent-shaped being, no bigger than a cashew, curled against my spine. That would be romantic, wouldn't it? A fitting response to all the death would be to bring in a new life. But it would not be true, which made me sad. Perhaps it was my Novemberish mood, but I couldn't help but ask myself why anyone would bring a person into this world. I don't mean just New Orleans, but any part of this world. Why do it? Just so you can set another person on the path toward death?

That's pretty much what life consists of, right? Strip away all the Christmas mornings and it's just a long walk to the end. Why bother? Sure, there are delicious moments, hot sauce and cannoli; however, the core truth that most of us don't want to think about is that the initiation into life is ultimately an initiation into death. How can responsible adults inflict that on another person? The only way I can see people doing that is if they pretend not to know this core truth. It's hard for me to turn off that part of my brain, the part that knows.

Yet, despite all good common sense, life continues to assert itself. In me and all around me, and in all sorts of surprising forms. Everything wants to live. There is a story about the Zen teacher Suzuki Roshi, who said of the cancer that was killing him, "It wants to live, too." Now, there's a brute, simple thought. If I were a hurricane, what would I do? I'd stretch myself to the fullest extent of my power permitted by the sea and the air and the land, and I'd do what my nature compelled me to do. I'd push as hard and as fast as I could, because that's what I was born to do. We may not like it, but just like the Loa, those archetypal forces of nature who possess us in Vodou, Katrina entered and possessed our city. And just like the Loa, she was not concerned with what we wanted. She had her own agenda. Where that leaves us, we are still trying to understand. Yet we must consider this strange truth, which is that it was the life force of Katrina that brought death. She lived out her life span on this earth. How can we resent something for doing what we all want to do?

Of course, many people are saying that the catastrophe in New Orleans resulted from the federal government's failure to provide appropriate flood protection, that it was a human-made disaster, not natural. These people have a good argument, which I don't dispute. Even so, we all know it started with a bad storm that came out of the sea and the sky, and no human made that.

Our return home to New Orleans depends on settling into and accepting that our tender, delicate lives will always exist in tension with powerful forces that could destroy us. And that it's not personal. No one owes us our Christmas mornings. The joy we receive along the path is a gift only. The best we can do is show proper gratitude until the gifts stop.

I went home to take care of myself, unresolved about life and death. However, it did occur to me that I would miss the cannoli after I'm gone.

When I got home, I went into the bathroom with a plastic Mardi Gras cup, sometimes known as "New Orleans china." These are the gaily decorated plastic cups that krewe members toss from the Mardi Gras floats to the cheering crowds. These cups proliferate during Carnival season because they hold a substantial amount of beer. No kitchen in New Orleans is complete without several dozen, and they serve many valuable functions beyond beer. This day I used a Mardi Gras cup to harvest my menstrual blood. I had a plan.

One method I use to cultivate such robust herbs and flowers in my garden is that from time to time I give them a drink from my own body. Iron-hungry gardenias and camellias enjoy a little menstrual blood during their growing season. The basil, the mint, the chives also flourish with a little of this rich nutrient. Note to gardeners: Always dilute your personal contributions to the garden with a good amount of water. Full-strength menstrual blood will overwhelm the plants. A few teaspoons go a long way.

The idea of fertilizing my garden this way came to me years ago when I was in New York. I had learned it was a witch's custom to pour her own menstrual blood into her houseplants. The magical combined with the earthy seized my imagination. Soon I left behind the concrete of New York to seek a greener place where I could plant a garden of my own to enact this ritual. Then when I arrived in New Orleans, I heard yet another menstrual blood–related story that added a new dimension to the custom.

Melanie, who lived across the street from my first home in New Orleans in the Irish Channel, told me that she could never eat spaghetti with tomato sauce. Her reason, she explained, was that in her neighborhood, ever since she was little, she'd been hearing the following story: When a woman wants to bind a man to her, she mixes some of her menstrual blood into a tomato sauce and serves it to him. When he eats it, he falls under her power forever. Melanie said she can't even look at a tomato sauce without thinking of menstrual blood, and the thought just puts her off her feed. Besides that, in many cases you don't know who made the tomato sauce, therefore you can't know the intentions of the cook, nor the unorthodox ingredients she might have added. A reckless eater of tomato sauce could unwittingly fall into a sorceress's web, one that was intended for some hapless other. And there you'd be—ensnared in a love spell for the rest of your life by a woman you don't even know.

Now, I should mention here that Melanie was a crack addict, and this fact may impugn her credibility as a source of information on folkloric arcana in New Orleans. However, the story got confirmation from another source, independent from Melanie. A woman I worked with named Justina—sober, intelligent, and reliable, who grew up in the Seventh Ward—told me she had the same problem with tomato sauce. Ever since she was a kid she had been hearing the same story about tricky women and the bloody spells they cast on their men from the kitchen.

Truly New Orleans is ripe ground, not just for camellias, jasmine, and basil, but stories and magic too. All these grow lush under my care. I feed my garden in this way not only because it helps the plants, but also because it's a way to put some of myself into the ground of this home that I love. There is no bond stronger than blood, no act of marriage more profound than giving this vital material of my body to the soil so that it may bring greater life. My specialty is basil pesto, not so much tomato sauce. So when I make pesto from the basil that I have nourished in the garden with my own blood, this vitality comes back to me transformed, and feeds my life force.

Years ago, I warned Sean: Don't come to dinner at my house unless you're prepared to fall in love. He did, anyway.

On this November morning in the season of death, as New Orleans moldered under a shroud of dust, one more of my cycles reached its end. I felt a familiar release, like a thick-knotted rope loosening itself in my pelvis. The cramps eased somewhat. The harvest took place over a water-filled bowl in the bathtub. I dropped a crimson cloud into this watery bed. I watched my blood and mucus swirl in the faint motion of the water. As I squatted, more of me sluiced out and plopped into the shimmering, now pinkening surface. Clumps of discrete matter—such a deep red, they were almost black—trailed long, feathery threads. I stared with my customary fascination.

Straightening slowly, I placed the bowl onto the floor and washed myself. My thighs looked as though I had been stabbed. When I finished my bath, I decanted the contents of the bowl into the Mardi Gras cup that was decorated with curling golden banners and the two masks of tragedy and comedy. How festive! Lance leaned his chin on the edge of the tub and observed this process without comment. By this point in our relationship, he had grown accustomed to my peculiar habits. It was also necessary for me to wait for Sean to leave town before I conducted this ritual. Although he would respect it, still he would ask a lot of questions. There are some things a woman can only get done with the wordless accompaniment of her dog. I dressed and headed out the door to the bayou.

Our street was empty. The low November sky made a gray cover for my work. When we stepped onto the grassy levee near the Magnolia Bridge, Lance trotted off on his own business. I knelt by the edge of the water with my cup of blood. The bayou seemed darker than usual. I couldn't see past a certain point. Even though the water was shallow by the edge, I could just make out a mossy stone before the bottom disappeared into murk. It might have been two feet or two hundred. Either way, it looked the same. When I looked into the bayou, I peered into a depthless well. I leaned closer to the water's surface and sniffed the funk. I caught that familiar fragrance of the bayou, not the sickening stench left behind by the storm. This was the smell of home.

"The soul loves the body," Meister Eckhart wrote seven hundred years ago. What do the mystics know, anyway? Well, they seem to know why we keep doing this. Why we ignite the candle of life again and again, despite the certainty of death. The body has its own hairy, humpy agenda, just wants to keep trying. Something—call it soul, if you like, or Loa—demands a fleshy doorway. We humans are the best candidates for that task. We didn't ask for it. We don't know what we're doing. Yet we do it.

I gazed into this snaky, twisting waterway, my bayou that curves like my own curious spinal cord, igniting life into my limbs and holding me strong and upright. The breeze pushed a slight movement on the water, making it clap against the grassy edge. The knees of my jeans now bore slowly spreading wet stains where I had knelt in the mud. The sunless day reflected little on the rippled surface of the water. I waited for a still moment in the air. Looked again. There was the dim, wavering outline of my own face. My eye looked back at me from the dark water. And then with the next quick shift in the bayou's surface, it was gone, warped out of recognition.

I lifted my cup and poured the contents onto the surface of this uncertain mirror. The stream of bloody water passed from my hand into the bayou's darkness. In an instant, it sank and disappeared, becoming the same as everything else. As the bayou took my gift, I sent my wishes into the water. *Come back, my lovely. I am not the same without you. Please come back to life.*

I stood up to leave and found Lance sitting behind me and watching with that patient and alert expression on his face that he wears when he's waiting for me to pay attention to him. I snapped on his leash and said, "Okay, let's go. Are you ready for another long car ride?"

Lance leaped up and wriggled with excitement. Either he had forgotten how much he hates long car rides, or he didn't understand what I had just said. Happiness is forgetting or not knowing. Since I can't do either, I'll never be a good dog. I walk with fear, death, and loss clinging to my back, while I look ahead. Just before we left, I turned to the bayou and bound my spell with rhyme. "See you later, alligator."

GETTING TO THE POINT

A YEAR AFTER KATRINA, IN AUGUST 2006, SEAN AND I WENT TO VISIT my parents at the Jersey shore, a welcome break from New Orleans. We had a carefree week of beach frolic and body surfing in the ocean. Yet, I experienced a cognitive dissonance. It happened whenever I traveled somewhere outside of New Orleans. I'd land in a "normal" town and realize how acclimated I had become to the sight back home of houses with roofs cracked open to the sky, jungly weed-choked yards, and rusted cars that would never run again parked in front. I was unaware that I had come to regard it as "normal" to look at a row of houses and absorb the sight as unremarkable that at least half of them were peppered with broken windowpanes and still bore the ugly tattoo of the storm: the big spray-painted X, giving names, dates, the lost and found, the dead. My tired eyes had grown numb to the signs of neglect and disintegration.

It was not until I stood somewhere else—my parent's tidy neighborhood or a street in Atlanta where I had gone for a friend's wedding—that I was startled by the sight of a whole street of houses, each clean and sharp, the paint stuck flat to the weatherboards, the rain gutters attached where they should be, the lawn trim, the fence upright. Imagine that! During that summer week, my South Jersey shore—so bright and shiny, where things worked and the streets were clear of trash remnants—felt like Shangri La.

Sean and I spent some of that time babysitting my two nephews, Harry and Danny, aged six and four, which was like herding porpoises. Sean provided most of the entertainment for the boys. They treated him like a large new toy sent all the way from New Orleans specifically for their use. Bearded and shaggy, Sean was exotic. It was not hard work for my husband to play at the beach with my nephews. He lit up like a Christmas tree whenever the kids appeared. All three threw themselves into the raucous surf, shrieking and tumbling ass over teakettle. They spent hours coasting the waves on boogie boards. (For the uninitiated: A boogie board is a Styrofoam mini-surfboard. No South Jersey shore child is completely dressed without one.) Then it was time for a mud-slinging contest. Harry and Danny attacked their uncle without mercy, and it was hard to tell who loved it more, Sean or the boys.

I wore a broad-brimmed hat and let my feet sink into the soft sand at the edge of the water, the baby waves foaming around my ankles. With my arms raised to keep my hat in place, I inhaled the fragrant mixture of Coppertone and my own sweat. With this scent, I came to my native self.

My job was to watch the children both large and small to make sure all their faces remained above water. As long as I kept my eyes on Harry's bleached towhead, Danny's red shirt, and Sean's pale freckled shoulders, then no one would drown, such was the power of my gaze. There were lifeguards, but I had no doubt they were still stoned from the night before. Would you trust the life of your nephew to a nineteen-year-old frat boy? No, I wouldn't either. I was good at this. I was anxious, sick to my stomach, and not having any fun. I would make a great mother some day.

My sister reclaimed her children later that day, and Sean and I were released from duty. So I took my husband on a long walk down the beach to the point in Longport. The point is a jetty at the southern end of Absecon Island. It is a long, skinny pile of jagged rocks that sticks far out into the deep water as the Atlantic Ocean makes a roiling turn into the Egg Harbor Inlet and the bay side of the island. When I was a kid, I used to come out to the point for all kinds of reasons. Mostly I came to escape from my family and the yelling. The point felt like the end of the world. It possessed an elemental savagery that could sweep the troubled thoughts from my mind.

Since that time of my childhood, the township had filled in the gaps between the rocks with cement, which made it an easy stroll to the end of the jetty. Back when I was twelve years old or so, it was a much less civilized place. I made it to the end by leaping the chasms, my bony toes clinging to the pointed wet rocks that were an unforgiving iron gray and slick with green sea moss. On either side of me the Atlantic Ocean threw all its might at the jetty, spraying salt water eight feet into the air before raining down on me. I'd crouch on one rock, tuck my head down, and wait for the last wave to pelt me, soaking me through to my skin. Then, in the small pause while the ocean rolled back to gather its fury to attack again, I'd uncurl myself and jump to the next rock. Would I make it? Each jump was a thrill, a leap into the unknown. There was always the chance I'd miscalculate, slip from my intended perch, crash, and slide down, down, down, into the broken shells and dark stinking water that pooled between the rocks. I loved this game. And had no idea how dangerous it was. I was invincible.

When I got to the end of the point, I'd stand with my back to the land and all that it held. Everything fell away in the face of the sea. The roar of its assault on the jetty filled my ears. I faced the ocean and stood with my arms outstretched, my palms open to the spray. I tasted the salt on my lips and caught the wind in my teeth. Sometimes, depending on what I was reading that summer, I liked to pretend I was the Witch of Cornwall. Other times I just stood there mesmerized by the monstrous swell of the ocean. It was bigger and more alive than anything I had left behind on earth. Each time the water pulled away and came rushing back at me in an immense foamy gray-blue wall, it seemed I might be swept into the depths. Then at the last moment, the ocean foundered on the rocks and stopped short of destroying me.

I imagined we had some sort of contract. That I was permitted to come this close so that I could sense the water's life force. But no closer. I didn't kid myself about the terms of our contract. We were not friends, this sea and me. It would kill me in an instant. Nonetheless I loved it. I brought my lonely soul to this tip of the world and let it fill me with wild joy.

On the day that Sean and I walked to the point, we were in a good mood and goofed along the way. Holding hands and side by side, I flipped up my heel and kicked him in the rear. Then he returned the smack to my butt with his heel. And then I got him back again. We traded stories about the funny characters we had met on the beach. A friend of my mother's had made a beeline for Sean and scrutinized him up and down, her sun-weathered face creased like a crumpled paper bag.

"You're very noticeable." She made this announcement as if she expected him to account for himself—how did he get here, and what was he doing on her beach?

Indeed he was noticeable. My freckled Irish city-kid husband was the whitest white man on earth. He got sunburned in candlelight. Sean looked nothing like the gleaming, oiled, rose-brown beach bums that populated my hometown. In South Jersey, your tan never completely faded in winter. It only lay dormant for a few months and then surged back to the surface on Memorial Day.

Sean told me about a conversation he had overheard between a woman and her son who had set up their towel camp next to ours. The mother had interrupted the young boy as he filled his pail with sand to tell him it was time to come home for lunch. The boy protested.

"But Daddy said he'd bring me later. For a hotdog."

"Your father is worthless. He will never take care of you." She apprised him of this fact with calm certainty.

As Sean told me this story, I could hear behind his laughter that he was experiencing a little dissonance of his own. He was both charmed and intimidated by these mouthy Yankee women and their casual contempt for men.

When we got to the point, it was late afternoon. The sun was hanging low and giving off its last blast before sinking below the line of houses behind us. I started walking toward the end of the jetty. Sean accompanied me for a bit, then stopped. I kept walking into the sound of the crashing waves, before noticing that my husband wasn't with me. I turned and squinted at the sun, looking for him. Sean's face wore sharp shadows. He dipped one toe into a puddle of water. Then he stood there with his hands on his hips.

"What's wrong?"

"What are we doing?" He was nervous about something.

"We're walking out to the end. C'mon, it's fun."

"You mean *all* the way? Are you sure it's safe?"

Now I was getting annoyed. "No, I can't say that I'm sure it's safe. But it is fun and exciting. It'll be a new experience, c'mon. Just walk with me."

"This is far enough for me. You go ahead if you want." His voice was hard.

"Will you please come with me? I promise nothing bad will happen."

"No, I really don't want to go out there, Connie." The lines in Sean's face deepened and set. He was not going to let me talk him into anything. He was too frightened to trust me.

I turned my back and left my husband. *City boy. It was a mistake to bring him here.* With each step away from the land and Sean, I went closer into the ocean's embrace. The thunder of the waves grew louder so that it drowned out what I had left behind. The water's presence surrounded me with the same merciless fury as ever before. Doused me in the same salty spray, as if I hadn't been gone for all those years.

I stood at the end with my toes holding fast to the last rock and opened my hands to the sea, my old lover.

I returned to Sean, waiting where I had left him. As we stepped off the rocks onto the sand to start the walk back home, Sean took my hand in his and remarked how much he loved taking care of my nephews. It was exhausting, he acknowledged, but still fun.

"Makes me feel like a kid." Sean laughed and kicked the sand.

"Doesn't it make you feel like a dad?" My mouth ran away with every opportunity it saw. Sean came to a halt.

"I mean, doesn't spending time with Harry and Danny and seeing how great that is . . . ? Does that make you feel any differently, any better about having a child?" Sean dropped my hand and stepped back. "With me," I added, perhaps unnecessarily.

"Ah, sure . . . it's nice to daydream about that."

"I want to do a lot more than daydream, Sean. I want to make it happen."

Sean inhaled and exhaled. "Look, I don't want a child. That isn't part of *my* vision for *my* life. We talked about this already." He walked off without me.

"Well, I'm not finished talking about it." I jogged to catch up to him. He was walking fast. He wouldn't look at me. I took his hand, and he squeezed my fingers too tight, grinding my knuckles. He didn't realize how painful this was. His face and body were rigid with anger, and something else. There it was again; I could see his fear.

As we walked away from the point, we engaged in yet another one of our bitter wrangles on this subject. Sean made his argument. I made mine. We back-and-forthed like that, while neither of us made a dent in the other's position. Even as we argued, we still held hands, and it hurt.

A rough wind came off the water. The sun had departed and made the sky a deeper blue on its way toward evening. The remaining light was soft, casting no shadows. It was dusk, that borderland between day and night, possessing some quality of each, but not entirely one or the other. The liminal space where magic happens.

Off in the distance, a crowd had gathered at the edge of the water. About thirty people faced the ocean. They all seemed to be looking at the same thing. There was a heightened energy in the way they stood as a group that didn't seem like casual lingering. Something was not right. Yet, I couldn't tell what they were doing. Then it hit me. It was late in the day. The lifeguards had gone off duty.

"Oh my God, someone has drowned!" I dropped our argument and started running toward the crowd.

"No!" Sean shouted. He stopped, his feet buried in the white sand. He tried to hold me back, but I kept running. I still don't know why I thought this was any of my business. Or what I would do once I got there. My feet took off on their own.

As I got closer, I slowed to a walk. I didn't see a dead body. Instead, I saw the crowd looking at a man standing up to his hips in the water. A wave smashed against his back, but he stood firm, facing the people on the beach. And waited. Nothing happened. Then a man broke from the crowd and ran to the water. He wore swim trunks and a T-shirt. He lifted his knees high to get over the incoming chop, while his large belly wobbled with every leap. The first man welcomed him with a hug. The second man turned to face the crowd on the beach and crossed his arms over his chest. The first man grasped the second man's head in a firm grip with one hand at the back of his neck and the other on his forehead. They stood like that for a moment or two, their faces close together, concentrating on something inward with their eyes shut. As a large swell came rolling in behind them, *bam!* The first man flipped the second man over backward right into the cresting wave. Held him there for a second and *whoosh!* Lifted him dripping, face-first, up and out of the water. The people on the beach broke into cheers and clapping. Someone snapped photos.

The breath came back into my body. My thoughts rearranged themselves. There was something else going on here at the edge of the sea. Not a drowning, but a baptism.

Sean caught up with me. "It's all right. No one died."

"Oh, good." He looked embarrassed and relieved.

We stood there and watched for a few minutes. The beach was deserted save for Sean and me and this gathering of the faithful. The fading light gave a blue theatrical aura to the scene. The people were so absorbed in what was transpiring before them in the ocean, they didn't notice us. It appeared to be a gang baptism. One by one, several of the people who were waiting on the beach ran out to meet the minister in the ocean and be bathed in Christ's blood. One woman came to the Lord in her bikini.

The near violence of these dunkings fascinated me. The minister intentionally slammed these people into the water. There was nothing gentle about their arrival in the Kingdom of Heaven. It wouldn't work otherwise. They had to be shocked out of their self-control, had to surrender to the minister's hands and let him take them through the doorway. An exercise in trust, and a reminder that birth was never supposed to be easy.

I wanted to stay and watch the whole thing. Sean wanted to get back. It was getting dark. We were late for dinner.

We left the baptism and continued down the beach. We walked side by side, but I walked backwards so I could watch a little longer. The bond in this crowd of people, their focus and tension, held me. I loved that they had come to the ocean not for idle frolic, but to conduct a vital transaction. I didn't want to take my eyes off them or their joy.

As well, my heart still raced a little over my jolting shift in perception of this scene. Here, I thought, was death, and it turned out to be new life. I misinterpreted the signs. I thought it had something to do with me.

SEASON OF MIRACLES

ON NEW YEAR'S EVE 2006, I SPENT MOST OF THE EVENING SITTING on our front porch, smoking cigarettes. I do this on the porch because, as we all know, smoking is a disgusting habit, and it stinks up the house. I smoke on just one day a year, December 31st. Then I give up smoking as my New Year's resolution. I try to set reasonable goals for myself. While offering a chance to pride myself on being disciplined, this maneuver also allows me to indulge my sneaky attraction to this filthy pastime without becoming fatally immersed.

I have always wished I could smoke as a regular thing. It's so damn sexy. All the busy hand work, the delicate finger poses, the flare of the match like an epiphany, illuminating the smoker's face in an expression of focused anticipation, pursed lips, maybe a little teeth, looking downward to watch that teardrop of flame come to the crisis point and burn a red crackling line upward. Then the inspiration of smoke. It's so alluring, this nonchalant death wish. It takes a certain amount of stupid, beautiful guts and a desire to engage in dangerous ephemera. What is smoke, anyway? The coiling gray stuff that hangs in the air but is so unlike air that it stings when we breathe it. It's not supposed to go up in there, and our noses and lungs know it. We have to force it on them for the sake of a killer style. They get used to it eventually.

The aesthetics of smoking appeal to me more than the execution. Since I

219

always give up cigarettes after one day, my nose and lungs never get used to the smoke. Each time I take it up again a year later, I am a virgin once more, and the smoke hurts the back of my throat so much that I never inhale all the way. Sure, everyone says that, but in my case it's true. I just drag in a mouthful of smoke, hold it for a second, and then propel it all out in a fancy stream like the amateur I am.

The vision of this gray cloud trailing from my lips fascinates me for the amount of time it takes to burn through three cigarettes. When the reek in my own hair and clothing overwhelms me, not to mention the ashy taste that coats the inside of my mouth, I make my New Year's resolution.

"I've just got to give these things up," I say out loud, gesturing with the butt end of my "Natural American Spirit 100% additive-free *natural* tobacco," as the packaging describes it, my crime of smoking tempered by the fact that these cigarettes are practically *organic.* I stub it out and go inside to strip and gargle and wash my hair. Refreshed, I face the year with strong resolve. Monkey off *my* back.

On this New Year's Eve, I sat in the dark and smoked and reflected on the past year, our return home after the hurricane, and everything else. New Year's Eve, if you manage not to be drunk, can be an opportune moment to take stock of things, whether you're in the mood or not. It was a cold night, and I was dateless for the holiday. Not that I care a whole lot about New Year's Eve. It is one of those made-up occasions, a meaningless turn of the calendar. Still I would have liked to spend it with my husband. Sean had arranged to give a concert somewhere far from New Orleans for this New Year's Eve. He was singing songs for other people, while I had been left to entertain myself, which I did by fouling the night air with cigarette smoke and wrapping myself in a cloak of resentment.

Until this night, the holidays had seemed a true season of miracles. The Saints made it into the playoffs, a cause for great joy across the land. They walked into it backwards, though, losing to the Carolina Panthers in the final game. The previous game had already put them in the playoffs by means of complicated mathematics that Sean had explained to me, which I then immediately slotted into the "nonessential information" drawer in my brain. Still, the Carolina game was heart-rending. To begin with, Payton took out the first string after six plays, a mistake in my view. Then, more crucially, in the third quarter with the score tied, Jamie Martin in for Drew Brees passed short right to Devery Henderson. Panther Chris Gamble intercepted at the New Orleans 18 and ran for a touchdown. From there the game devolved into a "cluster fuck," to borrow a phrase from my father-in-law. After it was over, I had to lie in a darkened room with a damp washcloth pressed to my eyelids for half an hour before Sean came to me and patted my wrist and explained the mathematics that allowed our boys into the playoffs. It was an inglorious finale to their best season in forty years. They were still the New Orleans Saints.

The team's abysmal history has long been attributed to the fact that the Superdome was built on an old graveyard that had been deconsecrated; yet many of the remains of those interred there had not been moved to make way for this super-duper civic project. The backhoes that broke ground for the building also unearthed some old coffins. There is a story that as they set the foundation for the Saints' new home, construction workers would stumble across the odd unclaimed skull in the dirt and toss it back and forth like a football. Man, you couldn't *beg* for worse mojo. In the winter of 2000, the Saints' management hired a Voodoo priestess (not Sallie Ann Glassman, but another well-known traveler in the spirit realm, Ava Kay Jones) to undo this damage. Jones conducted a banishing ritual in the home end zone, but to no avail. The Saints continued to be a disappointment to those who loved them the most.

My own theory, arising from my belief in the power of naming, is that it was just a bad idea to name a football team "The Saints." All the other teams have perfect macho-sounding names, appropriate given that the job requires them to be ruthless and aggressive. They have to hunt down and kill the other team, right? Even if it's in a playful way. So it makes sense to evoke these qualities in your football team by naming it after a bird of prey or some other fierce hunting animal, like Eagles, Falcons, Bears, or Lions. Or you might announce your football team's strength in battle by naming it after Raiders, Vikings, or Giants. Cowboys and Patriots are also totally butch. (Even Dolphins have a quality of assertiveness.) These names send the message: "Get out of my way, or I will step on you and crush you."

But *Saints*, for God's sake. This is not the right image for a football team. Saints love to suffer, die, and be buried. Their whole purpose is to take a beating, not give one to others. Saints never want to *cause* suffering. They want to imitate Christ by suffering themselves. Their glory comes in the *after*life. No one ever appreciates them while they're alive. Naming your football team "The Saints" is like saying: "Please come and kill me. Cut my throat so that I may bleed slowly into the ground. Set me on fire and dance around me while I scream in agony."

Yet, something clicked this year for "The Bless You Boys," as the banners around town have been calling them. The new coach could have something to do with it, but others more magically minded have suggested that all the suffering through Katrina burned off the residual karma that had been sticking to the Saints since the desecration of that graveyard beneath the Superdome. Maybe so.

Magical origins or not, it was a relief from all the aching sorrow in our city to have a winning team this year. No one was immune to the specter of hope. The optimism had overtaken even a cynic like me, although to be honest, my husband drew me into it. Sean may have grown up to be a Yoga Man—holistic and totally dedicated to nonviolence—but at his core there beats the passionate tribal heart of a New Orleans Saints Boy. All season, Sean was floating on air. There were some nights that he was so excited about a Saints victory, he couldn't fall sleep. We lay in bed on one such night. I drifted downward into the soft fog before dreaming. My husband was beside me. Or rather he was beside himself.

"Hey, Connie?" His voice had the wakeful clarity of a daytime chat.

"Yes."

"So who is your favorite Saints player? And why?"

If someone had interrupted my reading of *The Canterbury Tales* in the library at Smith College, over two decades ago, to tell me that I would one day participate in a serious discussion about my favorite football player, I would have spilled my grape soda from laughing so hard. Nonetheless, I found myself at home in my own bed in New Orleans, required to provide five reasons or more to support my choice. I told my husband that I liked Deuce McAllister because he looks a little bit Chinese, and because when he lies on his back in the grass while the assistant coach pulls out his hamstrings, he gazes to the sky with an expression on his sweet face that suggests he might cry real tears. Then I had to conclude that my true favorite was Michael Lewis, also known as "Beer Man" because he drove a beer truck before playing for the Saints. He is my favorite because he reminds me of Lance in that he is handsome and light on his feet. He has slender, delicate ankles, and he runs like a maniac. Plus, Lewis wears the number 84 on his jersey, and it just so happens that '84 is the year that I graduated from Smith College. So you see, it all came full circle right there.

(Six months later, Coach Sean Payton released Michael Lewis from the team. Payton also let go a reliable kicker, John Carney. If Payton had sent Carney to kick that field goal in the playoff game against the Bears this year instead of that other yutz, it might have been a whole different story. If you ask me, both these personnel decisions were a bad idea, but nobody asked me.)

Sean went off to his New Year's Eve gig, confident that the Saints would soon conquer the world, while I tried to have a jolly holiday by attending the annual bonfire and fireworks extravaganza that happens on the Orleans Avenue neutral ground, the local term for "wide grassy median." This New Year's Eve celebration is special because it is completely illegal and chaotic and dangerous. There are feral children running loose. Many of them have not had their shots. I always carry a Swiss Army knife with me in case one of them bites me and I have to open the wound to drain the infection.

The custom is for folks from the surrounding neighborhood to drag their now obsolete Christmas trees to the grassy center of the avenue to make a bonfire. On a typical New Year's Eve, there are probably a hundred trees or so, all gone stiff and dry with age, in a huge pile within a beer bottle's throw of the houses. At the stroke before midnight, I'm not sure who gives the signal, but someone who has put himself in charge lights the pile of trees. The needly branches flame up in a giant orange sky-licking dragon of a fire, so hot and intense that we all have to step back from it right away. In a flick, you feel your eyeballs cooking and your lashes curling to a black singe. It's a serious fire. Beautiful and terrible.

Then the drunks who are ambitious enough to attempt dancing hold hands and pull each other in a rough circle around the fire. No one has gotten a permit for the bonfire and the city would never issue one. The police are there from the start. They stand politely by the side and do not arrest anyone. Every year at about twenty minutes past midnight, the Fire Department shows up to put out the fire. They all know about it ahead of time. It's the same every year. The firemen give us twenty minutes of savage fire-dancing so we can feel like we got away with something risky. Then they roll in like indulgent uncles wearing big hats to put a stop to the nonsense.

On all sides of the bonfire for a couple of blocks, there are impromptu fireworks stations. Again, these are completely illegal, with no permits, and manned by amateurs who even when sober would not be competent to handle explosives. The only sober people setting off the fireworks are the feral children, who should not be trusted with a can opener, let alone gunpowder. As I walked among the crowd, I pulled up the collar of my coat and kept a low profile as flaming darts whizzed past my head. There was no telling where a firecracker might come from, as none of it was contained. Celebrants set off their own munitions wherever and however they liked. One guy accidentally set his friend's sleeve on fire by shooting a roman candle into it. No hard feelings, just New Year's Eve hijinks. Every so often there was a shattering blow in the sky that shook the fragile wooden weatherboards of the houses around us. These were the M-80s or "Cherry Bombs." Pretty name. Ugly sound. Who sells bombs to children?

For years now I have sunk deeply into this way of life, and I consider myself a New Orleanian in almost all regards. Yet, this easy, uncontrolled access to fireworks reveals a cultural divide that still disturbs my sense of order. I left the celebration when a remnant from the fireworks rained down from the sky and hit me in the forehead, leaving a bloody divot. A friend had just made a nervous joke, telling me to be careful of "falling shrapnel." We had both laughed, but then as I wiped a Kleenex on my forehead and found blood, I lost my party spirit. I went home to the haven of my porch and my smelly cigarettes.

Falling shrapnel naturally led to thoughts of Iraq. This New Year's Eve also marked the execution of Saddam Hussein. When the judge gave the death sentence, he let Saddam Hussein know that he would be permitted to smoke cigarettes before being hanged by the neck. How thoughtful. Had Hussein given up smoking while in jail? Here again, smoking makes its presence felt as the thing we all want to do but know we shouldn't. If the judge had given a life sentence, would the former dictator have given up cigarettes for good? Would he get in shape for the New York Marathon? Or just clean up his personal habits so as not to annoy the other prisoners? Oh, but when facing death, what the heck! Smoke away.

The other detail that leaped out from the mass of words surrounding this weirdly medieval disintegration of civility was that Saddam Hussein spent part of his final hours of life dyeing his hair. He went to the hangman's noose with a fresh coiffure, dark and virile. When I saw the photo in the newspaper, taken moments after he died, his face turned down with eyes closed as if sleeping, framed by the folds of the white shroud, I couldn't help but notice his neat dark hair. I tried to imagine the vanity crowding out his other thoughts as he underwent his beauty treatment the night before. I couldn't do it. I couldn't piece together a sense of the mind that could face his own execution for engineering the mass slaughter of human life and then fret about his hair.

Yet, when I saw his shrouded body finally, after all the blood shed over him, around him, because of him, by him, he looked like a regular dead man. Worm's meat, after all. Not unlike the other dead men I'd seen in the newspapers. When I looked at Saddam Hussein that way, I found his touch of vanity less galling. Instead I saw it as a desperate effort to hold onto a shred of identity. It was his final assertion: *This is who I am.*

Well, that's done with, isn't it? Now what?

We continue to count the dead. Around the same time that Saddam Hussein was executed, we passed another important milestone in Iraq. Three thousand American soldiers killed. The soldier whose death put the count over this mark was Dustin R. Donica. He came from Spring, Texas, and he was twenty-two years old when he received wounds from small-arms fire while conducting combat operations in Baghdad. His photo appears on CNN's website that keeps track of the dead in Iraq. His face is fair and stern. He looks like he just got his driver's license the day before and plays running back on his high school football team. Two or three more soldiers who were

225

killed almost immediately the following day quickly supplanted Donica's place at the top of CNN's list. There isn't time enough to document these events as fully as they deserve. Rough estimates put the death toll for Iraqi soldiers in the range of 15,000. God only knows how many Iraqi civilians. A hundred thousand? More? We'll never know for sure.

Saddam Hussein and Dustin Donica were not the only ones dead tonight. Two days ago, Dinerral Shavers, who was a drummer with the Hot 8 Brass Band and a music teacher at L.E. Rabouin High School, died of a gunshot wound to the head. He had been driving with his wife and step-children down Dumaine Street, not far from Bayou Saint John, when a young man ran toward the car and began firing a gun into the back window. Despite the bullet in his brain, Shavers managed to drive the car another four blocks before he collapsed—an apparent attempt to get his family out of danger. Shavers, too, asserted himself at the end: *This is who I am.*

Three men dead tonight for lots of bad reasons. All this to dwell on, and it was just New Year's Eve. None of our holidays would ever be simple again.

The number of people in Louisiana who died as a result of Katrina is a similarly moveable number. Nearly a year after the storm, the count reached 1,464 dead. There are about a hundred more bodies in the morgue that have not been identified or claimed by families. Still more are simply reported missing. That could increase. We wait and watch. Collectively holding our breath and taking nothing for granted, we walk lightly on this damaged ground. Our gaze moves among the splinters of what we knew as our home, searching for what's left behind, whether dead or salvageable. This process will take much longer than any of us imagined. As it goes on, the search becomes more refined because the things we're looking for become less tangible. Although the gross work of counting the dead has been largely finished, still we look, as though sensing that something vital remains buried somewhere underneath the mess. We are still searching for our way of life.

People outside of New Orleans always ask, "How are things going down there?" At the risk of sounding churlish, I am confident that I may speak for everyone when I say we are tired of answering that question. Tired of giving the status report. Tired of being defined in terms of this catastrophic thing that happened to us. We are grateful for the care and concern, but we just

226

want to return to regular days in our city, going about our business without serving as the poster children for disaster. Being a nationally televised victim is an energy-draining identity. We'd like to assert a new identity. Or have our old one back. We want a different story to tell.

Unfortunately, wanting doesn't make it so.

Okay, here is the status report. We are exhausted. We boomerang between hope and despair. Suicide has gone up, and many of the doctors who might help clinically depressed people have moved out of town. Divorce, domestic violence, and murder have also increased. The National Guard had to come back last summer because five people died by gunshot in one day in one neighborhood. There is a war here. Meanwhile the cops, the prosecutors, and judiciary are at war among themselves, each blaming the other for their numerous failures to protect us from thugs.

Thousands of people living in FEMA trailers, who want to rebuild their homes, have been stalled because the money they were promised by the federal government hasn't come through. The levees have still not been rebuilt to their pre-Katrina strength. The Army Corps of Engineers, in the mistaken belief that it was immune to litigation, published a 6,000-page document explaining that the levee failure resulted from the Corps' own flawed engineering.

A few months ago, the police stopped a man because he was driving erratically. One officer tapped on the driver's window, while another officer stood behind the car. According to the *Times-Picayune*, the man rolled down his window and said to the cop, "Just kill me! Get it over with, kill me!"

When the officer refused to comply with this request, the man put his car into a fast reverse and pinned the other officer against a car behind him. That cop tried to shoot out the man's tires but missed. Then the man sped off down the street, driving in wild swoops from side to side, intentionally slamming into the signs on the neutral ground that advertised construction contractors. (These quickie signs have proliferated like mushrooms since the storm.) When the cops caught up with him, he ran from his car. They wrestled him to the ground. All the while he begged the police to kill him.

Later we learned this man had gotten bad news from his insurance company. He would not receive the money he needed to repair his home.

The police spokesman stated without blushing that he considered it a great credit to the officers on the scene that they did not grant the man's wish, but instead apprehended him alive.

Most of us just get along nursing a chronic low-grade depression. We gathered at the New Orleans Museum of Art for an exhibit of photographs taken during and just after the storm. We clustered in small groups along the gallery wall filled with images of homes buckled and split, swollen bodies floating face down, thick dried mud crusted over children's toys scattered in the street. Many of these we had already seen too many times, but still we looked again and cried together in the museum. Strangers now often stand in public places, at community meetings, or sometimes in line at the grocery store and weep openly in each other's presence. No one apologizes, and no one explains.

I met our mailman, Cliff, on our front step and asked how he had made out. He told me he had three day's worth of clothing and that was it. Everything he owned had been washed out of his home in New Orleans East. He'd be moving to another city soon. I went back in the house and cried for half an hour. I didn't even know Cliff that well.

This was an unprecedented experience, to participate in a grief larger than my personal history. The storm was still taking a toll on my cognitive skills. I couldn't concentrate on anything, and my memory was like cheesecloth. One day as I was making up the bed, I spent a couple of long minutes staring at an object in my hand before I could remember the word "pillowcase."

The question keeps coming up: Why would anyone want to live in a place where this can happen? I found an answer from the people who had been in New Orleans during Hurricane Betsy in 1965. A few years ago I had interviewed a group of these folks for a story commemorating the anniversary of that storm. Each one of them vowed that they would never stay behind for another hurricane. But they also said they saw no reason to live somewhere else. The thought of facing an earthquake on the West Coast, blizzards in the Northeast, or tornados in the Midwest was far more frightening, because you can see a hurricane coming several days out, so you have time to prepare, while an earthquake or a tornado can attack without warning. And who needs all that snow?

"People out in California, they're crazy to live there with the earthquakes. *Those* scare me. I'll take a hurricane any day over an earthquake," said one man who lived in Saint Bernard Parish. "You stick with the devil you know."

The operative idea here is that there will always be some kind of devil lurking around our homes, no matter where we live. Absolute safety is an illusion. You just have to choose the threat that makes sense to you. I also think that New Orleanians hold a perverse fondness for their hurricanes. Certainly that was true in the stories I heard about Betsy, even though seventy-five people died in that storm. There is a strange intimacy we share with these storms, probably because when they do come upon us, we live with them for several days. Then, to underscore this intimacy, we give the storms a human name. By the time they're done with us, they're practically a member of the family. Every family has someone in it that everyone else wants to leave, right?

The difference I see with Hurricane Katrina is that people here are far more prone to refer to her as "the storm." We don't like to say her name. Too close, too painful. There may be a primitive fear that we will call her into being by speaking it aloud. Her name still reeks with the excruciating intimacy of death.

There have been a few things in addition to the Saints that have warmed our hearts this year in our funky, messy home. We put on a joyous Mardi Gras. One float carried a banner that read: "Hey Chirac! Buy us back!" I dressed as a mermaid. Sean was a pirate. There were a lot of water-themed costumes. The Frenchmen Street clubs have been jumping with music. There has been a shortage of stand-up bass players, and yet New Orleans musicians are performing valiantly to infuse the city with life again. The hurricane's wind and flood had scattered the contents of bird feeders, and the following spring, all over the city, big yellow fat-faced sunflowers popped up unexpectedly in our yards. A bumper crop of babies also arrived just about nine months after Katrina. See, this is what happens when people are holed up in cheap motel rooms for weeks on end with no jobs to go to and nothing to do but play cards and watch bad news on TV. Of course, many of the New Orleans public schools that those children will eventually attend are still a national embarrassment.

Back on the plus side, weekly garbage pickup has returned. Those of you who live in regular cities, I want you to pause as you drag your trash cans out to the curb. I want you to think deeply about what it might mean for you if no one came to take away your garbage for a few months. I want you to appreciate how fortunate you are that you can count on this vital service. How lucky you are to live in a city that works. Don't take that for granted. We don't.

Although we enjoyed more basics of civilized life than a year prior, and we were gradually seeing more houses returning to a fresh, repaired state, New Orleans still didn't work that well. It lurched along, trying to seem as though it worked, but that was a shadow play. To be honest, New Orleans didn't work that well before the storm, but it wasn't quite so obvious then. We all considered the city's general incompetence to be part of the charm. Just like those flawed levees that stood there untested for forty years and then couldn't stand up to the job they were supposedly built for, Katrina put an intolerable strain on weaknesses that the city had been living with for a long time. So that general incompetence degraded into criminal mayhem and negligence. The municipal chaos, the murders, the suicides, the looting, the hospital closings, and the schools that lack textbooks are more than anyone can bear. And the city's loosey-goosey, lighten-up, pour-a-cocktail, lower-your-expectations attitude isn't so adorable these days. We're tired, and we'd like things to work, please.

The loopy optimists among us say this shattering experience will make the city even better and stronger than before. That now we have a chance to do it again and this time do it right.

I distrust the big ideas, the puffy optimism. I have more faith in New Orleans's essential nature, which has been in place long before its birth three hundred years ago. That is: water, water everywhere. This element that so pervades the city ensures that its forms and structure will unravel eventually. Like the houses themselves in New Orleans, all the visionary proposals will be eaten away by slow damp rot. We do not stand on solid bedrock as New York, for example. That city, although rather dour, overserious, and not nearly as romantic or sexy as New Orleans, does function competently, and I think the hard stone that New York stands on imbues the functioning of the city with the reliability evoked by such a solid substance. By contrast, the wet sponge that New Orleans stands on is the thing that gives our city its character of soft yielding and falling to pieces. Nothing can change that. The water at the base of New Orleans's composition will undo any efforts to reform it into a sober, responsible city, comprised of right angles, punctual appointments, meaningful law enforcement. Why bother fixing the rain gutters, when they're just going to fall apart again? Humidity always defeats our best plans.

That said, I'd add that those of us who will stay in New Orleans and continue to call it home are the people who are good swimmers. I don't mean that literally, although actual swimming skills certainly can't hurt. No, I mean the people who can engage in the formless, dissolving nature of this place without fear of drowning. As you would in a body of water, when you're in New Orleans you have to move in concert with these fluid shifts, surrender to the otherness of the place, and meet it on its own terms. This is not your element. New Orleans is its own element with its own rules that change all the time. The only way to stay afloat is not to freak out when everything slips between your fingers. A lot of people think they can groove on the chaos and the shabby living standard, but they eventually go back to the place they came from, New York or Chicago, where the trains run on time.

My childhood in South Jersey prepared me to live in New Orleans. The house I grew up in, known locally as "the white elephant" with a soaring cathedral ceiling, stood precisely on the boundary between land and water. The foundation rested partly on the ground and partly on pilings that suspended it over the edge of the bay. I used to press my ear to the floor on the back porch and listen for the glup-glup of the water below. We were doomed, and it showed. Each year, the house tilted gently downward, a little closer to the bay, as the bulkhead shifted in the muddy bottom. There wasn't a single 90-degree angle in our home. Marbles rolled from one side of the room to the other. Certain doors refused to remain in one place but swung on their hinges according to their pitch in relation to the house's slide toward the water. It was like living in *The Cabinet of Dr. Caligari*. Now I can see that this grand, loose-limbed house formed my guiding sense that the rightness of things has little to do with the correctness of things.

Being a good swimmer also means being able to improvise as you go. If anything saves New Orleans from its own tragedy, it might be the people who have this skill. My sliver of optimism came alive on the day I worked with the Arabi Wrecking Krewe. This volunteer group started with a bunch of musicians, some of them from a band called Bonerama. It's an all-trombone ensemble, which I realize sounds improbable, but you'll have to take my word for it when I say Bonerama is a wicked hot band. One of the guys had a house in Arabi—a neighborhood farther east, past the Lower Ninth Ward, into Saint Bernard Parish—that was completely inundated by the flood. His friends and fellow musicians helped him gut the moldy, ruined interior of his house to get it ready for renovation. After that, they started taking requests from other musicians whose houses had been damaged. Before long they had weekly assignments to help a musician somewhere clean out a house. Arabi Wrecking Krewe came into existence because its members had realized that if they sat around and waited for help to show up, they'd wait an awfully long time. So they helped themselves and their "family," other musicians.

Although the process is in a technical sense "cleaning," in reality it's wrecking, because it requires tearing out all the interior walls and ceilings and bringing the house down to its bones. The day I volunteered with the Krewe, we worked on Al Belletto's house, which had been sitting empty for over a year. Al is a saxophonist and clarinetist, who has played with Louis Prima and the Dukes of Dixieland, also Woody Herman in the 1950s. Nowadays, Al was not in good health and was still living in Dallas, where he had gone after the storm put his house under eight feet of water.

That morning, I stopped Sean as he headed out the door with his harmonium in one hand, cell phone in the other, and asked him to join me for the wrecking. Since returning home, we had done little but look after ourselves, while volunteers from all over the country were pouring into New Orleans to help with the mountain of dirty work that still lay in the path toward the city's recovery.

"This would be good for us to do together," I said. "I want us to do something to help, even if it's just a little."

"I like the *idea* of that," Sean said. "But all the dust. It could be bad for my voice. I don't want to take the risk."

Okay. I was on my own again.

When I drove up to the house, I met Brian "Da Fiya Man." He wore a T-shirt that said: "New Orleans Fire Department. We stayed." Brian was the foreman on this job. He showed me the assorted sledgehammers, crowbars, and chisels I might use, and he offered me gloves, goggles, and a hazardous-materials mask with air filters on each side. In full gear I resembled some germ-phobic, outer-space freak. There was also a big cooler of lemonade. Everything one needs to wreck a house.

Soon two trombonists and an off-duty Marine joined us. More volunteers showed up, along with some of Belletto's family who were trying to salvage what remained of his record collection, hundreds of priceless 45s, along with some trophies. One bore the legend "Carnegie Hall 1946 Swing Competition, Award for Excellence" from Duke Ellington. Al's niece lined up the mud-tarnished trophies on the front porch and took pictures of them.

On the first sweep through, we found sheet music still glued to the floor where it had drifted down as the water receded and then baked into the floorboards as time and heat took over. I leaned down and picked at something with my fingernail. I peeled it up and found an old check Al had written to the IRS six years ago. A check that had been deposited, by the way, canceled, and returned to him for record keeping. Al paid his debt to the federal government, but they weren't doing much for him these days. We got the guts from Al's house out to the curb none too soon. The Army Corps of Engineers had just announced it would stop clearing away storm debris from the streets, as it had been doing for the past year. We went to work.

The house had old plaster walls that still showed the dark mud line about six feet up from the floor. The lath behind the plaster also had to come out to make way for the new wiring and plumbing. So, I picked up the sledgehammer. I had never handled one of these before. It weighed almost as much as I do. I took my first experimental swing with it and threw myself halfway across the room. Rick, one of the trombone players, leaped out of my way. The guys handed me a smaller hammer and sent me to the kitchen at the back of the house.

The kitchen had a big porcelain double sink bolted to the wall, and a brick chimney left over from an earlier century when the house was heated with coal. The chipped linoleum curled up at the edges. Vines that had found a way into the house grew along the ceiling. There was an assortment of mismatched teacups and saucers in the cabinet. A little wooden plaque, tacked to the wall, carried the message: "Bless This House."

We had to wreck this house. Not sure if there would be some blessing in that. I hoped there would be. As I lingered in the old kitchen, I imagined all the meals that had been cooked there, the countless buckets of red beans and rice, the chicken cutlets with sweet corn, the pecan pies. The decades of dishes that had been washed in that great white sink. There had probably been a Formica-topped table in the middle of the room where they ate their meals. I could see the past here, almost smell it cooking.

My job was to take down the walls. I balanced the hammer in one hand and hit the wall with what I thought was a good hard smack, yet my hammer left only a shallow dent in the plaster. I hit it again two or three times before I made a hole in the wall. This was going to be harder than I had anticipated, mainly because I was a little squeamish about damaging someone's home. I knew ultimately the house gutting would benefit Al and his family, but the actual process felt like treading on a taboo. Everything in my social conditioning had taught me *not* to destroy things. Putting holes in walls? It was rude to say the least, not to mention a violation of something sacred: the home, the kitchen, the heart and soul of a house. Maybe if I looked at this as something like surgery. We had to cut to be kind. Mine would be a ruthless compassion.

I threw the hammer at the wall with more vigor. *Bam!* That worked. A big hole opened up. I put a few more holes in a circle and then used the flat end of the hammerhead to pry off chunks of plaster. These fell to the floor in clouds of gray dust. Soon, I was swinging at the wall again; this time I started to enjoy it a little. *Bam!* and *Bam!* again. That was satisfying. Then I gave in and started whaling on the walls. I put my back into it, lunging at the wall with my hammer, bringing it around in a swift, shoulder-height arc . . . and then *smash*, hit the wall. Overhead. Underhand. Then I tried a two-handed grip like Chrissie Evert's backhand at the Wimbledon Open. Plaster rained down on my head so that my hair turned floury with dust. It trickled down inside my shirt and itched. As midday crept up on us, it became smothering hot in the house and inside my facemask. I had to stop every fifteen minutes or so and go outside to pull the mask away from my mouth and gulp in fresh air. I was drenched in sweat.

Even people with normal anger levels would find this work appealing. For someone with my unexpressed rage, it was a godsend. As my hammer cracked the plaster, I punched out all the things that didn't work. The unfairness. The dishonesty. The meanness. What an exhilarating outlet for aggression. I think everyone should wreck a house at least once. It's so healthy.

Each time I swung at the wall I could feel a ferocious wave of energy moving up from my gut, flashing across my shoulders, and rippling down my arms. I forgot why I was doing this. I forgot the images of chicken cutlets from the past. Forgot that a family had lived here. Now, this kitchen was an object that had to be taken down.

The guys were doing an even more ferocious job with the rest of the house. They tore at ceilings and lath, shattered the yellow tiled bathroom. Ghostly sunlight came through the smudged windows as the masked, goggled, and gloved men moved through a fog of dust. They worked without talking. Conversation was impossible in the noise of crashing junk. The men shoveled the piles of broken wood and chunks of plaster into wheelbarrows and trundled them down the ramp on the front steps, sending the contents flying onto the growing mountain of debris at the curb. And then back for more.

We worked like this for most of the day, pausing every now and then for lemonade and smoking. The guys wore facemasks to protect their lungs from the plaster dust while they worked. Then as soon as they went outside for a break, they'd pull off their masks to smoke a cigarette. This was September, so I had already kicked my habit and stuck to lemonade.

By the late afternoon, the house had been rendered nude on the inside. All the studs were exposed. I stood in the front door and could see all the way through to the back. I looked up through the attic to the roof, where sunshine glinted through the holes. The house looked vulnerable but cleaner than before. It looked ready for something new.

I relinquished my hammer back to Brian "Da Fiya Man" and looked around at the others' faces. To a man they were covered in grit and sopping wet with sweat. When they removed their goggles and masks, they wore black rings on their foreheads and cheeks. Rick won the "dirtiest shirt" contest.

Every particle of muscle in my body ached. It was a wonderful drained feeling. My body knew it had done as much as it could ever do. I would go home to a bath and a nap, but the others, who had worked even harder than I, were professional musicians. Today was a Saturday. They all had gigs tonight. They would go home, wash up, and then head out the door again to work until three in the morning. For now, Rick and Craig, another trombone player, leaned on the porch and barely said a word. They were so beat. But they looked happy, gleaming, and grimy. Heroic.

Later, when I got home, I curled up my creaky, worn-out body in a crescent on the floor. I'm just not used to this kind of effort. Lance joined me by pressing his back into my belly. I wasn't sure if I could do this again, not sure if I was as heroic as these others. Arabi Wrecking Krewe had a house-wrecking scheduled every weekend for a year, and that's just one volunteer group among many others. The number of houses that remained to be gutted went into the thousands. The most meaningful recovery work in this city was coming from volunteers, people who were fed up with waiting, so they put on a pair of gloves and went to work—for themselves, for other people, for whoever needed help. Many came to New Orleans from other cities, church groups being the most common. What impressed me about the Arabi Wrecking Krewe was that all those guys were locals. They had storm-related troubles of their own. Yet they were able to dig a little deeper and find the strength to do more.

My motive for volunteering with the Krewe was at least partly a sense of indebtedness. So many generous people had come to help clean things up, while I sat on my couch and ruminated on death and suffering. I had to do something to add my share, however small, to the effort. I had to get off the couch and put my body in motion. So that's how I ended up swinging that hammer all day. I got a lot of satisfaction from it. The other benefit

I received at the end of this house-wrecking was a sense of what might be possible in New Orleans if enough people show up for the city. And just dig a little deeper.

We were a depressed place, this New Orleans of mine. Most of us felt that our nerves were down to fine threads and that we couldn't take another minute beneath the weight of loss. What I've learned is that just when you think you can't give any more, that's when you have to give more. I didn't know where those resources were going to come from. Still, I think that is what New Orleans was asking from us now.

While I burned down my last cigarette on the porch and wished away the smoke and this dreadful New Year's Eve, I remembered an earlier New Year's celebration that had been much better. It happened on September 1, 2006, actually. The exact date is not so important. It was the spirit of the time.

This day was memorable because it had given us our first real break, slight but noticeable, from the summer's heat. Like a reprieve, a faint drying factor had taken over the atmosphere. Just a hint that our stalker August might have retreated a half step. Almost immediately, doors opened around my neighborhood. People came out of their houses, unafraid, not so dependent on air conditioning. I could see them looking around with relief. Maybe we could go outside and not suffocate. It was a lovely evening for a stroll along the bayou.

I took Lance with me to a wine tasting at the new shop called Swirl that had opened on the other side of Bayou Saint John near the Fair Grinds Coffeehouse. We crossed the Magnolia Bridge close to dusk. The bayou remained motionless. The evening felt like a light silk scarf on my skin.

At Swirl there was a crowd outside on the sidewalk. Beth, one of the shop's owners, had set up tables and chairs. They held these wine tastings every week, and it had become a regular social event for the neighborhood. Some of my dog-walking buddies were there. Les waved and shouted, "Lanque!" This is a pet name he had given Lance because Lance didn't have enough pet names. Rachel, who has a corgi named Arlene, was co-hosting the party and had made baked ziti. Beth poured a congenial glass of cabernet.

The party filled up the block, expanding to include the other shop fronts. Music drifted over to us from the Fair Grinds Coffeehouse. They still hadn't opened for coffee since the storm, but they were open for everything else: music, hanging out, talking. Tonight featured a fiddle duet with Tom and Daron. Tom, who lives on Moss Street near our house, was barefoot. It looked as though he had walked to this side of the bayou, about ten blocks or so, over streets and sidewalks, occasional grass and mud, without the benefit of shoes. For most of the summer, whenever I saw him, Tom lacked shoes. This appeared to be a lifestyle choice, not absent-mindedness.

Tom was also the constant companion to Pickle. "That's Pickle singular, not plural," Tom explained, referring to his dog, a grouchy golden-retriever/chow mutt. Tom did not take Pickle around on a proper leash, but on a length of electrical cord with a frayed end. Lance was afraid of Pickle and hid behind my legs at the coffeehouse. Pickle barked a sharp reprimand at Lance each time she saw him on the bayou or here or anywhere. It seemed there was nothing Lance could do to mollify Pickle. She was forever rebuking him. We couldn't figure out what he did to get on her bad side. I believed every side of Pickle was her bad side, but that's just me talking.

Tom said he and Daron would play a Beatles tune. Turned out to be a tune from George Harrison, the sweet one, the baby Beatle. Tom put aside his fiddle and settled his guitar in his lap. He brushed his fingertips along the strings and sang in a low, gentle voice, as if to himself, "Here Comes the Sun."

The song floated above our heads and hung on the air like the scent of sweet olive trees. *Little darling, it seems like years since it's been here.* My favorite Beatle and my favorite song. I have always been a bit embarrassed by how much I love this song, how quickly and deeply it moves me. Not awfully complex or revolutionary, this pretty song comes a hair short of mawkish. I'm embarrassed that such simple sentiment can put me under a spell. But then I guess the only sentiments worth having are the simple ones. That's the whole point, right? That any one of us can be swept to pieces with a few well-chosen words. One more item on the list of things I dread about being human.

"Happy New Year," Rachel said, and clinked her wine glass with mine.

New Year? It was a little early for Rosh Hashanah, wasn't it? Oh, *new* year. I got it. Here in New Orleans we had a new New Year now. Today was

September 1st. We had just passed the first anniversary of Katrina without mishap. We were in a new year now, thank God. A whole new life stretched before us. Until we got to the next hurricane season. We'd worry about that when the time came. In the meanwhile . . .

"Happy New Year," I offered back. Rachel slipped her arm around my waist and kissed my cheek.

I swirled the globe of my wine glass and breathed the fragrant wine. Didn't all this hurricane drama begin a year ago with a wine tasting? Here I was again, and glad that some things hadn't changed. I sipped the wine. Thank goodness we could still enjoy pleasures like these.

The evening was almost unbearably pleasant and simple. A palpable wave of good will swept through this small gathering of neighbors. Ham and Theresa went for ice cream at the market next door. Beth came out with a new Zinfandel she wanted us to try. Brianna was chasing the dogs, trying to make them take a ball from her hand. Normal things. Tom and Daron played on.

Sun, sun, sun, here it comes.

And I say . . . it's all right.

Seduced again by a pretty song, I felt a rising in my chest. A bubble of something lighter than air expanded and made me drift upward. My head floated at the top of my spine like a lotus on the surface of a pond. I smiled at everyone around me. My face couldn't help it. They smiled back. Warm and friendly, that's all. Here on the street where we lived.

We had no way of knowing how long this feeling would last. As I looked around, I struggled to absorb this happiness for its own sake. This evening was just a small pause from our troubles. There was so much destruction behind us, and so much work still lay ahead of us. Yet this evening was the flower that bloomed in the crack between past and future to show us that some respite from suffering was possible. None of us had manufactured the moment. It had landed on us with the same arbitrary flip of nature's whim as when the storm had descended on us. It was a gift.

Even as this pleasure rolled over me, I couldn't ignore the hint of it leaving. I felt I had to take it in and hold it. I wanted to eat the evening, drink the clear air, and inhale the music. If I didn't take this into my body and allow it to sink deep inside me, I would lose it. I had to memorize this time and this feeling. I was already losing it. No, I had it. There it was, coming over me in soft waves. Contentment. Safety. Ease of mind. Peace.

Later I was almost afraid to write it, afraid the act of capture would destroy it. Or that holding too tightly would smother it. Or perhaps I would over-imagine, make too much of it, and then be disappointed.

No, I'll do it right here, right now. I'll say it. We're going to be all right.

EPILOGUE: THE OTHER SHOE

I MARRIED THE YOGA KING OF NEW ORLEANS. AND I AM HERE TO TELL YOU he steps into his drawstring pants one leg at a time, just like any other man.

He wasn't the Yoga King when I met him. He was more of a duke or lesser lord. I helped Sean ascend to the heights of majesty he enjoys today, but I was never the Yoga Queen. I was the Prime Minister. The power behind the throne.

Being married to the Yoga King really made me want to smoke cigarettes. And drink whiskey. In fact, there is nothing like living with an inordinately limber man to make a woman lie on the couch and read magazines.

Still, we had a good marriage, I thought—one worth keeping. We were better together than apart. Yet, two years after Katrina swept through New Orleans, our marriage ended. The reason? I wanted to participate in a miracle, to see the soul enshrined in flesh. Sean maintained that was not for him.

It should have been clear where this was going. I hung in there, running my campaign, longer than good sense should have allowed, because I loved him. I didn't want to believe that he could make such a bad choice. And because Sean occasionally wavered enough to give me hope.

When we visited our friends and their daughter Lucie, who was one month old, Sean held Lucie during the entire visit and would not give her up. She fell asleep on his shoulder, and Sean melted into this warm little bundle, her gentle breath and soft heartbeat pulsing against his neck. On the way home, he wore a wistful smile.

"You know, holding Lucie felt so good . . ."

"Yes?"

"Makes me think it would be kinda nice to have a baby of our own."

I took these crumbs of encouragement and tried to make a cake. Didn't work. Whenever I got serious about it, Sean choked.

For a while, I tried to pretend I didn't see where this was going. That first time I brought up having a baby, Sean had slipped a knife into my heart. I let it stay there because I dreaded the implications of removing it. A knife hurts just as much coming out as it does going in. Finally, I couldn't ignore the pain any longer, so I tried to fix it.

I spent half our marriage trying to talk Sean out of his obdurate position. I wept and begged and cajoled. I made jokes and left smutty invitations on his pillow. He didn't object to sex, mind you. Just the baby that results from sex. Also, there was no margin for error with Sean. We were never going to have an "oops" baby. You know how some people have to check the stove four or five times to make sure they really, *really* turned off the gas? That's how Sean was with birth control.

I even tried backing off the topic to give him room to consider it without pressure. I hoped he would come around to my way of thinking on his own. Nope, he went about his business as though the topic was closed. He was genuinely shocked when I brought it up again.

During one of these agonizing dead-end conversations, we sat at the dining room table. I was wearing Sean's bathrobe, and I was crying. I wiped my nose with Sean's sleeve. It was the least he could grant me as he was once again telling me: No, he did not want to have a child.

"If you want a baby all that badly," Sean said, "then I think you should find a man who wants a baby and have one with him."

The air went out of my lungs. More tears piled up at the back of my throat. I squeaked out the words. "You can't mean that. You'd be willing to let me go? To some other man?"

Sean was a yogic master of composure. "Yes, I want you to be happy."

After such an exchange as this, some other woman would have put her husband out on the sidewalk with the garbage. I took mine to couple's therapy.

We made great progress in therapy. I talked at length about my hopes, my dreams, my desire for a family. Then Sean said again that he had no interest in being a father. At one point, the therapist asked if I would object to her having a session with Sean alone.

"No, for heaven's sake. Take him. Fix him."

"Well, it's good to see you still have your sense of humor." The therapist laughed because she thought I was joking.

After a few months of couple's therapy, Sean came to me and said he had changed his mind. He had spent the weekend sorting through boxes of stuff he had left in storage for years. A lot of it consisted of old diaries and photos from when he was in high school. This inventory of his own youth apparently inspired him to take a step toward fatherhood.

"Yes," my husband said. "I'm willing to have a child. I want to make you happy."

That was all I needed to hear. We tumbled into bed to do that thing that people do when they're trying to have a baby. Joyful! Exuberant! Abundant! Just like the old days. Sean whispered into my collarbone how much he loved me. Even as I drifted in the warm land of his hands, my busy mind filed away a distinct thought: *What a relief. Now I don't have to leave him.*

Three weeks later, Sean got cold feet. He told me he had changed his mind again. He was still not willing to have a child. When he broke the news, he pressed his spine a little deeper into the couch, as if bracing himself for a punch in the face.

I didn't hit him. I asked him to find someplace else to live.

A few months later, I found myself one night sprawled on the couch and talking on the phone with a friend of mine. I was trying to figure out what had gotten into Sean's head. I hoped she might have some insight.

Sean had left the house without a murmur of objection and called two weeks later to say, "I hope we can be friends." Seemed to me he had rushed awfully quickly to the I-hope-we-can-be-friends stage, but I let it go. Then we progressed through all the banal details of separation. The lawyers, the letters. At a certain point, Sean would only communicate through e-mail, and then later only through his attorney. He asked for some wigs he liked to wear on Mardi Gras that I had stashed in the back of my closet. Also he wanted some of the Christmas tree decorations and the television. I said sure, come and take those if you like. I wasn't going to quibble about a TV when I was mourning the loss of my chance to have a baby. All the while I wondered: Was this really how it was going to end? No bang, all whimper? The nothingness of his departure didn't make sense.

Then my friend helped me out. "There is something I have to tell you," she said. Her tone of voice sent my stomach plummeting. Good Christ, what next?

"Sean has been seeing somebody."

There was an audible *thunk*. A shoe fell from the sky. It all clicked into place. Of course. That explained everything. His absence. His disinterest. All that time I was moaning and crying about wanting a baby, Sean's mind was on someone else's uterus—or parts thereabout. The first words out of my mouth were "Oh, how . . . ordinary."

The precise timing of this affair didn't matter, because it amounted to the same thing for me. I had already made my decision about our marriage. I had tried to reconcile myself to spending the rest of my life with a man who refused to have a child with me, and I couldn't do it. Everything in me balked. Whenever I looked at Sean, I would think, "There is the reason we don't have a child." My path, although painful, had been clear. I didn't want to take it, but I had to force myself or live with a knife in my heart. Now, this new information about Sean's extramarital adventure was just insult heaped onto injury. More than betrayal, it was in poor taste.

As I sat there with the phone pressed into my ear and absorbed the concussion of this revelation, I saw that my beautiful husband, this man I had cherished and yes, idealized, was not who I thought he was. My brave man, nimble Sean had feet of clay after all. And his shoes rained down on my head that night.

More destruction. How much more destruction are we supposed to take? I ask that not merely for the sake of my own small world. But as a species, how many floods, cyclones, earthquakes, tsunamis, cancer, or divorce are we supposed to tolerate before we give up completely? This is a question for Job, and if he were here right now, he'd probably say we're supposed to take as much destruction as there is to give. Perhaps if we stop asking *Why?* or *How much more?* that might help us to see what's left and do something with it.

A year before the hurricane, my father suffered a massive stroke. A large portion of his brain died. My father is still alive. He walks and talks with some difficulty and has trouble recalling certain words. He can't sail his boat, but he still goes to the beach with his dogs. A few months after the hurricane, my sister was diagnosed with breast cancer. She had chemotherapy and radiation. Both her breasts are gone, but her hair came back. So far so good, she's cancer-free.

As for me, I am nearly done with the philosophical questions. I'll stick with walks and dogs and my sister's hair. Yet, I can't help but notice that more often than not, the pain we feel in the face of destruction is the pain of our illusions shattering. Our belief in safety, longevity, fidelity. These are hardly worth the paper they're written on. Perhaps we are better off without them. To be honest, I'm not so sure. I *like* my illusions. After the old ones had gone, I was sure I'd eventually replace them with new illusions. In the meantime, I had no choice but to breathe into this empty space left behind where my cherished beliefs used to be.

For some time I heard about other couples whose marriages ended in the aftermath of Hurricane Katrina. It became commonplace to blame the storm for these divorces, another way of demonizing this force of nature. There may be some truth to it. The storm put a tremendous pressure on all of us. It's only natural that under such pressure, we'd break wherever we were weak. So the storm didn't destroy us so much as she exposed the flaws in our composition. Our levees and canal walls and some of our marriages all had fissures in the foundations that might not have been visible were it not for all that wind and rain.

At a party during our first Christmas season home after the storm, I talked with a friend about the many relationships that were falling apart all around us. At the time, I thought: *Thank God, that will never happen to Sean and me.* My friend said that he envisioned the hurricane as a "social accelerator." He explained that whatever was in the process of happening in relationships at the time of the storm only accelerated that process afterward. The storm couldn't create something that wasn't already present in nascent form. That acceleration didn't just bring about the end of relationships that were doomed anyway. He also knew of a couple that had become engaged while they were gutting their flooded house. The guy had slipped a diamond ring onto his girlfriend's rubber-gloved finger. Then they kissed through sterile facemasks.

That's so cute. What a happy, romantic ending. I wish them well. How do we know they're not doomed? We don't.

I am not quite ready to thank Hurricane Katrina for accelerating the inevitable decline of my marriage. However, I am able to see finally that this was the ending I had been writing toward all along. I just didn't know it until I got to it. Other people who read the manuscript could see the problem and penciled notes in the margin: "Where is Sean in this scene? Why isn't he with you? Why are you so alone?" In the wake of my desolation, I was tempted to rewrite the earlier chapters, maybe give Sean a new name and treat him as a fictional character, since the man I wrote about in those lovely scenes of our courtship and our wedding was not the same man I knew now. In the end I decided to leave it as I wrote it. It was true at the time, and now it remains a document of its time. I can't deny its truth simply because I have uncovered more layers to the story.

One thing that I could do and have always done is take back the story and make it mine. I didn't have to leave it here with a whimper.

As if orchestrated by my design, the heavens provided an opening for my closure. On the night following that fateful shoe-falling phone conversation, there was going to be a full lunar eclipse. It would be visible in our sky between 8:00 and 10:00 in the evening. I gathered the things I needed. A thick packet of letters that Sean had written to me over the years, passionate love notes that now sounded obscene, too many adjectives. A copy of our marriage license. Photos from our wedding. A box of matches. A pillow. I planned to be sitting on the ground for a couple of hours.

When Lance saw me putting on my shoes, he jumped up from his bed, grabbed one of his squeaker toys, and met me at the door, his tail waving in anticipation of a late night walk. I made Lance stay home. He was disappointed, but I wanted to be alone.

I walked through the chilly February night to the Magnolia Bridge, the stage for so many passages. We had gotten engaged and married there. Tonight, I was making it *my* bridge. The sky didn't want to cooperate with viewing the lunar eclipse. The moon, gorgeous, fat, and full, slipped behind heavy clouds and then peeked out for a moment before disappearing again. There had been rain earlier, and now the air danced with a wafting mist.

I sat cross-legged on my pillow and leaned against the bridge's rusty stanchions. I wasn't quite ready to set up my business for the night. It was still a little early for the eclipse to begin. So I sat, breathing in the damp wind, and contemplated the empty space before me. I am not sure how long I sat there. My neighbor walked by with her dog Beau Jacques.

"Are you all right?" she asked. I told her I was fine. "Are you sure?" she asked again.

"Yes, really. I promise there is nothing wrong." Ten minutes later another woman with her dog came across the bridge and asked me the same thing. What was it with women and their dogs tonight? Okay, I guessed I better get started, because obviously I was unnerving people.

The wind blew a wide opening in the clouds at last, and the moon came into view. The eclipse had begun. A shadow shaped like a fingernail appeared at the edge. It was time. My plan was to conduct a purging ritual while the moon moved through her compressed cycle of death and rebirth.

I unpacked Sean's letters first and tucked them under my knee while I struggled to light the matches. First one sputtered out. Then another and another. The wet boards at my knees were soon littered with useless matchsticks. In addition to the problem of the wind, the weather had put a sheen of moisture on every surface. The letters had grown limp and the matches were spongy.

I made a wind barrier with my cupped hands and managed to get one grudging sliver of flame to catch on the letters. Slowly, slowly a swelling black crescent moved across the scribbled words, Sean's empty words, and ate them in a thin line of fire. I touched a fan of pages to this tender fire I'd started and got it going too. In a rush, it flared up in clouds of black smoke.

So I held it with my fingertips, down to the very end, as the cleansing fire demolished these false confessions. Then I dropped the burnt package into the water below. I ignited more pages and then our marriage license too, dropping them off the bridge at the last second before my fingers burned. Oddly the water did not immediately extinguish the flaming papers, but allowed them to float and burn for a moment. These fiery boats drifted on the surface of the bayou. They illuminated the flickering water, and at a brief glance they could have been mistaken for a celebration. They resembled a party favor for a wedding, or a baptism perhaps. Something joyful appeared to be in progress here. Then the bayou swallowed them whole.

I brushed ash from my lap and looked up over my shoulder. A police car had pulled up to the end of the bridge. Great. Just what I needed, a visit from the cops. It hadn't occurred to me until now that someone might object to my burning ritual. I waited in the wet dark. How will I explain this? Then a more pressing crime than my pyromania must have come in over the cop's radio because the police car peeled away from the bridge and sped down Moss Street.

I didn't want to take the chance that the police would return, so I decided to leave off burning stuff and just throw the rest in the trash. Not so ceremonial, but I had made my point.

I stood up and leaned on the bridge railing to watch the last minutes of the eclipse. The moon was almost black now. I had one remaining task, the hardest of all. I reached into my pocket and withdrew two rings. My engagement ring and my wedding ring. I held them in the palm of my hand and tried to look at them as if for the first time. My engagement ring was made of thick-ridged gold and graced with a raised green tourmaline cut in a triangular shape. The jewelry designer had dubbed this one part of her "shield series." Among the magical properties ascribed to green tourmalines is the power to strengthen hearts. My wedding band was an antique filigreed design with watery scrolls along the sides.

I loved these rings. I had always loved looking down at my hand and seeing them nested against each other. They gave off a greenish aura and had a medieval heft. They were perfect together, one strong and masculine, the other soft and feminine. The most beautiful rings I had ever seen in my life. I still loved the sight of them in my hand, even though I hadn't worn them in months. I hadn't known what to do with them. I felt like a fraud wearing them, so I put them out of sight, and yet had always been aware of their presence, glowing in the dark of my drawer. A rebuke or a reminder, I couldn't tell. It still made me angry that I had such beautiful rings but couldn't wear them because they represented something that was dead.

Now here they were at my purging ritual. They had to go. There has to be a sacrifice. And it has to hurt.

I stood beneath the dying moon and held my rings out over the water. This was it, and I couldn't do it. I stood there for a long time just contemplating what I was about to do. And I didn't want to. I wanted to keep these rings. If I let them go, there would be no return to my old life. No chance to recover the love. Even though I knew there was nothing for me in the past, still I wanted to hold on to these beautiful jeweled icons.

Oh, it hurts. It really hurts.

I tossed my engagement ring into the water first. I held my breath and forced my hand. Threw it ten feet out and then *plink*. It disappeared into the bayou. Then I threw my wedding ring after it.

There, that should do it.

I stared at the surface of the water, imagining my rings as they sank through the darkness and settled into the mud, their shine blunted by the murk. A turtle might find one and nose it around, wondering what it was for or how it got there, and then move on with his investigation of the mossy car parts and broken bottles that littered the bottom of the bayou. How long would it take for my golden rings to become worn away by this gentle destruction, the water's work? How long before they dissolved into the flow of all things? Perhaps I hadn't lost them entirely. In some form at least, they'd always be here, cradled in my bayou.

Clouds sailed overhead. The wind lifted my hair. I looked up and saw the thin golden edge of the moon reappearing. What good timing. The new moon was here. I gazed out over the dark water and inhaled the night. I savored these words on my tongue: I am wild and free.

ACKNOWLEDGMENTS

I OWE AN ENORMOUS DEBT OF GRATITUDE TO PATRICIA LEE LEWIS—poet, teacher, literary midwife—who held a manuscript workshop in her living room where *My Bayou* came into existence. Her love and intelligence have nourished this book and made it live. The other writers in the group, principally Eliza Williamson, Sheila Stuewe, Alyssa Lovell, Cherryl Jensen, and Betsy Loughran, deserve my heartfelt thanks for reading those early chapters with such enthusiasm and sharp feedback.

Thanks also go to my friend Shaun Hunter, who took time away from her own writing to help me with mine and has sent boundless encouragement. Excellent editing came from Dori Ostermiller, who clarified the gray areas, and Nancy Rowe, who wields a number two pencil like nobody's business.

This work first received recognition from *Bayou Magazine* (University of New Orleans), *Blackbird* (Virginia Commonwealth University), and *Oxford American,* and I am grateful to the editors of those journals for publishing chapters. Finally, I remain thankful to the editors of Michigan State University Press for bringing my book into the light of day, particularly Martha Bates, who said, "Yes."

None of this would be nearly as much fun, were it not for Geoff Stewart, my dance partner, who makes the good life so much happier.

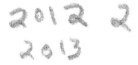